CODING

IN PYTHON

ROBERT C. MATTHEWS

Table of Contents

Coding in Python
A Comprehensive Beginners Guide to
Learn the Realms of Coding in Python

Coding in Python
Tips and Tricks to Coding with Python Using the Principles and Theories of Python Programming

Coding in Python
Advanced Guide to Coding Using
Python Programming Principles to Master the Art of Coding

CODING
IN PYTHON

A COMPREHENSIVE BEGINNERS GUIDE TO
LEARN THE REALMS OF CODING IN PYTHON

ROBERT C. MATTHEWS

Introduction

This book contains proven steps and strategies on how to code in Python. In this book, I have included all the basics of coding in Python, written in a lucid and easy-to-digest form. The book is divided into different chapters, each dealing with a specific topic. I started the book by explaining the process of downloading and installing Python on your operating system. As Windows is the most popular operating system in the world, I focused on Python installation on Windows.

After that, I moved on to Python variables and data types. I have explained them one by one. The most interesting of all the datatypes is the Python string, and it also is the most widely used in different Python programs that you will find in this book and that you will create yourself. Therefore, I emphasized it. Then I moved on to Python lists and tuples. I have tried to create a story in the book so that you find the content coherent, juicy, and highly valuable. To fulfill this purpose, I have created a game zone that is under development. The game revolves around a player who has a mission to equip an office with the cheapest in terms of price and with the most needed items so that the player can sell the office to the highest bidder. You can see the story kicking off with the start of the section on lists and tuples.

I will explain different Python codes regarding the game. As you find yourself inside the game development, you will learn different list methods such as the del method, the pop method, and list slicing. The game then moves on toward Python conditionals and dictionaries and gets more interesting. The conditionals add logic to the game, and dictionaries offer a way to store data most efficiently.

One of the most interesting programs you will see invites user input and integrates it into a while loop. You will also enjoy the chapter on functions that make the code smart and highly engaging. Functions are interesting because they can be easily paired up with different data types, and for and while loops.

Object-oriented programming will introduce to real programming. You will learn how to create classes, inheritance classes, and model real-life objects with the help of programming. You can create some very interesting programs with the help of Python classes.

I have clearly written the codes. Each code is coupled with its results. You can copy the code and paste it in the editor, do the edits of your choice, and get the result. This is how you can easily learn to code. I have written all the codes in Python 3.8 which is why I recommend you to download and install it. The process is already made a part of this book.

I wrote this book with the goal that a person who has to start Python coding from scratch can easily learn to code. The book is for those who are just getting started. I have explained each concept with due depth and comprehensiveness so that you beginners can understand it and digest it well. Even if you are just getting started in the world of coding, you can easily understand the concepts.

I recommend that you keep a notebook and a pen with you when you read this book so that you can note down the important points and code syntax to remember them and practice them. You also can bookmark them on a smart device and jump to the desired pages when you want to read them. Unlike other dry books of coding, this book will explain each step of the code so that you can easily reproduce what you have learned. I hope you have fun reading sessions once you get started. If you have got the fire to learn Python, this book should finish in five to six reading sessions.

Chapter One

Make a Start

This chapter will walk you through the process of making a start in Python coding. You will learn how to download and install Python on your operating system. You will also learn how to start the editor and write a code in Python text editor.

The first thing you should know about is setting up a Python environment on your operating system. Python is installed differently on different operating systems. There are currently two available versions of Python which are Python 2 and Python 3. Each programming language keeps evolving as developers add to it new concepts and ideas. Python developers have taken a step further by making regular developments to the language, making it more powerful and versatile as well. You can install both versions of your operating system.

Python 3 Installation

Python is one of the most widely used programming languages that were first launched in 1991. Since then Python has gained immense popularity. It also is considered one of the most popular as well as flexible programming languages. Unlike Linux, Windows operating systems don't have Python pre-installed by default. However, you always can install Python on the Windows operating system is a very easy step.

The prerequisites of installing Python 3 on your Windows system are that you must have Windows 10 installed on the system and have admin privileges. Also, you should have a command prompt running on the system. The next prerequisite is the availability of a remote desktop app. You can use it if you are planning to install Python on a remote Windows server.

The first step in the installation process is selecting the version you want to install. In this case, we are aiming at downloading Python 3. You should visit the official Python website python.org and download Python 3 installer for Windows. Now run the same on your system. As you are just getting started on learning the Python language, I recommend that you download and install Python 2 and Python 3 versions to test old and new projects simultaneously.

Executable Installer

You should download and install Python executable installer on your Windows operating system. The first step in this regard is to open your internet browser and move to the Downloads section of python.org. Make sure that you download and install only the version that has an executable installer available for Windows. The approximate download size is about 25 MB. If your Windows is a 32-bit operating system, you should select Windows x86 executable installer. If it is 64-bit, you should select Windows x86-64 executable installer. However, even if you install the wrong version, it is easy to uninstall it and reinstall it once again.

Run It

When the executable installer of Python has been downloaded, you need to run it. Select Install launcher for all users. This will ensure that all users on your system will be able to use it. Don't forget to tick Add Python 3.8 to the PATH box. This links the interpreter to the path of execution and facilitates programming. Older versions don't display this option.

In the next step, click on Install Now. When you have installed it, you will see that you will get Python IDLE and Pip. You also can verify Python on your system by navigating to the directory in which Python was installed or by entering the word Python in the search bar. You also can check it through Command Prompt by the name of the directory.

If you opt to install Python 2, you might not get Pip installed with it. Pip is a powerful package and is very helpful in building software and machine learning models. Therefore, you should make sure that the version you have installed has got Pip installed on it.

You can also confirm if Pip is installed on your operating system or not by opening the Start menu and typing the word cmb in the search bar. The command will open the Command Prompt application in which you can write pip –v. If the pip is installed on your system, you will see a line that starts with pip 19.0.3. Otherwise, the system will say that it doesn't recognize pip as an external or internal command. When you open the Python interpreter or IDLE, it will have text like the following:

Python 3.8.5 (tags/v3.8.5:580fbb0, Jul 20 2020, 15:57:54)
[MSC v.1924 64 bit (AMD64)] on win32
Type "help", "copyright", "credits" or "license()" for more information.
>>>

On the top is written the version of Python. If you have installed Python 2, the text will be as follows:

Python 2.7.8 (default, Jun 30 2014, 16:08:48) [MSC v.1500 64 bit (AMD64)] on win32
Type "copyright", "credits" or "license()" for more information.
>>>

Chapter Two

Python Variables and Data Types

When you run a file with the extension .py on Python, it suggests that you are running a Python program. The editor runs the program in a Python interpreter. The Python interpreter spots Python keywords, reads them, identifies them, and acts accordingly. Take the example of the print keyword. When the Python interpreter sees this keyword, it can print whatever you put in the parenthesis. When you write code in the Python editor, you will see that the Python editor highlights your code in different colors. That is how it recognizes different types of code. This feature of Python is known as syntax highlighting and is very useful as you learn to write Python programs.

Python Variables

Python variables are like containers that you can fill in with different types of data values. Python differs from other programming languages because it does not have any command for the declaration of a variable. You can create a variable just by assigning it a specific value. In the following example, I will create a variable and assign it some value. Please keep in mind that I am using a Python interpreter for the initial stages. I will move on to the Python editor in the later chapters.

```
>>> greetings = "Hello, I am here to learn Python."
>>> print(greetings)
Hello, I am here to learn Python.
>>>
```

The name of the variable is *greetings*. The variable holds a full sentence as its unique value. The print keyword, as I said, is used to display the value of the variable. The value of a variable can be easily replaced if you pack it up with another value. See the following example.

```
>>> greetings = "Hello, I am here to learn Python."
>>> print(greetings)
Hello, I am here to learn Python.
>>>
>>> greetings = "This is the world of Python."
>>> print(greetings)
This is the world of Python.
>>>
```

Naming Variables

When you are naming a variable, you must adhere to a couple of guidelines and rules. If you break some of the rules, you will see errors in the code. Even if missing out on the rules does not trigger errors, breaking the rules will make the code look vague and abstract. The success of a programmer is that his code should be easy to understand and read. You must keep the following rules in mind when you are creating variables.

- The names of variables may contain numbers, letters, and underscores. They may start with an underscore and a letter, but they cannot start with a number. For example, a variable can be written as greetings_77 but it cannot be written as 77_greetings.

- You must avoid the use of Python keywords while naming a variable. For example, you cannot name a variable as print because print is a Python keyword.

- If you can keep the names of variables as much descriptive as possible, it will help you better read and understand the code when you come back to at a later stage. For example, greetings are better than simply writing g.

Writing variable names is a continuous practice in Python. You will learn how to create better variable names as you move further into the world of coding.

When you are creating variables, it is common to get errors. You should make sure that you are not misspelling different words. Take a look at the possible errors and try to learn how to avoid them and fix them.

I will use the same variable greetings to show how you can end up getting an error message.

```
>>> greetings = "This is the world of Python."
>>> print(greeting)
Traceback (most recent call last):
  File "<pyshell#6>", line 1, in <module>
    print(greeting)
NameError: name 'greeting' is not defined
>>>
```

All I did was writing the wrong spelling in the code. What makes Python different from other programming languages is that it displays the error message which tells you the exact line on which you have made the error. This helps rectify the errors and clean the code.

By writing the wrong spelling, I don't suggest that Python recognizes the wrong or right spelling. I am trying to suggest that it reads the name of the variable and matches it with the command you have entered. In case of a mismatch, the error message pops up. So, even if you misspell the word while you allot a name to a variable, Python does not declare it an error.

```
>>> greetings = "This is the world of Python."
>>> print(gretings)
This is the world of Python.
>>>
```

I have deliberately misspelled the word greetings but still, Python read it and ran the code. A lot of programming errors happen just because of wrong spellings. You may call them typos. They can be easily managed if you read your code with close attention.

Python Datatypes

There are different types of data that you have to use in programming. Some are simple texts while others are integers or lists. Python supports a diversity of datatypes. However, you have to designate the datatype when you create one so that Python can recognize it easily and process it as per your wishes. In the following section, I will shed light on several data types that I will be using in various code snippets in the book.

Datatypes, in a brief look, are as under:

```
#This is Python list
>>> a = ["tomato, potato, garlic, ginger, pumpkin"]
>>> print(a)
['tomato, potato, garlic, ginger, pumpkin']
>>> #This is python frozenset
>>> a = frozenset({"tomato, potato, garlic, ginger, pumpkin"})
>>> print(a)
frozenset({'tomato, potato, garlic, ginger, pumpkin'})
>>> #This is python set
>>> a = {"tomato, potato, garlic, ginger, pumpkin"}
>>> print(a)
{'tomato, potato, garlic, ginger, pumpkin'}
```

```
>>> #This is python tuple
>>> a = ("tomato, potato, garlic, ginger, pumpkin")
>>> print(a)
tomato, potato, garlic, ginger, pumpkin
>>> #This is a dictionary
>>> a = {"fruit" : "tomato", "veg: potato", "veg" : "garlic",
"veg" : "ginger", "veg" : "pumpkin"}
SyntaxError: invalid syntax
>>> a = {"fruit" : "tomato", "veg": "potato", "veg" : "garlic",
"veg" : "ginger", "veg" : "pumpkin"}
>>> print(a)
{'fruit': 'tomato', 'veg': 'pumpkin'}
>>> a = {"fruit" : "tomato", "veg: potato", "veg1" : "garlic",
"veg2" : "ginger", "veg3" : "pumpkin"}
SyntaxError: invalid syntax
>>> a = {"fruit" : "tomato", "veg": "potato", "veg1" : "garlic",
"veg2" : "ginger", "veg3" : "pumpkin"}
>>> print(a)
{'fruit': 'tomato', 'veg': 'potato', 'veg1': 'garlic', 'veg2': 'ginger',
'veg3': 'pumpkin'}
```

In the above I have turned a string into different datatypes. In the dictionary section of the code, you will see some errors. One error is because of a missing quote marks while the other error is because of similar dictionary names. Dictionaries are important as they allow users to store their important data in the form of pairs. They are used in a number of ways.

Python Strings

The first data type is Python strings. Most of the Python programs have to collect and process the data, store it, and use it. One of the most common datatypes is known as strings. They appear to be simple at first glance, however they can be used in several ways. A string is popularly written in the form of characters. Anything that comes inside the quotation marks is dubbed as a string. You can use single or double quotes to create a string. The flexibility of using different types of quote marks is not without reason. It serves several purposes. See that in the following code snippet.

While single quotes allow you to write the code easily, double quotes allow you to use apostrophes in the text. In the following example, you will learn to use both types of quotes and their dos and don'ts.

```
>>> a = "I am learning Python."
>>> print(a)
I am learning Python.
>>> a = 'I am learning Python.'
>>> print(a)
I am learning Python.
>>> a = "I am learning Tack's book on Python."
>>> print(a)
I am learning Tack's book on Python.
```

>>> a = 'I am learning Tacky's book on Python.'

SyntaxError: invalid syntax

>>>

Strings are very interesting if you get a full grasp of the concept. You can change the text into lower and upper texts. I will use the same string example and experiment on it to see how we can change its case.

>>> a = "I am learning Python."

>>> print(a.title())

I Am Learning Python.

>>> print(a.upper())

I AM LEARNING PYTHON

>>> print(a.lower())

i am learning python.

>>>

One of the easiest tasks is changing the case as you have seen. There are three keywords: upper, lower, and title cases to change any string you have created for your code. You can see in the code that all the three keywords are accompanied by () brackets. It is called a method. A method can be defined as a kind of action that Python performs on a certain piece of data. Even a character as little as a dot is meaningful in Python coding. The dot that comes after the string's name directs Python to deploy the method, which can be the title, lower, upper cases. Each method has parenthesis at the end to fill in additional information. I have left the parenthesis empty in the above-mentioned code because I did not have to fill it in with additional information. However, in the next few chapters, I will explain how you can use the parenthesis to perform different types of tasks. They are quite interesting if you can use it in the right way.

Out of all the methods, the lower() method is specifically used to store data in Python programs. You might have browsed a website that asked you to write in small letters when you sought to enter some information on the database. Still, you very possibly might have entered the information in a capital case. The lower() method helps convert the strings into the lower case, even if a user like you entered the information in the capital case.

Many Python programs invite data for storage purposes and then use it. Sometimes you have two or more strings that you have to combine into one. The process is known as string concatenation. For example, you can combine the name of the state and the country's name after you receive them independently. The odds are high that you invite the users' information separately because usually you have to create two columns on your interface to facilitate the users. When you receive them separately, you can combine them with a simple method. See the following example.

```
>>> state_name = "california"
>>> country_name = "United States"
>>> Location_info = state_name + " " + country_name
>>> print(Location_info)
california United States
>>>
```

You can see that there is something wrong with the code. The display is good, but it is not neat. We can add a comma to the code and see how we can use it. From here, I will shift from Python IDLE to Python text editor to give you a feel of how you will write a program. Let us see how to switch from Python IDLE to the text editor.

The first step is to open Python IDLE or interpreter. Go to the File menu and click New File. A new window will pop up on your computer screen. This is a Python text editor. You can write the code on it. When you are done writing the code, you should click on Run on the top menu bar. The editor will ask you to save the code first and then run it. You need to save the code to your desired location and Python will run your code. One important point to note is that when you run the code, a new window of Python IDLE will pop up to display the result of the code. In the next code samples, you will see the code that is written in Python editor first, and attached to its tail will be the result of the code. The second result will start from the word Restart. This is how you will easily learn it and practice it on your computer system. Let us jump to the Python editor now.

```
state_name = "California"
country_name = "United States"
Location_info = state_name + " , " + country_name
print(Location_info)
= RESTART: C:/Users/saifia computers/Desktop/sample.py
California, United States
>>>
```

This code is neat and clean as I have added a comma to it. The most important thing to learn from this code sample is the plus operator used to combine the two strings. We can concatenate more than two strings as well. I will now add the name of the place to the concatenated string.

```
place_name = "Silicon Valley"
state_name = "California"
country_name = "United States"
location_info = place_name + " , " + state_name + " , " +
country_name
print(location_info)
= RESTART: C:/Users/saifia computers/Desktop/sample.py
Silicon Valley, California , United States
>>>
```

I will now use the same code to display a message to the user after he has entered his location information.

```
place_name = "Silicon Valley"
state_name = "California"
country_name = "United States"
location_info = place_name + " , " + state_name + " , " +
country_name
print("Hi, I want to visit " + location_info.title() + " in the next
month.")
= RESTART: C:/Users/saifia computers/Desktop/sample.py
```

Hi, I want to visit Silicon Valley, California, United States in the next month.

>>>

Let change the case of the strings and see how it works in the program.

```
place_name = "Silicon Valley"
state_name = "California"
country_name = "United States"
location_info = place_name + " , " + state_name + " , " +
country_name
print("Hi, I want to visit " + location_info.upper() + " in the
next month.")
print("Hi, I want to visit " + location_info.lower() + " in the
next month.")
= RESTART: C:/Users/saifia computers/Desktop/sample.py
```

Hi, I want to visit SILICON VALLEY, CALIFORNIA, UNITED STATES in the next month.

Hi, I want to visit silicon valley, california, united states in the next month.

>>>

You always have the option of creating a concatenated string and storing it in a variable so that you can use it later on as per your needs.

```
place_name = "Silicon Valley"
state_name = "California"
```

```
country_name = "United States"
location_info = place_name + " , " + state_name + " , " +
country_name
info = "Hi, I want to visit " + location_info.title() + " in the next
month."
print(info)
= RESTART: C:/Users/saifia computers/Desktop/sample.py
Hi, I want to visit Silicon Valley , California , United States in
the next month.
>>>
```

Python allows you to neatly format your strings by adding tabs, spaces and other symbols.

```
place_name = "Silicon Valley"
state_name = "California"
country_name = "United States"
location_info = place_name + " , " + state_name + " , " +
country_name
info = "\tHi, I want to visit " + location_info.title() + "\t in the
next month."
print(info)
= RESTART: C:/Users/saifia computers/Desktop/sample.py
Hi, I want to visit Silicon Valley , California , United States
in the next month.
>>>
```

The tab feature has worked perfectly. Now I will use the \n feature to start each word of the sentence on a new line.

```
place_name = "Silicon Valley"
state_name = "California"
country_name = "United States"
location_info = place_name + " , " + state_name + " , " +
country_name
info = "\nHi, \nI \nwant \nto \nvisit " + location_info.title() + "
\nin the \nnext month."
print(info)
= RESTART: C:/Users/saifia computers/Desktop/sample.py
Hi,
I
want
to
visit Silicon Valley, California, United States
in the
next month.
>>>
```

Python Numbers

Numbers are more often used in programming to do calculations or store data. For example, if you are developing a Python game, you need to keep the scores calculated. Python integers are the simplest form of numbers that you can use. I will do some calculations by using different mathematical operators.

```
a = 3 + 6
print(a)
a = 10 - 5
print(a)
a = 3 * 6
print(a)
a = 18 / 6
print(a)
a = 3 ** 6
print(a)
a = 15 ** 6
print(a)
= RESTART: C:/Users/saifia computers/Desktop/sample.py
9
5
18
3.0
729
11390625
>>>
```

In the next example, I will use multiple operators to see how Python maintains the order of mathematics.

```
a = 3 + 6 * 18
print(a)
a = 10 - 5 + 45
print(a)
a = 3 * 6 + 50 / 30
print(a)
a = 18 / 6 * 50
print(a)
a = (3 * 6 )- 23
print(a)
a = (15 ** 6) + 100
print(a)
= RESTART: C:/Users/saifia computers/Desktop/sample.py
111
50
19.666666666666668
150.0
-5
11390725
>>>
```

The next number type is float. This is the decimal form of integer. See how to use them.

```
a = 3.0 + 6.344 * 18.234
print(a)
a = 10.1 - 5.56 + 45.22
print(a)
a = 3.45 * 6.3 + 50.09 / 30.1
print(a)
a = 18.22 / 6.1 * 50.89
print(a)
a = (3.21 * 6.23 )- 23.22
print(a)
a = (15.123 ** 6.23) + 100.456
print(a)
= RESTART: C:/Users/saifia computers/Desktop/sample.py
118.67649600000001
49.76
23.399119601328902
152.00259016393443
-3.2216999999999985
22343252.55463075
>>>
```

When you mix up the datatypes without proper procedure, you get an error in return. For example, you have to mix up date with day to display a string statement. This will trigger an error if you do not fill in the code with the right datatype and through the right process.

```
place_name = "Silicon Valley"
state_name = "California"
country_name = "United States"
location_info = place_name + " , " + state_name + " , " +
country_name
date = 4
info = "Hi, I want to visit " + location_info.title() + " in the next
month on" + date + " th."
print(info)
= RESTART: C:/Users/saifia computers/Desktop/sample.py
Traceback (most recent call last):
  File "C:/Users/saifia computers/Desktop/sample.py", line 6, in
<module>
    info = "Hi, I want to visit " + location_info.title() + " in the
next month on" + date + " th."
TypeError: can only concatenate str (not "int") to str
>>>
```

The error is a type error. Python is unable to recognize the information you have put in. In simple words, the wrong method to fill in the code has confused Python. So, you have to turn the integer into a string first to display it in the right way. The technique is simple, but you will have to memorize it.

```
place_name = "Silicon Valley"
state_name = "California"
country_name = "United States"
location_info = place_name + " , " + state_name + " , " +
country_name
date = 4
info = "Hi, I want to visit " + location_info.title() + " on the " +
str(date) + "the of July"
print(info)
= RESTART: C:/Users/saifia computers/Desktop/sample.py
Hi, I want to visit Silicon Valley, California, United States on
the 4th of July
>>>
```

I have told python that I have to add an integer to the string statement.

Chapter Three

Python Lists and Tuples

This chapter will walk you through the concept of Python lists. I will explain what Python lists are and how you can use them in Python programs. Python lists are one of the most amazing features of Python programming. They allow you to fill in loads of information in a succinct manner. They allow you to pack up tons of information in an easy-to-access format. You can add millions of items to Python lists. Python lists are considered one of the robust features of Python programming.

A Python list is packed up with a streak of items that are adjusted in a specific order. A list can be filled with alphabets and digits. As a list may contain more than one element, the traditional naming practice for lists suggests that you give them a plural name. Let us assume that you are developing a game where a player has to set up an office with necessary items and sell the office to the highest bidder.

```
officeitems = ['printer', 'scanner', 'fan', 'table', 'chair', 'computer
system', 'table lights']
print(officeitems)
= RESTART: C:/Users/saifia computers/Desktop/sample.py
```

['printer', 'scanner', 'fan', 'table', 'chair', 'computer system', 'table lights']

>>>

The output is alright, except that you do not want your game users to see this output. It should be in an easy-to-digest form. Rather than printing the complete list, you can access certain elements in the list by a simple method. For example, the player in your game wants to see which item has been included in the office set up. To see that he should be able to access different items in the list. Here is the method you can include in your program to help your players confirm the inclusion of different items.

```
officeitems = ['printer', 'scanner', 'fan', 'table', 'chair', 'computer system', 'table lights']
print(officeitems[0])
print(officeitems[2])
print(officeitems[4])
print(officeitems[5])
print(officeitems[6])
= RESTART: C:/Users/saifia computers/Desktop/sample.py
printer
fan
chair
computer system
table lights
>>>
```

When you are writing the code for your game, you may run into a serious problem. Your player may want to access the item no 10 in the list, which does not exist in the first place as there are only seven items on the list. When the player tries to do that, the result will be an index error.

officeitems = ['printer', 'scanner', 'fan', 'table', 'chair', 'computer system', 'table lights']

print(officeitems[10])

= RESTART: C:/Users/saifia computers/Desktop/sample.py

Traceback (most recent call last):

  File "C:/Users/saifia computers/Desktop/sample.py", line 2, in <module>

    print(officeitems[10])

IndexError: list index out of range

>>>

You can deploy string methods to make the lists look neat and clean. I will use the title, lower and upper case methods to format the items from the list.

officeitems = ['printer', 'scanner', 'fan', 'table', 'chair', 'computer system', 'table lights']

print(officeitems[0].title())

print(officeitems[1].upper())

print(officeitems[2].lower())

= RESTART: C:/Users/saifia computers/Desktop/sample.py

Printer

SCANNER

fan

>>>

One important point to note regarding lists is that the first item in the list tends to start from zero. If you fill it in with 1, it means you are trying to access the second item on the list. If you want to access the fifth item on the list, you will have to use index number 3. There is another way to access items on the list. You can access the item by using negative indices. In the following example, I will access items both from positive and negative indices.

```
officeitems = ['printer', 'scanner', 'fan', 'table', 'chair', 'computer
system', 'table lights']
print(officeitems[0])
print(officeitems[1])
print(officeitems[2])
print(officeitems[-1])
print(officeitems[-2])
print(officeitems[-3])
= RESTART: C:/Users/saifia computers/Desktop/sample.py
printer
scanner
fan
table lights
```

computer system

chair

>>>

While the positive index starts from the left side, the negative index starts from the right side. It will pick the values from the end of the list and display them to the user.

Let us make the game more interesting by adding statements and using items from the list to build those statements. Each time your player buys something from the market and adds it to the office, he will receive a message on the screen that informs him how much he has achieved. I will use individual values from the list and apply the method of concatenation to create a message.

```
officeitems = ['printer', 'scanner', 'fan', 'table', 'chair', 'computer system', 'table lights']
comment = "Dear player! You have successfully purchased a " + officeitems[2].title() + "."
print(comment)
comment = "Dear player! You have successfully purchased a " + officeitems[0].upper() + "."
print(comment)
comment = "Dear player! You have successfully purchased a " + officeitems[2].lower() + "."
print(comment)
= RESTART: C:/Users/saifia computers/Desktop/sample.py
```

Dear player! You have successfully purchased a Fan.

Dear player! You have successfully purchased a PRINTER.

Dear player! You have successfully purchased a fan.

>>>

You can use the same items in different ways. All it needs a pinch of creativity. When the player has installed the items in the office, you can display a message on the screen to show that the items are operational.

officeitems = ['printer', 'scanner', 'fan', 'table', 'chair', 'computer system', 'table lights']

comment = "Dear player! The " + officeitems[2].title() + " is operational."

print(comment)

comment = "Dear player! The " + officeitems[0].title() + " is operational."

print(comment)

comment = "Dear player! The " + officeitems[6].title() + " are operational."

print(comment)

= RESTART: C:/Users/saifia computers/Desktop/sample.py

Dear player! The Fan is operational.

Dear player! The Printer is operational.

Dear player! The Table Lights are operational.

>>>

Modifying Lists

When you have created a list, you can easily change its items, add more items to it, and remove certain items. In this sense, lists are very flexible. Most of the lists that you create are dynamic. You can offer your player a choice to add different items to your list and remove items from the list of office items to increase or decrease the office's value. The faster he sells or the bigger he sells matter for the overall gaming score of the player.

officeitems = ['printer', 'scanner', 'fan', 'table', 'chair', 'computer system', 'table lights']

print(officeitems)

I will change the value of different items at different indices

officeitems[0] – 'water dispenser'

print(officeitems)

= RESTART: C:/Users/saifia computers/Desktop/sample.py

['printer', 'scanner', 'fan', 'table', 'chair', 'computer system', 'table lights']

['water dispenser', 'scanner', 'fan', 'table', 'chair', 'computer system', 'table lights']

>>>

Append Method

In the first line, I have displayed the original list. In the next line of code, I will change the first item's value and redisplay the list. The player has successfully replaced the item to boost the sale value of the office. You also can allow your player to keep adding more items to the office to beef up the value. One of the easiest and the most amazing way to add items to a list is by using the append method. This method is the simplest of adding new elements to a list. When you apply the append method, the element you want to add will be added to the end of the list. The player does not have a choice to add it to his favorite index.

```
officeitems = ['printer', 'scanner', 'fan', 'table', 'chair', 'computer system', 'table lights']
print(officeitems)
officeitems.append('water dispenser')
print(officeitems)
officeitems.append('multimedia projector')
print(officeitems)
officeitems.append('air conditioner')
print(officeitems)
officeitems.append('laptop')
print(officeitems)
= RESTART: C:/Users/saifia computers/Desktop/sample.py
['printer', 'scanner', 'fan', 'table', 'chair', 'computer system', 'table lights']
['printer', 'scanner', 'fan', 'table', 'chair', 'computer system', 'table lights', 'water dispenser']
```

['printer', 'scanner', 'fan', 'table', 'chair', 'computer system', 'table lights', 'water dispenser', 'multimedia projector']

['printer', 'scanner', 'fan', 'table', 'chair', 'computer system', 'table lights', 'water dispenser', 'multimedia projector', 'air conditioner']

['printer', 'scanner', 'fan', 'table', 'chair', 'computer system', 'table lights', 'water dispenser', 'multimedia projector', 'air conditioner', 'laptop']

>>>

The append method helps you build lists in perfect order. This is the most efficient way to build lists in a perfectly dynamic way. You can even start appending elements to an empty list. This is how your player will have more freedom to start right from scratch. He will see an empty office and equip it with the items he wants to add to it.

While the append method adds elements to the end of your lists, you can use the insert method to add items to the position of your choice. The first you need to do is to specify the index of each new element. See the following example.

```
officeitems = ['printer', 'scanner', 'fan', 'table', 'chair', 'computer system', 'table lights']
print(officeitems)
officeitems.insert(0, 'air conditioner')
print(officeitems)
officeitems.insert(2, 'multimedia projector')
```

```
print(officeitems)
officeitems.insert(3, 'water dispenser')
print(officeitems)
= RESTART: C:/Users/saifia computers/Desktop/sample.py
['printer', 'scanner', 'fan', 'table', 'chair', 'computer system', 'table
lights']
['air conditioner', 'printer', 'scanner', 'fan', 'table', 'chair',
'computer system', 'table lights']
['air conditioner', 'printer', 'multimedia projector', 'scanner', 'fan',
'table', 'chair', 'computer system', 'table lights']
['air conditioner', 'printer', 'multimedia projector', 'water
dispenser', 'scanner', 'fan', 'table', 'chair', 'computer system',
'table lights']
>>>
```

Del Method

There may be occasions in the game when a player wants to remove certain items from the office to adjust the office to his desires. You can easily remove different items from a list by a simple method. The first method is that of the del statement. Let us check how you can add this method to your code to make the game more interactive.

```
officeitems = ['printer', 'scanner', 'fan', 'table', 'chair', 'computer
system', 'table lights']
print(officeitems)
del officeitems[0]
```

```
print(officeitems)
del officeitems[1]
print(officeitems)
del officeitems[2]
print(officeitems)
= RESTART: C:/Users/saifia computers/Desktop/sample.py
['printer', 'scanner', 'fan', 'table', 'chair', 'computer system', 'table lights']
['scanner', 'fan', 'table', 'chair', 'computer system', 'table lights']
['scanner', 'table', 'chair', 'computer system', 'table lights']
['scanner', 'table', 'computer system', 'table lights']
>>>
```

Pop Method

While the del method demands from you that you mention the index number, you always have the choice to use another method, the pop() method, to remove items from your lists. This is helpful if you want to give your players the freedom to randomly remove items from the office setup.

The pop() method tends to eject items from the end of the list. However, you can use the item later on. This is why the pop() method is different from the del() method. Imagine that the office items are stacked up one upon another and you get the opportunity to pick and throw out from the top one by one. This is how the pop() method works.

I will use the pop() method until the list stands empty to show how a player can empty an office off the items if he wants to.

```
officeitems = ['printer', 'scanner', 'fan', 'table', 'chair', 'computer
system', 'table lights']
print(officeitems)
popped_officeitems = officeitems.pop()
print(officeitems)
print(popped_officeitems)
popped_officeitems = officeitems.pop()
print(officeitems)
print(popped_officeitems)
popped_officeitems = officeitems.pop()
print(officeitems)
print(popped_officeitems)
popped_officeitems = officeitems.pop()
print(officeitems)
print(popped_officeitems)
popped_officeitems = officeitems.pop()
print(officeitems)
print(popped_officeitems)
popped_officeitems = officeitems.pop()
print(officeitems)
print(popped_officeitems)
```

popped_officeitems = officeitems.pop()

print(officeitems)

print(popped_officeitems)

= RESTART: C:/Users/saifia computers/Desktop/sample.py

['printer', 'scanner', 'fan', 'table', 'chair', 'computer system', 'table lights']

['printer', 'scanner', 'fan', 'table', 'chair', 'computer system']

table lights

['printer', 'scanner', 'fan', 'table', 'chair']

computer system

['printer', 'scanner', 'fan', 'table']

chair

['printer', 'scanner', 'fan']

table

['printer', 'scanner']

fan

['printer']

scanner

[]

printer

>>>

Once there are no more items in the list but you still use the pop() method, it will return an error that will look like the following.

Traceback (most recent call last):

    File "C:/Users/saifia computers/Desktop/sample.py", line 24, in <module>

    popped_officeitems = officeitems.pop()

IndexError: pop from empty list

In the following section, I will show you how you can use the popped item in the code. If you want your player to explain to his boss why he removed an item from the item, you can add another line of code to your program.

officeitems = ['printer', 'scanner', 'fan', 'table', 'chair', 'computer system', 'table lights']

print(officeitems)

popped_officeitems = officeitems.pop()

print("I have sold " + popped_officeitems.title() + " because it was not adding the desired value to the office.")

= RESTART: C:/Users/saifia computers/Desktop/sample.py

['printer', 'scanner', 'fan', 'table', 'chair', 'computer system', 'table lights']

I have sold Table Lights because it was not adding the desired value to the office.

>>>

Unlike what most people think, the pop() method allows you to remove items from a list at specific positions of your choice. You have to fill in the parenthesis with the desired index number.

```
officeitems = ['printer', 'scanner', 'fan', 'table', 'chair', 'computer
system', 'table lights']

print(officeitems)

popped_officeitems = officeitems.pop(3)

print("I have sold the " + popped_officeitems.title() + " because
it was not adding the desired value to the office.")
```

= RESTART: C:/Users/saifia computers/Desktop/sample.py

['printer', 'scanner', 'fan', 'table', 'chair', 'computer system', 'table
lights']

I have sold the Table because it was not adding the desired
value to the office.

>>>

Remove Method

Another method to remove items from a list by using the remove
method. Many times you do not know the specific position of a value
that you want to remove. In that case, you can remove the item by
using the value of that item. To do that you have to fill in the
parenthesis of the remove() method with the value.

```
officeitems = ['printer', 'scanner', 'fan', 'table', 'chair', 'computer
system', 'table lights']

print(officeitems)

officeitems.remove('scanner')

print(officeitems)

officeitems.remove('table')
```

print(officeitems)

= RESTART: C:/Users/saifia computers/Desktop/sample.py

['printer', 'scanner', 'fan', 'table', 'chair', 'computer system', 'table lights']

['printer', 'fan', 'table', 'chair', 'computer system', 'table lights']

['printer', 'fan', 'chair', 'computer system', 'table lights']

>>>

Just like you used the popped value later on in the code, you can also use the removed value from the item.

officeitems = ['printer', 'scanner', 'fan', 'table', 'chair', 'computer system', 'table lights']

print(officeitems)

removeditem = 'scanner'

officeitems.remove(removeditem)

print("I have sold the " + removeditem.title() + " because it was not adding the desired value to the office.")

= RESTART: C:/Users/saifia computers/Desktop/sample.py

['printer', 'scanner', 'fan', 'table', 'chair', 'computer system', 'table lights']

I have sold the Scanner because it was not adding the desired value to the office.

>>>

List Organization

More often when you create lists, they flow in a kind of unpredictable order. You cannot always control the order in which the users provide data to the program. However, you can bring that information into perfect order later on. It may happen more often than you want to make the information presentable. This is the reason you should bring it into perfect order. There are several ways by which you can order lists in Python.

The sort() Method

The sort method of Python makes it fun to sort a list. I will use the same list of officeitems and experiment on it to see how the list gets organized. The sort() method sorts lists in an alphabetical order.

```
officeitems = ['printer', 'scanner', 'fan', 'table', 'table lights']
print(officeitems)
officeitems.sort()
print(officeitems)
= RESTART: C:/Users/saifia computers/Desktop/sample.py
['printer', 'scanner', 'fan', 'table', 'table lights']
['fan', 'printer', 'scanner', 'table', 'table lights']
>>>
```

The sort() method has changed the list into a perfect alphabetical order. You cannot revert to the original order once you have sorted your list. The sort() can also be used to order the list in the reverse alphabetical order.

```
officeitems = ['printer', 'scanner', 'fan', 'table', 'table lights']
print(officeitems)
officeitems.sort(reverse=True)
print(officeitems)
= RESTART: C:/Users/saifia computers/Desktop/sample.py
['printer', 'scanner', 'fan', 'table', 'table lights']
['table lights', 'table', 'scanner', 'printer', 'fan']
>>>
```

Coupled with the sort() method is the sorted() function. While the sort() method permanently reorders a list, the sorted() function makes temporary changes.

```
officeitems = ['printer', 'scanner', 'fan', 'table', 'table lights']
print(officeitems)
print(sorted(officeitems))
print(officeitems)
= RESTART: C:/Users/saifia computers/Desktop/sample.py
['printer', 'scanner', 'fan', 'table', 'table lights']
['fan', 'printer', 'scanner', 'table', 'table lights']
['printer', 'scanner', 'fan', 'table', 'table lights']
>>>
```

You can see that the sorted() function temporarily changed the order of the list. When I printed the list without the sorted() function, it comes back into its original order.

Index Errors

As errors are common in coding, you may run into index errors in lists. One of the most common types of errors with lists is the index error. You may confront this type of error more often when you work on lists. However, you can easily avoid that if you know at which point the index starts. Let us see first how the error message looks like.

officeitems = ['printer', 'scanner', 'fan', 'table', 'table lights']

print(officeitems[5])

= RESTART: C:/Users/saifia computers/Desktop/sample.py

Traceback (most recent call last):

  File "C:/Users/saifia computers/Desktop/sample.py", line 2, in <module>

    print(officeitems[5])

IndexError: list index out of range

>>>

The list contains five items, but when I invoke the index number 5, I get an error message. Just as for strings, the index for lists also starts at zero.

Index errors come up more often if the list is a long one. The best practice to work with long lists is to know the exact length of the list. Once you know the length, you can sort out each item's index number in the list. See the following method to check the length of the list.

officeitems = ['printer', 'scanner', 'fan', 'table', 'table lights']

len(officeitems)

Create A Loop

Python lists can be operated with loops. Coming back to the game. If you want your player to have the option of displaying all the items that he has set up in his office, you can run a loop through your list. This is helpful if you have added another character to your game who asks the player about the total number of items that he has bought for the office. Each item in the list will be neatly displayed. The *for* loop in Python will repeat the same action with each item.

I will use the same list of office items and print each item by looping the list with a for loop. Let us now create and build a *for* loop to print out each item you have bought for the office.

```
officeitems = ['printer', 'scanner', 'fan', 'table', 'table lights']
for officeitem in officeitems:
    print(officeitem)
= RESTART: C:/Users/saifia computers/Desktop/sample.py
printer
scanner
fan
table
table lights
>>>
```

Python *for* loop has looped through and printed each item on the list. When you are writing this code, you may hit an error which can be hard to explain because there will be no exact error message on the interpreter screen. See the following example.

```
officeitems = ['printer', 'scanner', 'fan', 'table', 'table lights']
for officeitem in officeitems:
    print(officeitems)
= RESTART: C:/Users/saifia computers/Desktop/sample.py
['printer', 'scanner', 'fan', 'table', 'table lights']
['printer', 'scanner', 'fan', 'table', 'table lights']
['printer', 'scanner', 'fan', 'table', 'table lights']
['printer', 'scanner', 'fan', 'table', 'table lights']
['printer', 'scanner', 'fan', 'table', 'table lights']
>>>
```

All I did was to add an s to officeitem in the last line of code. Python interpreted it differently and looped through the entire list and displayed it repetitively. Instead of getting an error message, Python changes the results.

What exactly I did in the code. In the first line of code, I have defined a list, namely officeitems. In the next line, I have defined a *for* loop. This line instructs Python to pick a name from the list and store it in the newly created variable officeitem. It is not necessary to name a variable in this way, but it is easy to remember. You can name it as you like. In the next line, I told Python to print each name that I had stored in the new variable. Python repeats lines for each item in the list. To kill the confusion about the name of the variable, I will now change the variable's name.

```
officeitems = ['printer', 'scanner', 'fan', 'table', 'table lights']
for things in officeitems:
    print(things)
= RESTART: C:/Users/saifia computers/Desktop/sample.py
printer
scanner
fan
table
table lights
>>>
```

Looping is an important concept in computer programming because it is used to automate some recitative tasks. If your list is packed up with a million items, Python loops will repeat the steps a million times and in a very fast manner.

The Python *for* loop is amazing because it allows you to experiment with the office items quickly. You have to set the code right and the entire list will be fully automated. I will now take each item from the list and display a message on the Python interpreter screen. If you want your player to tell his boss he has purchased each item at a discount price and from a quality production house, you can slightly change the code and display the message most uniquely.

```
officeitems = ['printer', 'scanner', 'fan', 'table', 'table lights']
```

```
for officeitem in officeitems:
    print("I have purchased the " + officeitem.lower() + " at a
discount price from TopQuality Productions.")
```

= RESTART: C:/Users/saifia computers/Desktop/sample.py

I have purchased the printer at a discount price from TopQuality Productions.

I have purchased the scanner at a discount price from TopQuality Productions.

I have purchased the fan at a discount price from TopQuality Productions.

I have purchased the table at a discount price from TopQuality Productions.

I have purchased the table lights at a discount price from TopQuality Productions.

\>\>\>

So, this is getting interesting now. This is how you can develop your game in a brilliantly interactive manner. If you want the player to speak more than one line, you can pair up more sentences to the reply. Each line will be executed in the order you write it in the code. I will now add a second line of code to the response of the player.

```
officeitems = ['printer', 'scanner', 'fan', 'table', 'table lights']
for officeitem in officeitems:
    print("I have purchased the " + officeitem.lower() + " at a
discount price from TopQuality Productions.")
```

```
    print ("I hope the " + officeitem.lower() + " will add more
value to the office.")
```

= RESTART: C:/Users/saifia computers/Desktop/sample.py

I have purchased the printer at a discount price from TopQuality Productions.

I hope the printer will add more value to the office.

I have purchased the scanner at a discount price from TopQuality Productions.

I hope the scanner will add more value to the office.

I have purchased the fan at a discount price from TopQuality Productions.

I hope the fan will add more value to the office.

I have purchased the table at a discount price from TopQuality Productions.

I hope the table will add more value to the office.

I have purchased the table lights at a discount price from TopQuality Productions.

I hope the table lights will add more value to the office.

>>>

This is how you can add a hundred lines if your program or game requires that. You also can add a finishing note to the end of a block of code. The finishing block of code executes without repetition. I will now add a reply from the boss in the game who has heard what the player said about purchasing items.

```
officeitems = ['printer', 'scanner', 'fan', 'table', 'table lights']
for officeitem in officeitems:
    print("I have purchased the " + officeitem.lower() + " at a discount price from TopQuality Productions.")
    print ("I hope the " + officeitem.lower() + " will add more value to the office.")
print("Thanks for making the purchase. Hope you will be able to sell out the office this month. After all, you won't like to be deprived of your bonus.")
```

= RESTART: C:/Users/saifia computers/Desktop/sample.py

I have purchased the printer at a discount price from TopQuality Productions.

I hope the printer will add more value to the office.

I have purchased the scanner at a discount price from TopQuality Productions.

I hope the scanner will add more value to the office.

I have purchased the fan at a discount price from TopQuality Productions.

I hope the fan will add more value to the office.

I have purchased the table at a discount price from TopQuality Productions.

I hope the table will add more value to the office.

I have purchased the table lights at a discount price from TopQuality Productions.

I hope the table lights will add more value to the office.

Thanks for making the purchase. Hope you will be able to sell out the office this month. After all, you won't like to be deprived of your bonus.

>>>

All I did was to remove the space before the print statement by which I want to end the *for* loop. This explains how crucial a role spaces play in Python programming. You miss out on an indentation and you will see an error on the screen.

```
officeitems = ['printer', 'scanner', 'fan', 'table', 'table lights']
for officeitem in officeitems:
print(officeitem)
Expected an indented block
```

List Slicing

You can slice a list to work with a portion of a list. This is helpful if you are building a long list of items and you have to work only with a handful of items. I will use the same list for slicing.

```
officeitems = ['printer', 'scanner', 'fan', 'table', 'table lights']
print(officeitems[1:4])
= RESTART: C:/Users/saifia computers/Desktop/sample.py
['scanner', 'fan', 'table']
>>>
```

The result contains only the items that I have sliced out of the original list. The output comes in the form of the original structure of the list.

The sliced part of the list can also be named as a subset of the list. If you omit the index's start, the subset of the list will start from the first item.

```
officeitems = ['printer', 'scanner', 'fan', 'table', 'table lights']
print(officeitems[:4])
= RESTART: C:/Users/saifia computers/Desktop/sample.py
['printer', 'scanner', 'fan', 'table']
>>>
```

Similarly, you can omit the second half of the range index.

```
officeitems = ['printer', 'scanner', 'fan', 'table', 'table lights']
print(officeitems[2:])
– RESTART: C:/Users/saifia computers/Desktop/sample.py
['fan', 'table', 'table lights']
>>>
```

The negative indexing is also available for Python lists.

```
officeitems = ['printer', 'scanner', 'fan', 'table', 'table lights']
print(officeitems[-2:])
= RESTART: C:/Users/saifia computers/Desktop/sample.py
['table', 'table lights']
>>>
```

You also can loop through the subset of a list or the slice of a list just like we did with a complete list.

```
officeitems = ['printer', 'scanner', 'fan', 'table', 'table lights']
```

```
print("Here are the items that have cost double the value of
others.")
for officeitem in officeitems[:4]:
    print(officeitem.title())
= RESTART: C:/Users/saifia computers/Desktop/sample.py
```
Here are the items that have cost double the value of others.

Printer

Scanner

Fan

Table

>>>

Copying

You can create a copy of the list based on the original list. This is helpful if you have packed up customer data in a list and you want to save it elsewhere to secure it in the wake of data breaches or any other kind of cyberattack. The most common way of making a copy of the list is to create a slice with no starting or ending values. This slice instructs Python to slice the list right from the starting value to the ending value. This is how you end up creating a copy of your list.

```
officeitems = ['printer', 'scanner', 'fan', 'table', 'table lights']
c_officeitems = officeitems[:]
print("Here is the list of items that I have purchased.")
print(officeitems)
```

```
print("\nHere is the exact copy of the same items.")
print(c_officeitems)
= RESTART: C:/Users/saifia computers/Desktop/sample.py
Here is the list of items that I have purchased.
['printer', 'scanner', 'fan', 'table', 'table lights']
Here is the exact copy of the same items.
['printer', 'scanner', 'fan', 'table', 'table lights']
>>>
```

Let us now check if you really have two lists and that if removing or modifying one list will affect the copied list or not.

```
officeitems = ['printer', 'scanner', 'fan', 'table', 'table lights']
c_officeitems = officeitems[:]
officeitems.append('computer system')
c_officeitems.append('blinds')
print("Here is the list of items that I have purchased.")
print(officeitems)
print("\nHere is the new list of office items.")
print(c_officeitems)
= RESTART: C:/Users/saifia computers/Desktop/sample.py
Here is the list of items that I have purchased.
['printer', 'scanner', 'fan', 'table', 'table lights', 'computer system']
Here is the new list of office items.
['printer', 'scanner', 'fan', 'table', 'table lights', 'blinds']
>>>
```

You can see that the two lists exist independently and that you can modify them separately. This is helpful if you are building data lists for a big financial institution.

You may create a copy of the list without using the slice method but you will not be able to modify the two lists independently of each other. They will not be able to exist independently of each other.

officeitems = ['printer', 'scanner', 'fan', 'table', 'table lights']

c_officeitems = officeitems

officeitems.append('computer system')

c_officeitems.append('blinds')

print("Here is the list of items that I have purchased.")

print(officeitems)

print("\nHere is the new list of office items.")

print(c_officeitems)

= RESTART: C:/Users/saifia computers/Desktop/sample.py

Here is the list of items that I have purchased.

['printer', 'scanner', 'fan', 'table', 'table lights', 'computer system', 'blinds']

Here is the new list of office items.

['printer', 'scanner', 'fan', 'table', 'table lights', 'computer system', 'blinds']

>>>

You can see that each list retained both newly added items. I will now add one item to one list only and see if the copied list retains that item or not.

officeitems = ['printer', 'scanner', 'fan', 'table', 'table lights']

c_officeitems = officeitems

officeitems.append('computer system')

print("Here is the list of items that I have purchased.")

print(officeitems)

print("\nHere is the new list of office items.")

print(c_officeitems)

= RESTART: C:/Users/saifia computers/Desktop/sample.py

Here is the list of items that I have purchased.

['printer', 'scanner', 'fan', 'table', 'table lights', 'computer system']

Here is the new list of office items.

['printer', 'scanner', 'fan', 'table', 'table lights', 'computer system']

>>>

So, as you can see that simply copying a list will not do the magic for you. Slicing helps you make the copy you desire for.

Python Tuples

While lists can be modified and are flexible, Python tuples are the opposite. Once you have created a tuple, you cannot change it. A tuple is similar to a list in the sense that you can fill it up with millions of items but at the same time, it is different from a list in the sense that you cannot add, remove or change the items in a tuple. This is helpful if you want to create a list that you do not want to be changed. The values in a tuple that cannot be changed are labeled as immutable in Python. So, you can label a rigid list or a tuple as an immutable list.

In appearance, a tuple looks mostly like a list except that you have to enclose the tuple items inside square brackets. Once you have created a tuple, you can easily access the tuples' items by using the index number. I will add a new feature to the game by creating a list of home items that the same player needs to sell. The difference is that the player cannot change the items of the house except in exceptional circumstances. He has to sell the house the way it is at the moment. He cannot add more items or remove the existing ones to tune the house's value as per the expectations and demands of buyers.

```
homeitems = ('dining table', 'cooking range', 'washing machine',
'refrigerator', 'air conditioner')
print(homeitems)
= RESTART: C:/Users/saifia computers/Desktop/sample.py
('dining table', 'cooking range', 'washing machine', 'refrigerator',
'air conditioner')
>>>
```

Let us see what happens when we try to change the value of an item in the tuple.

homeitems = ('dining table', 'cooking range', 'washing machine', 'refrigerator', 'air conditioner')

```
homeitems[0] = ('bed')
print(homeitems)
= RESTART: C:/Users/saifia computers/Desktop/sample.py
Traceback (most recent call last):
  File "C:/Users/saifia computers/Desktop/sample.py", line 2, in <module>
    homeitems[0] = ('bed')
TypeError: 'tuple' object does not support item assignment
>>>
```

You see an error because Python does not allow you to modify tuples. However, there is a way out by which you modify a tuple. You can do the modification by assigning new values to the same variable that carries the tuple. In the following code snippet, I will redefine the tuple.

```
homeitems = ('dining table', 'cooking range', 'washing machine', 'refrigerator', 'air conditioner')
print("Original items in the tuple:")
for homeitem in homeitems:
    print(homeitem)
homeitems = ('chairs', 'carpets', 'plates', 'oven')
print("Modified items in the tuple:")
for homeitem in homeitems:
```

```
    print(homeitem)
```

= RESTART: C:/Users/saifia computers/Desktop/sample.py

Original items in the tuple:

dining table

cooking range

washing machine

refrigerator

air conditioner

Modified items in the tuple:

chairs

carpets

plates

oven

>>>

Tuples are data structures that can be used to store values that cannot be changed through a program.

Looping

Just like lists, you can create a loop through your tuple.

```
homeitems = ('dining table', 'cooking range', 'washing machine', 'refrigerator', 'air conditioner')
for homeitem in homeitems:
    print(homeitem)
```

= RESTART: C:/Users/saifia computers/Desktop/sample.py

dining table

cooking range

washing machine

refrigerator

air conditioner

>>>

Chapter Four

Python Conditionals

A key part of programming is about examining a set of conditions and then taking appropriate action based on the conditions. The if statement in Python lets you test the state of a program and act on it appropriately. This chapter will walk you through the process of writing conditionals and checking them as well. The chapter will encompass simple and complex if statements. I will explain how you can pair up an if statement with lists.

```
homeitems = ['dining table', 'cooking range', 'washing machine',
'refrigerator', 'air conditioner']
for homeitem in homeitems:
    if homeitem == 'dining table':
        print(homeitem.upper())
    else:
        print(homeitem.title())
= RESTART: C:/Users/saifia computers/Desktop/sample.py
DINING TABLE
Cooking Range
Washing Machine
Refrigerator
```

Air Conditioner

>>>

The simplest conditional test tends to check if a particular variable's value stands equal to your value of interest. Sometimes you need to check if a value exists in a list or not. The player in the game might want to check if a certain item has been purchased or not before he lists the office for sale.

```
officeitems = ['printer', 'scanner', 'fan', 'table', 'table lights']
'scanner' in officeitems
```

You can use the conditional statements to check if a certain item appears in a list. You also can use the item to display a message or comment.

```
officeitems = ['printer', 'scanner', 'fan', 'table', 'table lights']
item = 'scanner'
item1 = 'table'
item2 = 'extension cable'
if item in officeitems:
    print(item.title() + " exists in the office.")
if item1 in officeitems:
    print(item1.title() + " exists in the office.")
if item2 not in officeitems:
    print(item2.title() + " is not exist in the office. You should
buy it as soon as possible.")
= RESTART: C:/Users/saifia computers/Desktop/sample.py
```

Scanner exists in the office.

Table exists in the office.

Extension Cable does not exist in the office. You should buy it as soon as possible.

>>>

Let us see what more you can do with the conditional statements. You can add the conditional statement to tell the player when the office will be ready for listing in the game.

```
officeitems = 10
if officeitems >= 10:
    print("You can list the office for sale")
= RESTART: C:/Users/saifia computers/Desktop/sample.py
You can list the office for sale
>>>
```

See the following example with an additional print statement.

```
officeitems = 12
if officeitems >= 10:
    print("You can list the office for sale")
    print("Have you listed it yet.")
= RESTART: C:/Users/saifia computers/Desktop/sample.py
You can list the office for sale
Have you listed it yet?
>>>
```

The if-else Statement

The condition can be interesting if you add to it the else statement to print a statement if the count of items has not matured yet. The if-else statement allows you to test the conditions in both ways. The else statement defines an action when a particular condition fails.

```
officeitems = 11
if officeitems >= 10:
    print("You can list the office for sale")
    print("Have you listed it yet?")
else:
    print("Sorry, you cannot list the office for sale.")
    print("Please buy and add more items to the office and list it
again for sale.")
= RESTART: C:/Users/saifia computers/Desktop/sample.py
You can list the office for sale
Have you listed it yet?
>>>
```

As the items are more than 10, the condition has been tested passed. Now I will reduce the count of the items to test the else-statement.

```
officeitems = 9
if officeitems >= 10:
    print("You can list the office for sale")
    print("Have you listed it yet?")
```

```
else:
    print("Sorry, you cannot list the office for sale.")
    print("Please buy and add more items to the office and list it
again for sale.")
= RESTART: C:/Users/saifia computers/Desktop/sample.py
Sorry, you cannot list the office for sale.
Please buy and add more items to the office and list it again for
sale.
>>>
```

The if-elif-else Chain

The elif statement allows you to add one more condition to the block of code.

```
officeitems = 5
if officeitems < 10:
    print("You still can list the office but it will not bring you the
desired amount of money.")
elif officeitems < 15:
    print("You can list the office for sale")
    print("Have you listed it yet?")

else:
    print("Sorry, you cannot list the office for sale.")
```

```
print("Please buy and add more items to the office and list it
again for sale.")
```

= RESTART: C:/Users/saifia computers/Desktop/sample.py

You still can list the office, but it will not bring you the desired
amount of money.

>>>

You can test multiple conditions with conditional statements.

```
officeitems = ['printer', 'scanner', 'fan', 'table', 'table lights']
if 'printer' in officeitems:
    print("I have purchased the printer.")
if 'fan' in officeitems:
    print("I have purchased the fan.")
if 'scanner' in officeitems:
    print("I have purchased the scanner.")
```

= RESTART: C:/Users/saifia computers/Desktop/sample.py

I have purchased the printer.

I have purchased the fan.

I have purchased the scanner.

>>>

When the player has checked if he has purchased all the desired
items, the game will give him a green signal to list the office. You
can add a print statement at the end of the block of code.

```
officeitems = ['printer', 'scanner', 'fan', 'table', 'table lights']
```

```
if 'printer' in officeitems:
    print("I have purchased the printer.")
if 'fan' in officeitems:
    print("I have purchased the fan.")
if 'scanner' in officeitems:
    print("I have purchased the scanner.")
print("\nYou can list the office now.")
```

= RESTART: C:/Users/saifia computers/Desktop/sample.py

I have purchased the printer.

I have purchased the fan.

I have purchased the scanner.

You can list the office now.

>>>

The same code cannot work with an elif statement. It will stop working. See what happens when we remove the simple if statement and add an elif statement.

```
officeitems = ['printer', 'scanner', 'fan', 'table', 'table lights']
if 'printer' in officeitems:
    print("I have purchased the printer.")
elif 'fan' in officeitems:
    print("I have purchased the fan.")
elif 'scanner' in officeitems:
    print("I have purchased the scanner.")
```

```
print("\nYou can list the office now.")
```

= RESTART: C:/Users/saifia computers/Desktop/sample.py

I have purchased the printer.

You can list the office now.

>>>

If Statements and Lists

You can pair up if statements with lists. You can actually combine the two and do some amazing things. In the next example, I will pair up a loop with a list to make the game more interactive.

```
officeitems = ['printer', 'scanner', 'fan', 'table', 'table lights']
for officeitem in officeitems:
    print("I have purchased the " + officeitem + ".")
print("\nBoss: You can list the office for sale now.")
```

= RESTART: C:/Users/saifia computers/Desktop/sample.py

I have purchased the printer.

I have purchased the scanner.

I have purchased the fan.

I have purchased the table.

I have purchased the table lights.

Boss: You can list the office for sale now.

>>>

You have a straightforward result because the code contains a simple for loop. However, you can add a bit more complexity to the code.

The boss may ask the employee about a certain item that must be included in the office set up before the office is put on sale. The employee has to handle the situation in the most appropriate way. I will add an if-else statement along with the for loop to make the code more flexible.

```
officeitems = ['printer', 'scanner', 'fan', 'table', 'table lights']
for officeitem in officeitems:
    if officeitem == 'cupboard':
        print("Sorry Boss, I have not purchased it yet.")
    else:
        print("However, I have purchased the " + officeitem + ".")
print("\nBoss: You can list the office for sale only after you purchase the cupboard and set it up in the office.")
= RESTART: C:/Users/saifia computers/Desktop/sample.py
However, I have purchased the printer.
However, I have purchased the scanner.
However, I have purchased the fan.
However, I have purchased the table.
However, I have purchased the table lights.
Boss: You can list the office for sale only after purchasing the cupboard and setting it up in the office.
>>>
```

Now, the Python interpreter checks each office item before it displays the message. The code confirms if the boss has asked for the cupboard. When he asks for the item, he gets a different response from the employee. The else block makes sure that the response is in affirmative for all the other items.

Multiple Lists

Up till now, we have worked with a single list. In this code sample, I will work on multiple lists. I will add a list of optional items that may or may not be purchased. However, purchasing these items will help increase the value of the office.

```
officeitems = ['printer', 'scanner', 'fan', 'table', 'table lights']
optionalitems = ['pen', 'paper', 'drafting pads', 'books', 'water dispenser']
for optionalitem in optionalitems:
    if optionalitem in officeitems:
        print("The office has been set up will all the essential and optional items.")
    else:
        print("Sorry, I have not purchased the " + optionalitem + ".")
print("\nBoss: You can list the office for sale only after you purchase the optional items and set them up in the office.")
= RESTART: C:/Users/saifia computers/Desktop/sample.py
Sorry, I have not purchased the pen.
Sorry, I have not purchased the paper.
Sorry, I have not purchased the drafting pads.
```

Sorry, I have not purchased the books.

Sorry, I have not purchased the water dispenser.

Boss: You can list the office for sale only after purchasing the optional items and setting them up in the office.

>>>

I defined the list of office items and optional items. I created a loop through the optional items to check if they also are added to the office or not. Upon the checking of each item, a message is displayed. In the end, the boss gives his verdict on whether to list the office or not. In the code mentioned above, the office does not contain any item from the list of optional items, therefore it displayed the same message. You can change that by including one or two optional items in the list of office items. See the following code.

```
officeitems = ['printer', 'paper', 'drafting pads', 'scanner', 'fan', 'table', 'table lights']
optionalitems = ['pen', 'paper', 'drafting pads', 'books', 'water dispenser']
for optionalitem in optionalitems:
    if optionalitem in officeitems:
        print("I have purchased the " + optionalitem + ".")
    else:
        print("Sorry, I have not purchased the " + optionalitem + ".")
print("\nBoss: You can list the office for sale only after you purchase all the optional items and set them up in the office.")
```

= RESTART: C:/Users/saifia computers/Desktop/sample.py

Sorry, I have not purchased the pen.

I have purchased the paper.

I have purchased the drafting pads.

Sorry, I have not purchased the books.

Sorry, I have not purchased the water dispenser.

Boss: You can list the office for sale only after purchasing all the optional items and setting them up in the office.

>>>

Chapter Five

Python Dictionaries

This chapter will walk you through the concept of Python dictionaries, which are the most important part of Python coding. You can store information in a dictionary in the form of pairs. You can easily access the information, modify it, and delete it at will. Dictionaries are amazing in the sense that they allow you to store unlimited information. Just like lists, I will explain how you can pair up a dictionary with a loop.

When you have a good grasp of Python dictionaries, you will learn how to model an object with a dictionary's help. Creating a dictionary is simple, but updating it and using it in a code can be tricky. I will move through this chapter step by step. In the first code sample, I will create a simple dictionary.

```
officeitems = {'printer' : 'HP', 'paper': 'A4', 'drafting pads':
'blank', 'scanner': 'hybrid', 'table': 'wood', 'table lights': 'LED'}
print(officeitems)
= RESTART: C:/Users/saifia computers/Desktop/sample.py
{'printer': 'HP', 'paper': 'A4', 'drafting pads': 'blank', 'scanner':
'hybrid', 'table': 'wood', 'table lights': 'LED'}
>>>
```

There is another way to access and display selected information from a dictionary. You can use one of the pairs' values and use them to access the other value of the pair. See the following code example.

```
officeitems = {'printer' : 'HP', 'paper': 'A4', 'drafting pads':
'blank', 'scanner': 'hybrid', 'table': 'wood', 'table lights': 'LED'}
print(officeitems['printer'])
print(officeitems['paper'])
print(officeitems['table lights'])
print(officeitems['table'])
print(officeitems['drafting pads'])
= RESTART: C:/Users/saifia computers/Desktop/sample.py
HP
A4
LED
wood
blank
>>>
```

Dictionaries are more complex than lists, therefore you need more programming practice to handle them. You can see that a dictionary contains key-value pairs where each key is automatically connected to its value. Each key's value can be a string or an integer or even a list in some cases. It also can be a dictionary in a more complex code form. You have to wrap up a dictionary in curly braces or the dictionary will display an error. A key has directed association with its value.

Accessing values from a dictionary is easy. As you have seen in the above code sample, I tried to access each value with the help of a key or a dictionary. Dictionaries are also very dynamic, and they allow you to add as many key-value pairs to the dictionary as you desire. I will now take an empty dictionary and fill it up with key-value pairs of my choice.

```
officeitems = {}
officeitems['printer'] = 'HP'
officeitems['paper'] = 'A4'
officeitems['drafting pads'] = 'blank'
officeitems['scanner'] = 'hybrid'
officeitems['table lights'] = 'LED'
print(officeitems)
= RESTART: C:/Users/saifia computers/Desktop/sample.py
{'printer': 'HP', 'paper': 'A4', 'drafting pads': 'blank', 'scanner': 'hybrid', 'table lights': 'LED'}
>>>
```

You also can modify the value of a key as you deem fit. In order to do that, you have to mention the name of the dictionary and write the key in square brackets. Then you have to write the new value for the same key.

```
officeitems = {'printer' : 'HP', 'paper': 'A4', 'drafting pads':
'blank', 'scanner': 'hybrid', 'table': 'wood', 'table lights': 'LED'}
print("I have purchased a printer by " + officeitems['printer'] +
".")
officeitems['printer'] = 'dell'
print("However, I have also purchased one more now by " +
officeitems['printer'] + ".")
= RESTART: C:/Users/saifia computers/Desktop/sample.py
I have purchased a printer by HP.
However, I have also purchased one more now by dell.
>>>
```

Removing Pairs

When you don't need a certain key-value pair, you can remove it easily. You can apply the del statement to remove the key-value pair. All you have to do is to mention the name of your dictionary and key. I will remove different items from the dictionary I have created earlier on.

```
officeitems = {'printer' : 'HP', 'paper': 'A4', 'drafting pads':
'blank', 'scanner': 'hybrid', 'table': 'wood', 'table lights': 'LED'}
print(officeitems)
del officeitems['printer']
print(officeitems)
del officeitems['paper']
print(officeitems)
```

```
del officeitems['drafting pads']
print(officeitems)
del officeitems['scanner']
print(officeitems)
del officeitems['table']
print(officeitems)
del officeitems['table lights']
print(officeitems)
```

= RESTART: C:/Users/saifia computers/Desktop/sample.py

{'printer': 'HP', 'paper': 'A4', 'drafting pads': 'blank', 'scanner': 'hybrid', 'table': 'wood', 'table lights': 'LED'}

{'paper': 'A4', 'drafting pads': 'blank', 'scanner': 'hybrid', 'table': 'wood', 'table lights': 'LED'}

{'drafting pads': 'blank', 'scanner': 'hybrid', 'table': 'wood', 'table lights': 'LED'}

{'scanner': 'hybrid', 'table': 'wood', 'table lights': 'LED'}

{'table': 'wood', 'table lights': 'LED'}

{'table lights': 'LED'}

{}

>>>

You can see that when all the pairs are removed, the result is an empty dictionary. One important thing to keep in mind is that the del statement removes a pair completely from the dictionary. Therefore, only use the del statement when you are sure that you do not need a certain key-value pair.

A dictionary allows you to use the values in a print statement to display certain messages.

officeitems = {'printer' : 'HP', 'paper': 'A4', 'drafting pads': 'blank', 'scanner': 'hybrid', 'table': 'wood', 'table lights': 'LED'}

print("I bought a printer by " + officeitems['printer'] + ".")

print("I also bought a scanner by " + officeitems['scanner'] + ".")

print("The paper if of the size " + officeitems['paper'] + ".")

print("The drafting pads are " + officeitems['drafting pads'] + ".")

= RESTART: C:/Users/saifia computers/Desktop/sample.py

I bought a printer by HP.

I also bought a scanner by hybrid.

The paper if of the size A4.

The drafting pads are blank.

>>>

I have used the print keyword in the code. Then I added the appropriate statement to the code. After that came the part of the concatenation operator. This is how you can use the values of a dictionary to display messages in your code.

Looping

Just like we formed a loop through a list, we can form the same through a dictionary as well. A Python dictionary may contain a few millions of key-value pairs. As a dictionary carries big amounts of data, Python allows you to create a loop through it to easily see each key-value pair and use it in a program. In the first example, I will loop through each item in your dictionary.

```
officeitems = {'printer' : 'HP', 'paper': 'A4', 'drafting pads':
'blank', 'scanner': 'hybrid', 'table': 'wood', 'table lights': 'LED'}
for key, value in officeitems.items():
    print("\nThe Key: " + key)
    print("The Value: " + value)
= RESTART: C:/Users/saifia computers/Desktop/sample.py
The Key: printer
The Value: HP
The Key: paper
The Value: A4
The Key: drafting pads
The Value: blank
The Key: scanner
The Value: hybrid
The Key: table
The Value: wood
The Key: table lights
```

The Value: LED

>>>

There is another method to display the values of each key-value pair. See the following example.

```
officeitems = {'printer' : 'HP', 'paper': 'A4', 'drafting pads': 'blank', 'scanner': 'hybrid', 'table': 'wood', 'table lights': 'LED'}
for k, v in officeitems.items():
    print("\nThe Key: " + k)
    print("The Value: " + v)
```

= RESTART: C:/Users/saifia computers/Desktop/sample.py

The Key: printer

The Value: HP

The Key: paper

The Value: A4

The Key: drafting pads

The Value: blank

The Key: scanner

The Value: hybrid

The Key: table

The Value: wood

The Key: table lights

The Value: LED

>>>

One important thing to consider before moving on is the order in which Python stores the key-value pairs. When you create and run a loop through a dictionary, Python does not care about the order in which you had created the dictionary. It only tracks down the keys and their respective values.

```
officeitems = {'printer' : 'Produced by HP', 'paper': 'A4 type',
'drafting pads': 'It is blank', 'scanner': 'it is hybrid', 'table': 'made
of wood', 'table lights': 'They are LED'}
for items, features in officeitems.items():
    print(items.title() + " carries the following feature: " +
features.title())
```

= RESTART: C:/Users/saifia computers/Desktop/sample.py

Printer carries the following feature: Produced By Hp

Paper carries the following feature: A4 Type

Drafting Pads carries the following feature: It Is Blank

Scanner carries the following feature: It Is Hybrid

Table carries the following feature: Made Of Wood

Table Lights carries the following feature: They Are Led

>>>

The code instructs Python to loop through the key-value pairs inside of the dictionary. As the code loops through each pair, Python first stores each key inside the variable named items. It stores each value inside the variable named features. The same variables are then added to the print statement that runs and displays related messages.

You can opt for looping through all the keys or values separately. For example, sometimes you need to work just with the keys and only want to display them. There is a way out. See the following example.

officeitems = {'printer' : 'Produced by HP', 'paper': 'A4 type', 'drafting pads': 'It is blank', 'scanner': 'it is hybrid', 'table': 'made of wood', 'table lights': 'They are LED'}

for items in officeitems.keys():

    print(items.title())

= RESTART: C:/Users/saifia computers/Desktop/sample.py

Printer

Paper

Drafting Pads

Scanner

Table

Table Lights

>>>

Now I will form a loop through each key's values and display the result in the interpreter.

officeitems = {'printer' : 'Produced by HP', 'paper': 'A4 type', 'drafting pads': 'It is blank', 'scanner': 'it is hybrid', 'table': 'made of wood', 'table lights': 'They are LED'}

for items in officeitems.values():

    print(items.title())

= RESTART: C:/Users/saifia computers/Desktop/sample.py

Produced By Hp

A4 Type

It Is Blank

It Is Hybrid

Made Of Wood

They Are Led

>>>

The sorted() Method

To make your loops more interesting, you can add to them the sorted() method. A dictionary is not in order, therefore you need to bring it up in the order you want it to be. You can use the sorted() method to make that happen.

officeitems = {'printer' : 'Produced by HP', 'paper': 'A4 type', 'drafting pads': 'It is blank', 'scanner': 'it is hybrid', 'table': 'made of wood', 'table lights': 'They are LED'}

for items in sorted(officeitems.keys()):

    print(items.title() + " has been purchased at a discount price. I hope it will help earn a handsome amount from the sale of the office")

= RESTART: C:/Users/saifia computers/Desktop/sample.py

Drafting Pads has been purchased at a discount price. I hope it will help earn a handsome amount from the sale of the office

Paper has been purchased at a discount price. I hope it will help earn a handsome amount from the sale of the office

Printer has been purchased at a discount price. I hope it will help earn a handsome amount from the sale of the office

Scanner has been purchased at a discount price. I hope it will help earn a handsome amount from the sale of the office

Table has been purchased at a discount price. I hope it will help earn a handsome amount from the sale of the office

Table Lights have been purchased at a discount price. I hope it will help earn a handsome amount from the sale of the office

>>>

You can see that the result is in perfect alphabetical order.

Nesting

Ever wondered if you can make a dictionary more complex than it already is. You can nest a long dictionary inside another dictionary. The process is dubbed as nesting. You also can nest more than one dictionaries in a list. You can diversify the process of nesting by several methods.

I am going to pack up multiple dictionaries inside a list. Coming to the back, I will create three different dictionaries about different items of an office and then cram them all inside a list.

officeitem1 = {'printer' : 'Produced by HP', 'scanner': 'it is hybrid', 'laptop': 'dell'} officeitem2 = {'paper': 'A4 type', 'drafting pads': 'It is blank', 'pen': 'parker'}

officeitem3 = {'table': 'made of wood', 'table lights': 'They are LED', 'office chair': 'boss'}

officeitems = [officeitem1, officeitem2, officeitem3]

for officeitem in officeitems:

   print(officeitem)

= RESTART: C:/Users/saifia computers/Desktop/sample.py

{'printer': 'Produced by HP', 'scanner': 'it is hybrid', 'laptop': 'dell'}

{'paper': 'A4 type', 'drafting pads': 'It is blank', 'pen': 'parker'}

{'table': 'made of wood', 'table lights': 'They are LED', 'office chair': 'boss'}

>>>

The three dictionaries denote each section of the office items. One deals with IT set up, the second denotes stationary while the third section denotes office furniture.

Random Dictionary Methods

Dictionaries are flexible in the sense that they allow you to do several things. For example, you can check if a certain key exists in the dictionary or not. I will use the if statement in the code.

officeitem1 = {'printer' : 'Produced by HP', 'scanner': 'it is hybrid', 'laptop': 'dell', 'paper': 'A4 type', 'drafting pads': 'It is blank', 'pen': 'parker', 'table': 'made of wood', 'table lights': 'They are LED', 'office chair': 'boss'}

```
if "scanner" in officeitem1:
    print("Yes, I have got 'scanner' in the office.")
else:
    print("Sorry, I do not have that item.")
```

= RESTART: C:/Users/saifia computers/Desktop/sample.py

Yes, I have got 'scanner' in the office.

>>>

There is another method known as the clear() method that will empty your dictionary. See the following code sample.

```
officeitem1 = {'printer' : 'Produced by HP', 'scanner': 'it is hybrid', 'laptop': 'dell', 'paper': 'A4 type', 'drafting pads': 'It is blank', 'pen': 'parker', 'table': 'made of wood', 'table lights': 'They are LED', 'office chair': 'boss'}
print(officeitem1)
officeitem1.clear()
print(officeitem1)
```

= RESTART: C:/Users/saifia computers/Desktop/sample.py

{'printer': 'Produced by HP', 'scanner': 'it is hybrid', 'laptop': 'dell', 'paper': 'A4 type', 'drafting pads': 'It is blank', 'pen': 'parker', 'table': 'made of wood', 'table lights': 'They are LED', 'office chair': 'boss'}

{}

>>>

You can see that the clear method has emptied the dictionary. Python allows you to create perfect copies of your dictionary. You can create as many copies as you want to. The method is dubbed as the copy() method. It is a built-in Python method.

```
officeitem1 = {'printer' : 'Produced by HP', 'scanner': 'it is
hybrid', 'laptop': 'dell', 'paper': 'A4 type', 'drafting pads': 'It is
blank', 'pen': 'parker', 'table': 'made of wood', 'table lights': 'They
are LED', 'office chair': 'boss'}
print(officeitem1)
officeitem2 = officeitem1.copy()
print(officeitem2)
= RESTART: C:/Users/saifia computers/Desktop/sample.py
{'printer': 'Produced by HP', 'scanner': 'it is hybrid', 'laptop':
'dell', 'paper': 'A4 type', 'drafting pads': 'It is blank', 'pen':
'parker', 'table': 'made of wood', 'table lights': 'They are LED',
'office chair': 'boss'}
{'printer': 'Produced by HP', 'scanner': 'it is hybrid', 'laptop':
'dell', 'paper': 'A4 type', 'drafting pads': 'It is blank', 'pen':
'parker', 'table': 'made of wood', 'table lights': 'They are LED',
'office chair': 'boss'}
>>>
```

There is another built-in method to create copy of the dictionary. The method is labeled as the dict() method.

```
officeitem1 = {'printer' : 'Produced by HP', 'scanner': 'it is
hybrid', 'laptop': 'dell', 'paper': 'A4 type', 'drafting pads': 'It is
```

blank', 'pen': 'parker', 'table': 'made of wood', 'table lights': 'They are LED', 'office chair': 'boss'}

print(officeitem1)

officeitem2 = dict(officeitem1)

print(officeitem2)

= RESTART: C:/Users/saifia computers/Desktop/sample.py

{'printer': 'Produced by HP', 'scanner': 'it is hybrid', 'laptop': 'dell', 'paper': 'A4 type', 'drafting pads': 'It is blank', 'pen': 'parker', 'table': 'made of wood', 'table lights': 'They are LED', 'office chair': 'boss'}

{'printer': 'Produced by HP', 'scanner': 'it is hybrid', 'laptop': 'dell', 'paper': 'A4 type', 'drafting pads': 'It is blank', 'pen': 'parker', 'table': 'made of wood', 'table lights': 'They are LED', 'office chair': 'boss'}

>>>

We had the exact copy of the same dictionary. There is a bit of difference in writing the code.

If you have to create a dictionary from scratch, you can use the dict() constructor to do that. I will take an empty dictionary and fill it in with the keys and values by using the dict() constructor.

officeitem1 = dict(printer = 'Produced by HP', scanner = 'it is hybrid', laptop = 'dell', paper = 'A4 type', draftingpads = 'blank', pen = 'parker', table = 'made of wood')

print(officeitem1)

= RESTART: C:/Users/saifia computers/Desktop/sample.py

{'printer': 'Produced by HP', 'scanner': 'it is hybrid', 'laptop': 'dell', 'paper': 'A4 type', 'draftingpads': 'blank', 'pen': 'parker', 'table': 'made of wood'}

>>>

The keys should not contain any spaces while you are constructing a dictionary by the dict() constructor. Please take a look at how I wrote drafting pads. If you leave any spaces between the keys, Python interpreter will return syntax error.

Chapter Six

Input and Python Loops

Programs are written to solve different problems. Some programs are made to collect information from users. These programs demand special functions that could collect the information and process it to the system's database. When you put your office on sale, you can introduce a special function that invites the buyers' quotations. The user input program will take the input, analyze it, and respond to the user.

In this chapter, I'll explain how you can build a program that accepts user input and processes it. I will use the input() function to develop the program. The user input and while loop will be explained together as it is the while loop that keeps the program running. The while loop runs the program as long as a particular condition stands true.

The input() Function

It is an interesting function and very helpful in program building. The function pauses your program and allows the user to fill in the program with the requisite information. Once the function receives the information, it forwards it to a variable for storage purposes.

```
pgm = input("This program repeats whatever you write: ")
```

print(pgm)

This program repeats whatever you write: I am learning Python and I am enjoying it well.

I am learning Python and I am enjoying it well.

>>>

This program repeats whatever you write: Do you know Python can be used to educate robots.

Do you know Python can be used to educate robots.

>>>

I entered some statements which the program repeats as they are. The important point is that you have to rerun the program once it has repeated one statement. When you run the program, it pauses and waits for the user to write something. Once the program senses input, it waits for the user to press Enter. After that, it displays the results. I will create a program that asks users to enter the bidding price to buy the office that has already been set up by the player in your game.

```
pgm = input("Please enter the bidding price at which you want
to buy the office: ")
print("I want to buy the office at " + pgm + " million dollars.")
```

Please enter the bidding price at which you want to buy the office: five

I want to buy the office for five million dollars.

>>>

The program is suitable only if the user enters the value in the form of string. Therefore you will have to leave a note, instructing the user to write only in words. However, there is a way out to solve this problem. You can allow users to enter the price in numbers without causing an error.

```
pgm = input("Please enter the bidding price at which you want to buy the office: ")
print("I want to buy the office at " + str(pgm) + " million dollars.")
```

= RESTART: C:/Users/saifia computers/Desktop/sample.py

Please enter the bidding price at which you want to buy the office: 5

I want to buy the office for 5 million dollars.

>>>

In the next sample, I will create a program that has more than lines.

```
pgm = input("If you are interested in buying the office, please proceed to fill in the price box. ")
pgm += "\nPlease enter the bidding price at which you want to buy the office. "
username = input(pgm)
```

print("I want to buy the office for " + username + " million dollars.")

= RESTART: C:/Users/saifia computers/Desktop/sample.py

If you are interested in buying the office, please proceed to fill in the price box.

Please enter the bidding price at which you want to buy the office. 3

I want to buy the office for 3 million dollars.

>>>

This is how you can easily build a multiline string in the user input function.

While Loops

This section will shed light on how you can create and use Python while loops. You have already encountered the for loop which runs through a list of items and applies the code to each item in the list. The while loop is a bit different. It runs through a set of items as long as a certain condition stands true. While loop is interesting in the sense that you can use it to execute different interesting mathematical functions. The simplest and the most interesting thing is counting the numbers.

```
my_number = 1
while my_number <= 15:
    print(my_number)
    my_number += 1
```

= RESTART: C:/Users/saifia computers/Desktop/sample.py

1

2

3

4

5

6

7

8

9

10

11

12

13

14

15

>>>

See another mathematical example of the use of a while loop.

```
my_number = 1
while my_number <= 100:
    print(my_number)
    my_number += 5
```

= RESTART: C:/Users/saifia computers/Desktop/sample.py

```
1
6
11
16
21
26
31
36
41
46
51
56
61
66
71
76
81
86
91
96
>>>
```

I set the value to numbers 1 and 5, respectively. The while loop reads it and keeps running until it reaches 15 and 100, respectively. The code guides the loop to calculate the numbers and display the result on the interpreter. The loops get repeated as long as its condition remains true. Your player needs a while loop to exit the game. Only a while loop helps you end a game and shutdown it properly. Otherwise, it will hang the system each time you try to shut it down.

This demands that you let the users quit the game when they want to. I will not pack up the program in a while loop and then define the quit value for the same so that users can exit it by entering the quit value.

```
pgm = input("This program repeats whatever you tell it: ")
pgm += "\nYou have to enter 'q' to exit the program. "
msg = ""
while msg != 'q':
    msg = input(pgm)
    print(msg)
```

= RESTART: C:/Users/saifia computers/Desktop/sample.py
This program repeats whatever you tell it: I am determined to learn Python in six months.

I am determined to learn Python in six months.

You have to enter 'q' to exit the program. I am determined to build my programs in the first month of learning.

I am determined to build my programs in the first month of learning.

I am determined to learn Python in six months.

You have to enter 'q' to exit the program. q

q

>>>

I defined the prompt namely pgm in the first line of code. It gives the user two options; one to enter a message and another to quit the program. I also set a variable that stored the information the user enters. The while loop runs until the user enters q and breaks the loop. It can run a million times on end if the user does not end it.

```
pgm = input("This program repeats whatever you tell it: ")
pgm += "\nYou have to enter 'q' to exit the program. "
msg = ""
while msg != 'q':
    msg = input(pgm)
    print(msg)
```

= RESTART: C:/Users/saifia computers/Desktop/sample.py
This program repeats whatever you tell it: hi

hi
You have to enter 'q' to exit the program. how are you

how are you
hi

You have to enter 'q' to exit the program. What is your name?

What is your name?

hi

You have to enter 'q' to exit the program. Are you fine?

Are you fine?

hi

You have to enter 'q' to exit the program. I am looking forward to doing business with you.

I am looking forward to doing business with you.

hi

You have to enter 'q' to exit the program. q

q

>>>

You can see that the while loop ran until I entered the keyword q that broke the loop. The program is perfect except for the fact that it displays q as an actual message. If I add an *if* clause to the code, it will work just fine.

```
pgm = input("This program repeats whatever you tell it: ")
pgm += "\nYou have to enter 'q' to exit the program. "
msg = ""
while msg != 'q':
    msg = input(pgm)
```

```
if msg != 'q':
    print(z
```

= RESTART: C:/Users/saifia computers/Desktop/sample.py

This program repeats whatever you tell it: Hi

Hi

You have to enter 'q' to exit the program. My name is Jack.

My name is Jack.

Hi

You have to enter 'q' to exit the program. I am here to do business with you.

I am here to do business with you.

Hi

You have to enter 'q' to exit the program. I want to sell an office to the highest bidder. Have a look at the pictures.

I want to sell an office to the highest bidder. Have a look at the pictures.

Hi

You have to enter 'q' to exit the program. I think you are not interested. Thank you!

I think you are not interested. Thank you!

Hi

You have to enter 'q' to exit the program. q

>>>

The program did not display the word q as a message. It simply lets the user exit the program.

The Break Keyword

If you want to exit the loop without running the code that remains, you can add a break statement to the program. The break statement tends to redirect the flow of a program and allow you to execute the code of your choice.

```
pgm = input("Please enter the name of the office item that you
have purchased:")
pgm +- "\n(You have to enter 'q' to exit the program.) "
while True:
    item = input(pgm)
    if item == 'q':
        break
    else:
        print("I have purchased the " + item.title())
= RESTART: C:/Users/saifia computers/Desktop/sample.py
Please enter the name of the office item that you have
purchased:table
table
(You have to enter 'q' to exit the program.)
```

I have purchased the

table

(You have to enter 'q' to exit the program.) laptop

I have purchased the Laptop

table

(You have to enter 'q' to exit the program.) computer system

I have purchased the Computer System

table

(You have to enter 'q' to exit the program.) stack of paper.

I have purchased the Stack Of Paper.

table

(You have to enter 'q' to exit the program.) air conditioner

I have purchased the Air Conditioner

table

(You have to enter 'q' to exit the program.) q

>>>

You have another choice as well. Instead of breaking out of the loop, you can integrate into the block of code a continue statement that will take the code back to the start after the condition stands tested. See the following mathematical example.

```
num = 0
while num < 40:
    num += 1
```

```
    if num %4 == 0:

        continue

    print(num)
```

= RESTART: C:/Users/saifia computers/Desktop/sample.py

1

2

3

5

6

7

9

10

11

13

14

15

17

18

19

21

22

23

25

26

27

29

30

31

33

34

35

37

38

39

>>>

You can see that the continue statement returned the code after a pause at the point Python tested the condition. The num started at 0. I kept the figure under 40 so the loop ran until 4, checked if the current number is divisible by 4 and then executed the rest of the code because the number was not divisible by 4. Let us try another example to clear the concept fully.

```
num = 4
while num < 80:
    num += 3
    if num %4 == 0:
        continue
    print(num)
```

= RESTART: C:/Users/saifia computers/Desktop/sample.py

7

10

13

19

22

25

31

34

37

43

46

49

55

58

61

67

70

73

79

82

>>>

Loops, Lists, Dictionaries

The three go side by side. I have already given some code snippets that showed what a while loop could be used for. I will give a comprehensive overview of how you can pair up loops, lists, and dictionaries. The examples will be a bit more complex than the previous examples.

```
items_tobuy = ['printer', 'scanner', 'laptop', 'paper', 'drafting
pads', 'pen', 'table', 'table lights', 'office chair']
items_bought = []
while items_tobuy:
    officeitems = items_tobuy.pop()
    print("I am purchasing the " + officeitems.title())
    items_bought.append(officeitems)
    print("\nI have purchased the following items:")
    for item_bought in items_bought:
        print(item_bought.title())
```

= RESTART: C:/Users/saifia computers/Desktop/sample.py

I am purchasing the Office Chair

I have purchased the following items:

Office Chair

I am purchasing the Table Lights

I have purchased the following items:

Office Chair

Table Lights

I am purchasing the Table

I have purchased the following items:

Office Chair

Table Lights

Table

I am purchasing the Pen

I have purchased the following items:

Office Chair

Table Lights

Table

Pen

I am purchasing the Drafting Pads

I have purchased the following items:

Office Chair

Table Lights

Table

Pen

Drafting Pads

I am purchasing the Paper

I have purchased the following items:

Office Chair

Table Lights

Table

Pen

Drafting Pads

Paper

I am purchasing the Laptop

I have purchased the following items:

Office Chair

Table Lights

Table

Pen

Drafting Pads

Paper

Laptop

I am purchasing the Scanner

I have purchased the following items:

Office Chair

Table Lights

Table

Pen

Drafting Pads

Paper

Laptop

Scanner

I am purchasing the Printer

I have purchased the following items:

Office Chair

Table Lights

Table

Pen

Drafting Pads

Paper

Laptop

Scanner

Printer

>>>

When a player purchases an item, he will get a clear message that an item has been bought and added to the office. So, this has definitely made the game more interesting.

While loop can also help you in removing multiple instances of a particular value. If an item's value is being repeated in the list, you can set up a while loop to remove all instances of the same. For a small list, manually removing it is not a problem. However, this feature of the while loops becomes a must when you are dealing with long lists.

```
officeitems = ['printer', 'scanner', 'laptop', 'paper', 'drafting pads', 'scanner', 'pen', 'table', 'scanner', 'table lights', 'office chair']
print(officeitems)
while 'scanner' in officeitems:
```

```
    officeitems.remove('scanner')
print(officeitems)
= RESTART: C:/Users/saifia computers/Desktop/sample.py
['printer', 'scanner', 'laptop', 'paper', 'drafting pads', 'scanner',
'pen', 'table', 'scanner', 'table lights', 'office chair']
['printer', 'laptop', 'paper', 'drafting pads', 'pen', 'table', 'table
lights', 'office chair']
>>>
```

In the next example, I will build a dictionary with the user input with a while loop. I will create a program that will ask the user to tell about the office items he wants to buy and the brand name. The input will be forwarded to a dictionary and used to create the desired output for the user. The program will display purchase statistics in a neat and summarized way.

```
officeitems = {}
buying = True
while buying:
    buyer_item = input("\nWhat do want to buy? ")
    officeitem = input("Of what brand do you want to buy? ")
    officeitems[buyer_item] = officeitem
    repeat = input("Would you like to buy another item for the
office? (yes/ no ")
    if repeat == 'no':
        buying = False
```

```
print("\nPurchase Statistics")
for buyer_item, officeitem in officeitems.items():
    print("I have purchased " + buyer_item + " from the brand "
+ officeitem + ".")
```

= RESTART: C:/Users/saifia computers/Desktop/sample.py

What do you want to buy? table

Of what brand do you want to buy? interwood

Would you like to buy another item for the office? (yes/ noyes

What do you want to buy?

= RESTART: C:/Users/saifia computers/Desktop/sample.py

What do you want to buy? table

Of what brand do you want to buy? interwood

Would you like to buy another item for the office? (yes/ no yes

What do you want to buy? air conditioner

Of what brand do you want to buy? orient

Would you like to buy another item for the office? (yes/ no yes

What do you want to buy? laptop

Of what brand do you want to buy? dell

Would you like to buy another item for the office? (yes/ no yes

What do you want to buy? office chair

Of what brand do you want to buy? boss

Would you like to buy another item for the office? (yes/ no no

Purchase Statistics

I have purchased a table from the brand interwood.

I have purchased an air conditioner from the brand orient.

I have purchased a laptop from the brand dell.

I have purchased an office chair from the brand boss.

>>>

The same program can be redesigned to collect names and email IDs of users who visit your eCommerce website. You can then use the information to send your prospects direct mail ads and boost your business. All you need is a bit of tweaking to the existing code and your program will be ready to boost your marketing campaign.

```python
users_id = {}
info = True
while info:
    user_name = input("\nWhat is your name? ")
    user_id = input("what is your email id? ")
    users_id[user_name] = user_id
    repeat = input("Would you like to add another username or id? (yes/ no ")
    if repeat == 'no':
        info = False
print("\nUser Info")
for user_name, user_id in users_id.items():
    print("My name is " + user_name + " and my email ID is " + user_id + ".")
= RESTART: C:/Users/saifia computers/Desktop/sample.py
```

What is your name? johnson

what is your email id? johnson@gmail.com

Would you like to add another username or id? (yes/ no yes

What is your name? emily

what is your email id? emily@yahoo.com

Would you like to add another username or id? (yes/ no yes

What is your name? emilia

what is your email id? emilia@outlook.com

Would you like to add another username or id? (yes/ no yes

What is your name? mark

what is your email id? mark@rocketmail.com

Would you like to add another username or id? (yes/ no yes

What is your name? jasmine

what is your email id? jasmine@gmail.com

Would you like to add another username or id? (yes/ no

User Info

My name is johnson and my email ID is johnson@gmail.com.

My name is emily and my email ID is emily@yahoo.com.

My name is emilia and my email ID is emilia@outlook.com.

My name is mark and my email ID is mark@rocketmail.com.

My name is jasmine and my email ID is jasmine@gmail.com.

>>>

You can see how easy it is to build a program with a while loop and user input function to collect crucial prospect data that can ultimately help you shape your marketing campaign. You can give this program a brilliant interface and run it as part of your landing page design. As I have defined an empty dictionary at the start, you can fill it with as much information as you want to. It can carry over a million items.

Chapter Seven

Python Functions

This chapter will walk you through the process of writing functions. Functions can be defined as blocks of code that have just one job to perform. When you want to do a simple task that you have defined in your function, you can just call the function you have written to do the job. If you are looking forward to performing the same task more than once throughout the program, you can just make a call to the same function and Python will execute the entire block of code. Functions make your programs simple and easy to write and run.

In this chapter, I will explain how you can create functions, pass crucial information to the same, and repeat multiple times the task that functions perform. I will also explain how you can store a function in the form of modules.

Defining Functions

Defining a function is a simple job. The keyword I will use is called *def*. The keyword will be followed by the name of the function and parenthesis. Parenthesis is a function that is very important as it can be used for different purposes, like adding default information and passing information to functions at a later stage of writing a program.

```
def user_info():
    print("My name is Joe and I am a new user.")
user_info()
= RESTART: C:/Users/saifia computers/Desktop/sample.py
My name is Joe and I am a new user.
>>>
```

In the first line of code, I have defined the function. The second line carries the usual print statement while the last line is where I made a function call to display the function's information. This can be dubbed as the simplest structure of a function. The def keyword defines the function.

From this point, I will make it a bit complex by passing information to the function. I will have to modify it a little bit to suit our needs. The parenthesis now will no longer be empty. I will fill them up with some information.

```
def user_info(username):
    print("My name is " + username.title() + " and I am a new user.")
user_info('Joe')
user_info('Jimmy')
user_info('Emily')
user_info('Emilia')
user_info('Mark')
= RESTART: C:/Users/saifia computers/Desktop/sample.py
```

My name is Joe and I am a new user.

My name is Jimmy and I am a new user.

My name is Emily and I am a new user.

My name is Emilia and I am a new user.

My name is Mark and I am a new user.

>>>

The most important point to note here is that functions help you cut short the block of code. You do not have to rewrite a block of code again and again to do the same job. All you need is to call the function and use the parenthesis to use new information for the same block of code. Programmers love functions because they save their time and energy when they write lengthy programs.

Arguments and Parameters

I have packed up the variable inside the parenthesis and named it as the username; this is labeled as a parameter. The values Joe and Emily that I have put in the parenthesis function are known as arguments. Arguments and parentheses are often confused with each other. People use them interchangeably. That is not the right thing to do.

There can be multiple arguments for a function; you can pass them to the function in many ways and put them in a position. They are called positional arguments and they are also known as keyword arguments. Each argument may include the name of a variable, a list, or a dictionary.

Positional Arguments

When you make a function call, Python ought to watch the arguments with a specific parameter in the definition of a function. The matching of values are dubbed as positional arguments.

```
def user_info(username, email_id):
    print("My name is " + username.title() + " and I am a new user.")
    print("My email ID is " + email_id.title() + ".")
user_info('Joe', 'joe@gmail.com')
user_info('Jimmy', 'jimmy@outlook.com')
user_info('Emily', 'emily@gmail.com')
user_info('Emilia', 'emilia@yahoo.com')
user_info('Mark', 'mark@outlook.com')
= RESTART: C:/Users/saifia computers/Desktop/sample.py
My name is Joe and I am a new user.
My email ID is Joe@Gmail.Com.
My name is Jimmy and I am a new user.
My email ID is Jimmy@Outlook.Com.
My name is Emily and I am a new user.
My email ID is Emily@Gmail.Com.
My name is Emilia and I am a new user.
My email ID is Emilia@Yahoo.Com.
My name is Mark and I am a new user.
My email ID is Mark@Outlook.Com.
>>>
```

The output neatly displays the name of the user and his or her email ID. In the above code sample, I have called the function more than once. Multiple function calls are the most efficient way to do a job. As soon as a new user fills in the information and you make a function call, the entire block of code will run and execute the information. There is virtually no limit to the number of function calls. One important thing to keep in mind while making a function call is to remember the position of arguments. If you change the position, you are likely to get funny results.

```
def user_info(username, email_id):
    print("My name is " + username.title() + " and I am a new user.")
    print("My email ID is " + email_id.title() + ".")
user_info('joe@gmail.com', 'Joe')
user_info('jimmy@outlook.com', 'Jimmy' )
user_info('emily@gmail.com', 'Emily')
user_info('Emilia', 'emilia@yahoo.com')
user_info('Mark', 'mark@outlook.com')
>>>= RESTART: C:/Users/saifia computers/Desktop/sample.py
My name is Joe@Gmail.Com and I am a new user.
My email ID is Joe.
My name is Jimmy@Outlook.Com and I am a new user.
My email ID is Jimmy.
```

My name is Emily@Gmail.Com and I am a new user.

My email ID is Emily.

My name is Emilia and I am a new user.

My email ID is Emilia@Yahoo.Com.

My name is Mark and I am a new user.

My email ID is Mark@Outlook.Com.

>>>

I have changed the position for the first three function calls and the results are ridiculous.

Keyword Arguments

There is another way out. You can use keyword arguments to avoid this kind of mix up. A keyword argument is like a name-value pair that is passed to a function. A keyword argument allows you to create a link between the name and the value inside an argument. When you pass the argument to the function, Python cannot mistake it. It eliminates the confusion and you do not have to worry about bringing your arguments in order.

```
def user_info(username, email_id):
    print("My name is " + username.title() + " and I am a new user.")
    print("My email ID is " + email_id.title() + ".")
user_info(email_id = 'joe@gmail.com', username = 'Joe')
user_info( email_id = 'jimmy@outlook.com', username = 'Jimmy' )
```

user_info(email_id = 'emily@gmail.com', username = 'Emily')

user_info(username = 'Emilia', email_id = 'emilia@yahoo.com')

user_info(username = 'Mark', email_id = 'mark@outlook.com')

= RESTART: C:/Users/saifia computers/Desktop/sample.py

My name is Joe and I am a new user.

My email ID is Joe@Gmail.Com.

My name is Jimmy and I am a new user.

My email ID is Jimmy@Outlook.Com.

My name is Emily and I am a new user.

My email ID is Emily@Gmail.Com.

My name is Emilia and I am a new user.

My email ID is Emilia@Yahoo.Com.

My name is Mark and I am a new user.

My email ID is Mark@Outlook.Com.

>>>

I have changed the positions of the arguments and it hardly affected the results. Keyword arguments help you create a functional program.

Default Values

When you are writing a program, you may come up with information that you have to use repeatedly. This means that you will have to fill in the function call with the required arguments each you need that information to be executed. This may result in a waste of time and energy, and may also cause frustration. If you create default values for the function, you will be able to execute the excessively used information fast and efficiently. When you leave the function call empty, it will use the default arguments. You can use the default information as many times as you want to. The default values tend to simply a program and declutter the code. I will fill in the same example with the default arguments and also use the default values multiple times.

```
def user_info(username = 'Dora', email_id =
'dora@outlook.com'):
    print("My name is " + username.title() + " and I am a new
user.")
    print("My email ID is " + email_id.title() + ".")
user_info(email_id = 'joe@gmail.com', username = 'Joe')
user_info()
user_info( email_id = 'jimmy@outlook.com', username =
'Jimmy' )
user_info()
user_info( email_id = 'emily@gmail.com', username = 'Emily')
user_info(username = 'Emilia', email_id = 'emilia@yahoo.com')
user_info(username = 'Mark', email_id = 'mark@outlook.com')
user_info()
= RESTART: C:/Users/saifia computers/Desktop/sample.py
My name is Joe and I am a new user.
My email ID is Joe@Gmail.Com.
```

My name is Dora and I am a new user.

My email ID is Dora@Outlook.Com.

My name is Jimmy and I am a new user.

My email ID is Jimmy@Outlook.Com.

My name is Dora and I am a new user.

My email ID is Dora@Outlook.Com.

My name is Emily and I am a new user.

My email ID is Emily@Gmail.Com.

My name is Emilia and I am a new user.

My email ID is Emilia@Yahoo.Com.

My name is Mark and I am a new user.

My email ID is Mark@Outlook.Com.

My name is Dora and I am a new user.

My email ID is Dora@Outlook.Com.

>>>

You can use the keyword arguments, the positional arguments and the default values at the same time.

```
def user_info(username = 'Dora', email_id =
'dora@outlook.com'):
    print("My name is " + username.title() + " and I am a new
user.")
    print("My email ID is " + email_id.title() + ".")
user_info(email_id = 'joe@gmail.com', username = 'Joe')
user_info()
```

```
user_info( username = 'Jimmy' )
user_info()
user_info( email_id = 'emily@gmail.com', username = 'Emily')
user_info('Emilia', email_id = 'emilia@yahoo.com')
user_info('Mark', 'mark@outlook.com')
user_info()
= RESTART: C:/Users/saifia computers/Desktop/sample.py
My name is Joe and I am a new user.
My email ID is Joe@Gmail.Com.
My name is Dora and I am a new user.
My email ID is Dora@Outlook.Com.
My name is Jimmy and I am a new user.
My email ID is Dora@Outlook.Com.
My name is Dora and I am a new user.
My email ID is Dora@Outlook.Com.
My name is Emily and I am a new user.
My email ID is Emily@Gmail.Com.
My name is Emilia and I am a new user.
My email ID is Emilia@Yahoo.Com.
My name is Mark and I am a new user.
My email ID is Mark@Outlook.Com.
My name is Dora and I am a new user.
My email ID is Dora@Outlook.Com.
>>>
```

The most important thing to note in the code mentioned above is that in one function call when I missed out on writing the email ID, the program picked it up from the default values and ran it. If you leave one argument in the function call but have a default argument in place, you will have it covered by the default values.

You may run an error if you fail to fill in the function call with the arguments.

```
def user_info(username, email_id ):
    print("My name is " + username.title() + " and I am a new user.")
    print("My email ID is " + email_id.title() + ".")


user_info()
= RESTART: C:/Users/saifia computers/Desktop/sample.py
Traceback (most recent call last):
  File "C:/Users/saifia computers/Desktop/sample.py", line 6, in <module>
    user_info()
TypeError: user_info() missing 2 required positional arguments: 'username' and 'email_id'
>>>
```

Returning Values

A function does not have to display the output in a direct form. You can make the function process a bunch of data and return the value in an indirect form. The return statement picks up a value from the function and forwards it to the line that made a function call.

```
def user_info(username, email_id ):
    info = "My name is " + username.title() + " and I am a new user, and my email ID is " + email_id.title() + "."
    return info.title()
newuser = user_info('Dora', 'dora@gmail.com')
print(newuser)
newuser1 = user_info('John', 'john@gmail.com')
print(newuser1)
newuser2 = user_info('Jimmy', 'jimmy@gmail.com')
print(newuser2)
```

= RESTART: C:/Users/saifia computers/Desktop/sample.py

My Name Is Dora And I Am A New User, And My Email Id Is Dora@Gmail.Com.

My Name Is John And I Am A New User, And My Email Id Is John@Gmail.Com.

My Name Is Jimmy And I Am A New User, And My Email Id Is Jimmy@Gmail.Com.

>>>

In the next code sample, I will add another argument to the code. I will also experiment on making an argument optional so that the users who do not want to fill in a value, can leave it without running an error in the program.

```
def user_info(username, email_id, gender ):
    info = "My name is " + username.title() + " and I am a new
user, and my email ID is " + email_id.title() + ". My gender is "
+ gender.title() + "."
    return info.title()
newuser = user_info('Dora', 'dora@gmail.com', 'female')
print(newuser)
newuser1 = user_info('John', 'john@gmail.com', 'male')
print(newuser1)
newuser2 = user_info('Jimmy', 'jimmy@gmail.com', 'male')
print(newuser2)
= RESTART: C:/Users/saifia computers/Desktop/sample.py
My Name Is Dora And I Am A New User, And My Email Id Is
Dora@Gmail.Com. My Gender Is Female.
My Name Is John And I Am A New User, And My Email Id Is
John@Gmail.Com. My Gender Is Male.
My Name Is Jimmy And I Am A New User, And My Email Id
Is Jimmy@Gmail.Com. My Gender Is Male.
>>>
```

Suppose someone wants to leave the email option aside. You can add a conditional statement to the existing code to allow users to make a choice at will.

```python
def user_info(username, gender, email_id=" "):
    if email_id:
        info = "My name is " + username.title() + " and I am a new user, and my email ID is " + email_id.title() + ". My gender is " + gender.title() + "."
    else:
        info = "My name is " + username.title() + " and my gender is " + gender.title() + "."
    return info.title()
newuser = user_info('Dora', 'female')
print(newuser)
newuser1 = user_info('John', 'john@gmail.com', 'male')
print(newuser1)
newuser2 = user_info('Jimmy', 'jimmy@gmail.com', 'male')
print(newuser2)
```

= RESTART: C:/Users/saifia computers/Desktop/sample.py

My Name Is Dora And My Gender Is Female.

My Name Is John And I Am A New User, And My Email Id Is Male. My Gender Is John@Gmail.Com.

My Name Is Jimmy And I Am A New User, And My Email Id Is Male. My Gender Is Jimmy@Gmail.Com.

>>>

Function and Dictionary

You can pair up a dictionary with a function. Take the example of the following function.

```
def user_info(username, gender, email_id):
    user = {'uname': username, 'gender': gender, 'email address': email_id}
    return user
newuser = user_info('Johnson', 'johnson@gmail.com', 'male')
print(newuser)
newuser1 = user_info('John', 'john@gmail.com', 'male')
print(newuser1)
newuser2 = user_info('Jimmy', 'jimmy@gmail.com', 'male')
print(newuser2)
newuser3 = user_info('Dora', 'dora@gmail.com', 'female')
print(newuser3)
= RESTART: C:/Users/saifia computers/Desktop/sample.py
{'uname': 'Johnson', 'gender': 'johnson@gmail.com', 'email address': 'male'}
{'uname': 'John', 'gender': 'john@gmail.com', 'email address': 'male'}
{'uname': 'Jimmy', 'gender': 'jimmy@gmail.com', 'email address': 'male'}
{'uname': 'Dora', 'gender': 'dora@gmail.com', 'email address': 'female'}
>>>
```

The function user_info takes the requisite information about the name, gender and email address of a user, and fill them up into a dictionary. Each value is stored in the designated key. The function receives information in raw form and turns it into textual information in a meaningful data structure. Up till now, I have stored and processed the information in the form of strings. You may confront situations where you have to store data in numerical form as well. There is an easy way out.

```
def user_info(username, gender, email_id, age="):
    user = {'uname': username, 'gender': gender, 'email address':
email_id}
    if age:
        user['age'] = age
    return user
newuser = user_info('Johnson', 'johnson@gmail.com', 'male',
age=55)
print(newuser)
newuser1 = user_info('John', 'john@gmail.com', 'male', age=33)
print(newuser1)
newuser2 = user_info('Jimmy', 'jimmy@gmail.com', 'male',
age= 54)
print(newuser2)
newuser3 = user_info('Dora', 'dora@gmail.com', 'female', age=
24)
print(newuser3)
```

{'uname': 'Johnson', 'gender': 'johnson@gmail.com', 'email address': 'male', 'age': 55}

{'uname': 'John', 'gender': 'john@gmail.com', 'email address': 'male', 'age': 33}

{'uname': 'Jimmy', 'gender': 'jimmy@gmail.com', 'email address': 'male', 'age': 54}

{'uname': 'Dora', 'gender': 'dora@gmail.com', 'email address': 'female', 'age': 24}

>>>

I have added a new parameter to the function's definition and have also assigned this parameter a kind of empty default value.

Function and While Loop

You can pair up a function with a while loop. Let us jump to the text editor to see how you can do that.

```
def user_info(username, email_id, gender ):
    info = "My name is " + username.title() + " and I am a new
user, and my email ID is " + email_id.title() + ". My gender is "
+ gender.title() + "."
    return info.title()
while True:
    print("\nPlease tell me about yourself.")
    user_name = input("Please enter your name: ")
    email = input("Please enter your email address: ")
```

133

```python
    gen = input("Please enter your gender: ")

newuser = user_info(user_name, email, gen)
print("\n The user information is as follows: " + newuser + ".")
```

= RESTART: C:/Users/saifia computers/Desktop/sample.py

Please tell me about yourself.

Please enter your name: John

Please enter your email address: john@gmail.com

Please enter your gender: male

Please tell me about yourself.

Please enter your name: jimmy

Please enter your email address: jimmy@gmail.com

Please enter your gender: male

Please tell me about yourself.

Please enter your name: dora

Please enter your email address: dora@gmail.com

Please enter your gender: female

Please tell me about yourself.

Please enter your name:

The while loop lacks a quit condition therefore it will run on end and will keep asking about the name of users even after all the users have filled in their personal information. I will add a break statement in the same code so that users can exit the program when they have entered all the information.

```python
def user_info(username, email_id, gender ):
    info = "My name is " + username.title() + " and I am a new
user, and my email ID is " + email_id.title() + ". My gender is "
+ gender.title() + "."
    return info.title()
while True:
    print("\nPlease tell me about yourself.")
    print("(If you want to exit the program, enter 'q')")
    uname = input("Please enter your name: ")
    if uname == 'q':
        break

    uemail = input("Please enter your email address: ")
    if uemail == 'q':
        break
    ugen = input("Please enter your gender: ")
    if ugen == 'q':
        break


    newuser = user_info(uname, uemail, ugen)
    print("\n The user information is as follows: " + newuser + ".")
```

This program will keep running until someone enters 'q.' Functions are flexible in inviting and using different types of data structures. You can easily pass a list to a specific function. Whether the list is of numbers, names, and even complex objects like dictionaries. When you do that, the function gets access to the specific contents of the list.

```
def user_info(usersinfo):
    for userinfo in usersinfo:
        mg = "Hi, My name is " + userinfo.title() + ". I am here to take a walk-in interview."
        print(mg)
candidate_names = ['jimmy', 'john', 'dora', 'johnson', 'james']
user_info(candidate_names)
= RESTART: C:/Users/saifia computers/Desktop/sample.py
Hi, My name is Jimmy. I am here to take a walk-in-interview.
Hi, My name is John. I am here to take a walk-in-interview.
Hi, My name is Dora. I am here to take a walk-in-interview.
Hi, My name is Johnson. I am here to take a walk-in-interview.
Hi, My name is James. I am here to take a walk-in-interview.
>>>
```

If you run into an error, it can possibly be due to a missing argument. See the following error type.

```
def user_info(usersinfo):
    for userinfo in usersinfo:
        mg = "Hi, My name is " + userinfo.title() + ". I am here to take a walk-in interview."
```

```
    print(mg)
candidate_names = ['jimmy', 'john', 'dora', 'johnson', 'james']
user_info()
```

= RESTART: C:/Users/saifia computers/Desktop/sample.py

Traceback (most recent call last):

File "C:/Users/saifia computers/Desktop/sample.py", line 7, in <module>

user_info()

TypeError: user_info() missing 1 required positional argument: 'usersinfo'

>>>

Therefore, you should not leave the parenthesis of the function empty.

Functions allow you to modify different data types such as lists. You can first pass a list and then modify it as well. The changes you introduce to a list are permanent and allow a person to work efficiently. The following will pass the list without functions.

```
to_buy_items = ['printer', 'scanner', 'fan', 'table', 'chair',
'computer system', 'table lights']
bought_items = []
while to_buy_items:
    office = to_buy_items.pop()
    print("I am buying the " + office)
    bought_items.append(office)
```

```
print("\nI have purchased and set up the following items in the office:")
for bought_item in bought_items:
    print(bought_item)
```

= RESTART: C:/Users/saifia computers/Desktop/sample.py

I am buying the table lights

I am buying the computer system

I am buying the chair

I am buying the table

I am buying the fan

I am buying the scanner

I am buying the printer

I have purchased and set up the following items in the office:

table lights

computer system

chair

table

fan

scanner

printer

>>>

Now I will write two functions for two separate jobs. The code will be more efficient and interactive.

```python
def officeitems (to_buy_items, bought_items):
    while to_buy_items:
        office = to_buy_items.pop()
        print("I am buying the " + office)
        bought_items.append(office)
def o_bought_items(bought_items):
    print("\nI have purchased and set up the following items in
the office:")
    for bought_item in bought_items:
        print(bought_item)
to_buy_items = ['printer', 'scanner', 'fan', 'table', 'chair',
'computer system', 'table lights']
bought_items = []
officeitems(to_buy_items, bought_items)
o_bought_items(bought_items)
```

= RESTART: C:/Users/saifia computers/Desktop/sample.py

I am buying the table lights

I am buying the computer system

I am buying the chair

I am buying the table

I am buying the fan

I am buying the scanner

I am buying the printer

I have purchased and set up the following items in the office:

table lights

computer system

chair

table

fan

scanner

printer

>>>

Chapter Eight

Object-Oriented Programming

Object-oriented programming is the spirit of Python. It is one of the most effective approaches to develop software. Object-oriented programming suggests that you write effective classes to represent real-world situations and objects. While writing a class, you get the actual feel of automation. You get to build an object from a class and add appropriate personality traits to the same. The process of building objects from a class is dubbed as instantiation.

In this chapter, I will explain how to write Python classes and how to create a lot of instances in a single class. I will also define the actions that I want to attribute to an object. You will also be able to store the classes in the form of modules and then import them to your program files.

Python classes help you build complex programs and give you a feel for programming. You will get to know your code and the bigger concepts behind these codes. Classes can help you wrap up a lot of work in a short amount of time and meet complex challenges in the simplest ways. A class can turn a random program into sophisticated software.

You can model any real-world object with the help of Python classes. In the next code snippet, I will write a code that will be modeled on a leopard. I will give the leopard a name, age, and color. I will add behavioral attributes to the class as well.

Leopard Class

After writing the leopard class, I will add instances to the same that will store the name, age and color of the object.

```
class Leopard():
    """This class will build the model of a leopard."""
    def __init__(self, lname, lage, lcolor):
        """here I will initialize the name, age and color attributes
of the class."""
        self.lname = lname
        self.lage = lage
        self.lcolor = lcolor
    def run(self):
        print(self.lname.title() + " is running fast out in the wild.")
    def attack(self):
        print(self.lname.title() + " is now attacking a deer who is
grazing in the meadow.")
```

This is how you can write a class and add attributes to it. I have created the class and add a couple of functions.

Explaining the __init__() Method

It is a special method that is automatically run by Python when you create a new instance from the main Leopard class. The method two underscores in the front and two in the trail.

I have defined the __init__() method and given it three attributes for the name, age, and the color of the leopard. Then I added two more methods that are about the behavioral traits of the leopard we are creating. These methods will print messages about the running and attacking of the leopard. If you want to understand it in a simpler form, you can consider the leopard a robot leopard. This will help you understand how Python helps in automating machines by modeling them on real-life objects.

Now that we have the structure of the class, we can move on to create different objects. I will add an instance to the Leopard class.

```
class Leopard():
    """This class will build the model of a leopard."""


    def __init__(self, lname, lage, lcolor):
        """here I will initialize the name, age and color attributes
of the class."""
        self.lname = lname
        self.lage = lage
        self.lcolor = lcolor
    def run(self):
```

```
        print(self.lname.title() + " is running fast out in the wild.")
    def attack(self):
        print(self.lname.title() + " is now attacking a deer who is
grazing in the meadow.")
leopard1 = Leopard('Tame', 9, 'yellow')
print("The name of the leopard is " + leopard1.lname.title() +
".")
print("The age of the leopard is " + str(leopard1.lage) + ".")
print("The color of the leopard is " + leopard1.lcolor.title() +
".")
```

= RESTART: C:/Users/saifia computers/Desktop/sample.py

The name of the leopard is Tame.

The age of the leopard is 9.

The color of the leopard is Yellow.

>>>

Now I will add more instances to the same class.

```
class Leopard():
    """This class will build the model of a leopard."""

    def __init__(self, lname, lage, lcolor):
        """here I will initialize the name, age and color attributes
of the class."""
        self.lname = lname
        self.lage = lage
```

```python
        self.lcolor = lcolor
    def run(self):
        print(self.lname.title() + " is running fast out in the wild.")
    def attack(self):
        print(self.lname.title() + " is now attacking a deer who is
grazing in the meadow.")
leopard1 = Leopard('Tame', 9, 'yellow')
print("The name of the leopard is " + leopard1.lname.title() +
".")
print("The age of the leopard is " + str(leopard1.lage) + ".")
print("The color of the leopard is " + leopard1.lcolor.title() +
".")
leopard2 = Leopard('Fame', 8, 'snow white')
print("The name of the leopard is " + leopard2.lname.title() +
".")
print("The age of the leopard is " + str(leopard2.lage) + ".")
print("The color of the leopard is " + leopard2.lcolor.title() +
".")
leopard3 = Leopard('Storm', 11, 'yellow')
print("The name of the leopard is " + leopard3.lname.title() +
".")
print("The age of the leopard is " + str(leopard3.lage) + ".")
print("The color of the leopard is " + leopard3.lcolor.title() +
".")
```

= RESTART: C:/Users/saifia computers/Desktop/sample.py

The name of the leopard is Tame.

The age of the leopard is 9.

The color of the leopard is Yellow.

The name of the leopard is Fame.

The age of the leopard is 8.

The color of the leopard is Snow White.

The name of the leopard is Storm.

The age of the leopard is 11.

The color of the leopard is Yellow.

>>>

Now that I have created an instance for the Leopard class, I will now add to it some additional methods that will make the robot leopard run wildly and attack the prey to hunt his meal. This is going to be quite interesting.

```
class Leopard():
    """This class will build the model of a leopard."""
    def __init__(self, lname, lage, lcolor):
        """here I will initialize the name, age and color attributes
of the class."""
        self.lname = lname
        self.lage = lage
        self.lcolor = lcolor
    def run(self):
```

```python
    print(self.lname.title() + " is running fast out in the wild.")
  def attack(self):
    print(self.lname.title() + " is now attacking a deer who is
grazing in the meadow.")
leopard1 = Leopard('Tame', 9, 'yellow')
print("The name of the leopard is " + leopard1.lname.title() +
".")
print("The age of the leopard is " + str(leopard1.lage) + ".")
print("The color of the leopard is " + leopard1.lcolor.title() +
".")
leopard1.run()
leopard1.attack()
leopard2 = Leopard('Fame', 8, 'snow white')
print("The name of the leopard is " + leopard2.lname.title() +
".")
print("The age of the leopard is " + str(leopard2.lage) + ".")
print("The color of the leopard is " + leopard2.lcolor.title() +
".")
leopard2.run()
leopard2.attack()
leopard3 = Leopard('Storm', 11, 'yellow')
print("The name of the leopard is " + leopard3.lname.title() +
".")
print("The age of the leopard is " + str(leopard3.lage) + ".")
```

print("The color of the leopard is " + leopard3.lcolor.title() + ".")

leopard3.run()

leopard3.attack()

= RESTART: C:/Users/saifia computers/Desktop/sample.py

The name of the leopard is Tame.

The age of the leopard is 9.

The color of the leopard is Yellow.

Tame is running fast out in the wild.

Tame is now attacking a deer who is grazing in the meadow.

The name of the leopard is Fame.

The age of the leopard is 8.

The color of the leopard is Snow White.

Fame is running fast out in the wild.

Fame is now attacking a deer who is grazing in the meadow.

The name of the leopard is Storm.

The age of the leopard is 11.

The color of the leopard is Yellow.

Storm is running fast out in the wild.

Storm is now attacking a deer who is grazing in the meadow.

>>>

Python creates two separate instances if you keep the name, age and color of the leopard same. See the following example.

```python
class Leopard():
    """This class will build the model of a leopard."""

    def __init__(self, lname, lage, lcolor):
        """here I will initialize the name, age and color attributes
of the class."""
        self.lname = lname
        self.lage = lage
        self.lcolor = lcolor
    def run(self):
        print(self.lname.title() + " is running fast out in the wild.")
    def attack(self):
        print(self.lname.title() + " is now attacking a deer who is
grazing in the meadow.")
leopard1 = Leopard('Tame', 9, 'yellow')
print("The name of the leopard is " + leopard1.lname.title() +
".")
print("The age of the leopard is " + str(leopard1.lage) + ".")
print("The color of the leopard is " + leopard1.lcolor.title() +
".")
leopard2 = Leopard('Tame', 9, 'yellow')
print("The name of the leopard is " + leopard2.lname.title() +
".")
print("The age of the leopard is " + str(leopard2.lage) + ".")
```

```
print("The color of the leopard is " + leopard2.lcolor.title() +
".")
```

= RESTART: C:/Users/saifia computers/Desktop/sample.py

The name of the leopard is Tame.

The age of the leopard is 9.

The color of the leopard is Yellow.

The name of the leopard is Tame.

The age of the leopard is 9.

The color of the leopard is Yellow.

>>>

The Fish Class

```
class Fish():
    """This class will build the model of a leopard."""

    def __init__(self, fname, fage, fcolor):
        """here I will initialize the name, age and color attributes
of the class."""
        self.fname = fname
        self.fage = fage
        self.fcolor = fcolor
    def swim(self):
        print(self.fname.title() + " is swimming at a fast pace
against the current.")
```

```python
    def hunt(self):
        print(self.fname.title() + " is hunting smaller fish to feed itself.")
fish1 = Fish('Tuna', 2, 'yellow')
print("The name of the fish is " + fish1.fname.title() + ".")
print("The age of the fish is " + str(fish1.fage) + ".")
print("The color of the fish is " + fish1.fcolor.title() + ".")
fish1.swim()
fish1.hunt()
fish2 = Fish('whale', 50, 'blue & white')
print("The name of the fish is " + fish2.fname.title() + ".")
print("The age of the fish is " + str(fish2.fage) + ".")
print("The color of the fish is " + fish2.fcolor.title() + ".")
fish2.swim()
fish2.hunt()
```

= RESTART: C:/Users/saifia computers/Desktop/sample.py

The name of the fish is Tuna.

The age of the fish is 2.

The color of the fish is Yellow.

Tuna is swimming at a fast pace against the current.

Tuna is hunting smaller fish to feed itself.

The name of the fish is Whale.

The age of the fish is 50.

The color of the fish is Blue & White.

Whale is swimming at a fast pace against the current.

Whale is hunting smaller fish to feed itself.

>>>

The Bike Class

In this code sample, I will create bike class. I will add the model name, make, color and year of manufacturing to the class and display the information in a neatly formatted form.

```
class Bike():
    """This class will build the model of a bike."""

    def __init__(self, bmodel, bmake, bcolor, byear):

        self.bmodel = bmodel
        self.bmake = bmake
        self.bcolor = bcolor
        self.byear = byear
    def fullname(self):
        fullbikename = str(self.byear) + ' ' + self.bmodel + ' ' +
self.bmake + ' ' + self.bcolor
        return fullbikename.title()

bike1 = Bike('CG-125', 'Honda', 'blue', 2012)
print(bike1.fullname())
```

2012 Cg-125 Honda Blue

>>>

The process is similar to that of the creation of a Leopard class. I have defined the __init__ () method and the self-parameters. Four parameters will define the make, model, color and year of making of the bike. When you are creating a new instance to the bike class, you will have to define the make, model, year and color of the bike. If you miss one of the parameters while creating an instance, you will see an interpreter error just like the following.

```python
class Bike():
    """This class will build the model of a bike."""
    def __init__(self, bmodel, bmake, bcolor, byear):
        self.bmodel = bmodel
        self.bmake = bmake
        self.bcolor = bcolor
        self.byear = byear
    def fullname(self):
        fullbikename = str(self.byear) + ' ' + self.bmodel + ' ' +
self.bmake + ' ' + self.bcolor
        return fullbikename.title()
bike1 = Bike('CG-125', 'blue', 2012)
print(bike1.fullname())
```

```
>>>= RESTART: C:/Users/saifia
computers/Desktop/sample.py
Traceback (most recent call last):
  File "C:/Users/saifia computers/Desktop/sample.py", line 16,
in <module>
    bike1 = Bike('CG-125', 'blue', 2012)
TypeError: __init__() missing 1 required positional argument:
'byear'
>>>
```

Just like the Leopard class, you can create as many instances for the Bike class as you need. This program is helpful if you are looking forward to owning a bike showroom. You can fill in the bike class with the latest information whenever a new bike gets registered with the showroom for sale. This is how you allow your customers to view each bike and its specifications in a fast and efficient way. I will now add more instances to the Bike class to show how you can store more information to the database through a working Bike class.

```
class Bike():
    """This class will build the model of a bike."""
        self.bmodel = bmodel
        self.bmake = bmake
        self.bcolor = bcolor
        self.byear = byear
    def fullname(self):
```

```python
        fullbikename = "We have a bike that hit the markets in " +
str(self.byear) + ". The model is " + self.bmodel + ". The bike is
manufactured by " + self.bmake + ". Its color is " + self.bcolor
+ "."
        return fullbikename.title()
bike1 = Bike('CG-125', 'Honda', 'blue', 2012)
print(bike1.fullname())
bike2 = Bike('F 900 R', 'BMW', 'black', 2014)
print(bike2.fullname())
bike3 = Bike('F 900 XR', 'BMW', 'blue', 2014)
print(bike3.fullname())
bike4 = Bike('R 1250 RT', 'BMW', 'brown', 2016)
print(bike4.fullname())
bike5 = Bike('Heritage Classic', 'Harley Davidson', 'black',
2018)
print(bike4.fullname())
```

= RESTART: C:/Users/saifia computers/Desktop/sample.py

We Have A Bike That Hit The Markets In 2012. The Model Is
Cg-125. The Bike Is Manufactured By Honda. Its Color Is Blue.

We Have A Bike That Hit The Markets In 2014. The Model Is
F 900 R. The Bike Is Manufactured By BMW. Its Color Is
Black.

We Have A Bike That Hit The Markets In 2014. The Model Is
F 900 Xr. The Bike Is Manufactured By BMW. Its Color Is
Blue.

We Have A Bike That Hit The Markets In 2016. The Model Is R 1250 Rt. The Bike Is Manufactured By BMW. Its Color Is Brown.

We Have A Bike That Hit The Markets In 2016. The Model Is R 1250 Rt. The Bike Is Manufactured By BMW. Its Color Is Brown.

>>>

Each attribute in the Bike class demands an initial value. You can set the initial value at zero. It also can be an empty string. When you are running a showroom, you need to tell your customers how many kilometers the bike has run on the road. To achieve this objective, you can integrate a method into the program. See the changes in the code. I will include an odometer reading method for the Bike class.

```
class Bike():
    """This class will build the model of a bike."""

    def __init__(self, bmodel, bmake, bcolor, byear):

        self.bmodel = bmodel
        self.bmake = bmake
        self.bcolor = bcolor
        self.byear = byear
        self.odometer_reading = 0
    def fullname(self):
```

```python
        fullbikename = "We have a bike that hit the markets in " +
str(self.byear) + ". The model is " + self.bmodel + ". The bike is
manufactured by " + self.bmake + ". Its color is " + self.bcolor
+ "."
        return fullbikename.title()
    def read_odometer(self):
        print("This bike has run " + str(self.odometer_reading) + "
kilometers on the road.")
bike1 = Bike('CG-125', 'Honda', 'blue', 2012)
print(bike1.fullname())
bike1.read_odometer()
bike2 = Bike('F 900 R', 'BMW', 'black', 2014)
print(bike2.fullname())
bike2.read_odometer()
bike3 = Bike('F 900 XR', 'BMW', 'blue', 2014)
print(bike3.fullname())
bike3.read_odometer()
bike4 = Bike('R 1250 RT', 'BMW', 'brown', 2016)
print(bike4.fullname())
bike4.read_odometer()
bike5 = Bike('Heritage Classic', 'Harley Davidson', 'black',
2018)
print(bike4.fullname())
bike5.read_odometer()
```

= RESTART: C:/Users/saifia computers/Desktop/sample.py

We Have A Bike That Hit The Markets In 2012. The Model Is Cg-125. The Bike Is Manufactured By Honda. Its Color Is Blue.

This bike has run 0 kilometers on the road.

We Have A Bike That Hit The Markets In 2014. The Model Is F 900 R. The Bike Is Manufactured By BMW. Its Color Is Black.

This bike has run 0 kilometers on the road.

We Have A Bike That Hit The Markets In 2014. The Model Is F 900 Xr. The Bike Is Manufactured By BMW. Its Color Is Blue.

This bike has run 0 kilometers on the road.

We Have A Bike That Hit The Markets In 2016. The Model Is R 1250 Rt. The Bike Is Manufactured By BMW. Its Color Is Brown.

This bike has run 0 kilometers on the road.

We Have A Bike That Hit The Markets In 2016. The Model Is R 1250 Rt. The Bike Is Manufactured By BMW. Its Color Is Brown.

This bike has run 0 kilometers on the road.

>>>

Python calls the __init__() method to form a new instance. It stores the values in the form of attributes just as it did for the past example. Python has now created a new attribute and adjusts its value to zero. Coupled with the attribute comes a new method, namely read_odometer(). This is how your customers can easily read the mileage of the bike. It is also helpful for you, as you can easily track how many miles your car has run.

You have the power to change the value of the attributes in different ways. You can directly change the value of the attribute by an instance. You can set its value with the help of a method or increment the same by a method. In the following code sample, I will test how we can make the above-mentioned changes. I have also changed the read_odometer() method to reading_odometer() method to make more current and interactive.

```
class Bike():
    """This class will build the model of a bike."""
    def __init__(self, bmodel, bmake, bcolor, byear):
        self.bmodel = bmodel
        self.bmake = bmake
        self.bcolor = bcolor
        self.byear = byear
        self.odometer_reading = 0
    def fullname(self):
        fullbikename = "We have a bike that hit the markets in " +
str(self.byear) + ". The model is " + self.bmodel + ". The bike is
manufactured by " + self.bmake + ". Its color is " + self.bcolor
+ "."

        return fullbikename.title()
```

```python
    def reading_odometer(self):
        print("This bike has run " + str(self.odometer_reading) + " kilometers on the road.")
bike1 = Bike('CG-125', 'Honda', 'blue', 2012)
print(bike1.fullname())
bike1.odometer_reading = 21
bike1.reading_odometer()
bike2 = Bike('F 900 R', 'BMW', 'black', 2014)
print(bike2.fullname())
bike2.odometer_reading = 27
bike2.reading_odometer()
bike3 = Bike('F 900 XR', 'BMW', 'blue', 2014)
print(bike3.fullname())
bike3.odometer_reading = 30
bike3.reading_odometer()
bike4 = Bike('R 1250 RT', 'BMW', 'brown', 2016)
print(bike4.fullname())
bike4.reading_odometer()
bike5 = Bike('Heritage Classic', 'Harley Davidson', 'black', 2018)
print(bike4.fullname())
bike5.reading_odometer()
>>>= RESTART: C:/Users/saifia computers/Desktop/sample.py
```

We Have A Bike That Hit The Markets In 2012. The Model Is Cg-125. The Bike Is Manufactured By Honda. Its Color Is Blue.

This bike has run 21 kilometers on the road.

We Have A Bike That Hit The Markets In 2014. The Model Is F 900 R. The Bike Is Manufactured By BMW. Its Color Is Black.

This bike has run 27 kilometers on the road.

We Have A Bike That Hit The Markets In 2014. The Model Is F 900 Xr. The Bike Is Manufactured By BMW. Its Color Is Blue.

This bike has run 30 kilometers on the road.

We Have A Bike That Hit The Markets In 2016. The Model Is R 1250 Rt. The Bike Is Manufactured By BMW. Its Color Is Brown.

This bike has run 0 kilometers on the road.

We Have A Bike That Hit The Markets In 2016. The Model Is R 1250 Rt. The Bike Is Manufactured By BMW. Its Color Is Brown.

This bike has run 0 kilometers on the road.

>>>

You can also change the default value at 50 kilometers to manage the difference of mileage consumed in transporting the bike from one place to another.

```
class Bike():
    """This class will build the model of a bike."""
```

```python
    def __init__(self, bmodel, bmake, bcolor, byear):
        self.bmodel = bmodel
        self.bmake = bmake
        self.bcolor = bcolor
        self.byear = byear
        self.odometer_reading = 50
    def fullname(self):
        fullbikename = "We have a bike that hit the markets in " + str(self.byear) + ". The model is " + self.bmodel + ". The bike is manufactured by " + self.bmake + ". Its color is " + self.bcolor + "."
        return fullbikename.title()
    def reading_odometer(self):
        print("This bike has run " + str(self.odometer_reading) + " kilometers on the road.")


bike1 = Bike('CG-125', 'Honda', 'blue', 2012)
print(bike1.fullname())
bike1.odometer_reading = 100
bike1.reading_odometer()
bike2 = Bike('F 900 R', 'BMW', 'black', 2014)
print(bike2.fullname())
bike2.odometer_reading = 500
bike2.reading_odometer()
```

```
bike3 = Bike('F 900 XR', 'BMW', 'blue', 2014)

print(bike3.fullname())

bike3.odometer_reading = 700

bike3.reading_odometer()

bike4 = Bike('R 1250 RT', 'BMW', 'brown', 2016)

print(bike4.fullname())

bike4.reading_odometer()

bike5 = Bike('Heritage Classic', 'Harley Davidson', 'black', 2018)

print(bike4.fullname())

bike5.reading_odometer()
```

= RESTART: C:/Users/saifia computers/Desktop/sample.py

We Have A Bike That Hit The Markets In 2012. The Model Is Cg-125. The Bike Is Manufactured By Honda. Its Color Is Blue.

This bike has run 100 kilometers on the road.

We Have A Bike That Hit The Markets In 2014. The Model Is F 900 R. The Bike Is Manufactured By BMW. Its Color Is Black.

This bike has run 500 kilometers on the road.

We Have A Bike That Hit The Markets In 2014. The Model Is F 900 Xr. The Bike Is Manufactured By BMW. Its Color Is Blue.

This bike has run 700 kilometers on the road.

We Have A Bike That Hit The Markets In 2016. The Model Is R 1250 Rt. The Bike Is Manufactured By BMW. Its Color Is Brown.

This bike has run 50 kilometers on the road.

We Have A Bike That Hit The Markets In 2016. The Model Is R 1250 Rt. The Bike Is Manufactured By BMW. Its Color Is Brown.

This bike has run 50 kilometers on the road.

>>>

Proper Modification of Values

It is quite helpful to have a bunch of methods that would update different attributes of your program. Instead of directly accessing multiple attributes, you can pass the latest value to a newly added method and let it handle updating the program. The program will do the updating internally and you do not have to worry about it anymore. The new method will be dubbed as updating_the_odometer().

```
class Bike():
    """This class will build the model of a bike."""
    def __init__(self, bmodel, bmake, bcolor, byear):
        self.bmodel = bmodel
        self.bmake = bmake
        self.bcolor = bcolor
        self.byear = byear
```

```python
        self.odometer_reading = 50
    def fullname(self):
        fullbikename = "We have a bike that hit the markets in " +
str(self.byear) + ". The model is " + self.bmodel + ". The bike is
manufactured by " + self.bmake + ". Its color is " + self.bcolor
+ "."
        return fullbikename.title()
    def reading_odometer(self):
        print("This bike has run" + str(self.odometer_reading) + "
kilometers on the road.")
    def updating_the_odometer(self, bmileage):
        self.odometer_reading = bmileage
bike1 = Bike('CG-125', 'Honda', 'blue', 2012)
print(bike1.fullname())
bike1.updating_the_odometer(100)
bike1.reading_odometer()
bike2 = Bike('F 900 R', 'BMW', 'black', 2014)
print(bike2.fullname())
bike2.updating_the_odometer(1000)
bike2.reading_odometer()
bike3 = Bike('F 900 XR', 'BMW', 'blue', 2014)
print(bike3.fullname())
bike3.updating_the_odometer(700)
bike3.reading_odometer()
```

bike4 = Bike('R 1250 RT', 'BMW', 'brown', 2016)

print(bike4.fullname())

bike4.reading_odometer()

bike5 = Bike('Heritage Classic', 'Harley Davidson', 'black', 2018)

print(bike4.fullname())

bike5.reading_odometer()

= RESTART: C:/Users/saifia computers/Desktop/sample.py

We Have A Bike That Hit The Markets In 2012. The Model Is Cg-125. The Bike Is Manufactured By Honda. Its Color Is Blue.

This bike has 100 kilometers on the road.

We Have A Bike That Hit The Markets In 2014. The Model Is F 900 R. The Bike Is Manufactured By BMW. Its Color Is Black.

This bike has 1000 kilometers on the road.

We Have A Bike That Hit The Markets In 2014. The Model Is F 900 Xr. The Bike Is Manufactured By BMW. Its Color Is Blue.

This bike has 700 kilometers on the road.

We Have A Bike That Hit The Markets In 2016. The Model Is R 1250 Rt. The Bike Is Manufactured By BMW. Its Color Is Brown.

This bike has 50 kilometers on the road.

We Have A Bike That Hit The Markets In 2016. The Model Is R 1250 Rt. The Bike Is Manufactured By BMW. Its Color Is Brown.

This bike has 50 kilometers on the road.

>>>

You can make further experiments with the odometer method. A major problem in a showroom is keeping tabs on who is reversing the odometer of the motorbikes. If you are a true businessman, you will not like to dupe your customers. However, sometimes it is not that you who want to dupe the customers. It is your employees who are trying to bag extra profit in addition to their commission. You must stop this practice if you want to live up to your customers' expectations and keep your reputation intact. You can add some logic to your program to ensure no rolling back of the odometer by anyone. I will integrate an if-else statement to the Bike class and do a few changes to make it possible.

```
class Bike():
    """This class will build the model of a bike."""
    def __init__(self, bmodel, bmake, bcolor, byear):
        self.bmodel = bmodel
        self.bmake = bmake
        self.bcolor = bcolor
        self.byear = byear
        self.odometer_reading = 0
    def fullname(self):
```

```
        fullbikename = "We have a bike that hit the markets in " +
str(self.byear) + ". The model is " + self.bmodel + ". The bike is
manufactured by " + self.bmake + ". Its color is " + self.bcolor
+ "."
        return fullbikename.title()
    def reading_odometer(self):
        print("This bike has run " + str(self.odometer_reading) + "
kilometers on the road.")
    def updating_the_odometer(self, bmileage):
        self.odometer_reading = bmileage
        if bmileage >= self.odometer_reading:
            self.odometer_reading = bmileage
        else:
            print("You are not authorized to roll back the reading of
the odometer.")
bike1 = Bike('CG-125', 'Honda', 'blue', 2012)
print(bike1.fullname())
bike1.updating_the_odometer(100)
bike1.reading_odometer()
bike2 = Bike('F 900 R', 'BMW', 'black', 2014)
print(bike2.fullname())
bike2.updating_the_odometer(1000)
bike2.reading_odometer()
bike3 = Bike('F 900 XR', 'BMW', 'blue', 2014)
```

```
print(bike3.fullname())

bike3.updating_the_odometer(700)

bike3.reading_odometer()

bike4 = Bike('R 1250 RT', 'BMW', 'brown', 2016)

print(bike4.fullname())

bike4.updating_the_odometer(40)

bike4.reading_odometer()

bike5 = Bike('Heritage Classic', 'Harley Davidson', 'black', 2018)

print(bike5.fullname())

bike5.updating_the_odometer(0)

bike5.reading_odometer()
```

= RESTART: C:/Users/saifia computers/Desktop/sample.py

We Have A Bike That Hit The Markets In 2012. The Model Is Cg-125. The Bike Is Manufactured By Honda. Its Color Is Blue.

This bike has run 100 kilometers on the road.

We Have A Bike That Hit The Markets In 2014. The Model Is F 900 R. The Bike Is Manufactured By BMW. Its Color Is Black.

This bike has run 1000 kilometers on the road.

We Have A Bike That Hit The Markets In 2014. The Model Is F 900 Xr. The Bike Is Manufactured By BMW. Its Color Is Blue.

This bike has run 700 kilometers on the road.

We Have A Bike That Hit The Markets In 2016. The Model Is R 1250 Rt. The Bike Is Manufactured By BMW. Its Color Is Brown.

This bike has run 40 kilometers on the road.

We Have A Bike That Hit The Markets In 2018. The Model Is Heritage Classic. The Bike Is Manufactured By Harley Davidson. Its Color Is Black.

This bike has run 0 kilometers on the road.

>>>

You can increase the value of an attribute by introducing a simple method to the program. I will another method to the class to make it work. I will add incremental values to each of the five instances I have created. The method will tell Python to add up the incremental value to the existing value and run the program. The incremented value will be displayed in a separate print statement in the code.

```
class Bike():
    """This class will build the model of a bike."""

    def __init__(self, bmodel, bmake, bcolor, byear):

        self.bmodel = bmodel
        self.bmake = bmake
        self.bcolor = bcolor
        self.byear = byear
```

```
        self.odometer_reading = 0
    def fullname(self):
        fullbikename = "We have a bike that hit the markets in " +
str(self.byear) + ". The model is " + self.bmodel + ". The bike is
manufactured by " + self.bmake + ". Its color is " + self.bcolor
+ "."
        return fullbikename.title()
    def reading_odometer(self):
        print("This bike has run " + str(self.odometer_reading) + "
kilometers on the road.")
    def updating_the_odometer(self, bmileage):
        self.odometer_reading = bmileage
        if bmileage >= self.odometer_reading:
            self.odometer_reading = bmileage
        else:
            print("You are not authorized to roll back the reading of
the odometer.")
    def incrementing_odometer(self, bmileage):
        self.odometer_reading += bmileage


bike1 = Bike('CG-125', 'Honda', 'blue', 2012)
print(bike1.fullname())
bike1.updating_the_odometer(100)
bike1.reading_odometer()
```

```python
bike1.incrementing_odometer(1000)
bike1.reading_odometer()
bike2 = Bike('F 900 R', 'BMW', 'black', 2014)
print(bike2.fullname())
bike2.updating_the_odometer(1000)
bike2.reading_odometer()
bike2.incrementing_odometer(500)
bike2.reading_odometer()
bike3 = Bike('F 900 XR', 'BMW', 'blue', 2014)
print(bike3.fullname())
bike3.updating_the_odometer(700)
bike3.reading_odometer()
bike3.incrementing_odometer(1000)
bike3.reading_odometer()
bike4 = Bike('R 1250 RT', 'BMW', 'brown', 2016)
print(bike4.fullname())
bike4.updating_the_odometer(40)
bike4.reading_odometer()
bike4.incrementing_odometer(1000)
bike4.reading_odometer()
bike5 = Bike('Heritage Classic', 'Harley Davidson', 'black',
2018)
print(bike5.fullname())
bike5.updating_the_odometer(0)
```

bike5.reading_odometer()

bike5.incrementing_odometer(10000)

bike5.reading_odometer()

= RESTART: C:/Users/saifia computers/Desktop/sample.py

We Have A Bike That Hit The Markets In 2012. The Model Is Cg-125. The Bike Is Manufactured By Honda. Its Color Is Blue.

This bike has run 100 kilometers on the road.

This bike has run 1100 kilometers on the road.

We Have A Bike That Hit The Markets In 2014. The Model Is F 900 R. The Bike Is Manufactured By BMW. Its Color Is Black.

This bike has run 1000 kilometers on the road.

This bike has run 1500 kilometers on the road.

We Have A Bike That Hit The Markets In 2014. The Model Is F 900 Xr. The Bike Is Manufactured By BMW. Its Color Is Blue.

This bike has run 700 kilometers on the road.

This bike has run 1700 kilometers on the road.

We Have A Bike That Hit The Markets In 2016. The Model Is R 1250 Rt. The Bike Is Manufactured By BMW. Its Color Is Brown.

This bike has run 40 kilometers on the road.

This bike has run 1040 kilometers on the road.

We Have A Bike That Hit The Markets In 2018. The Model Is Heritage Classic. The Bike Is Manufactured By Harley Davidson. Its Color Is Black.

This bike has run 0 kilometers on the road.

This bike has run 10000 kilometers on the road.

>>>

Chapter Nine

The Inheritance Class

Now that you have learned how to write a class, it is pertinent to mention that Python classes are well known for the ease of use they offer to programmers. Once you have written a class, you can reuse it multiple times. There is a process called inheritance in which a subclass is inherited from the parent class. The inherited class is named that way because it inherits the attributes of the parent class. The inherited class is dubbed as the child class. It can use each attribute and method of the parent class. However, you also can create new attributes only for the child class.

Just as you did for the parent class, you will also have to use the __init__() method for the child class. I will create a child class of racer bikes.

```python
class Bike():
    """This class will build the model of a bike."""
    def __init__(self, bmodel, bmake, bcolor, byear):
        self.bmodel = bmodel
        self.bmake = bmake
        self.bcolor = bcolor
        self.byear = byear
```

```python
        self.odometer_reading = 0
    def fullname(self):
        fullbikename = "We have a bike that hit the markets in " +
str(self.byear) + ". The model is " + self.bmodel + ". The bike is
manufactured by " + self.bmake + ". Its color is " + self.bcolor
+ "."
        return fullbikename.title()
    def reading_odometer(self):
        print("This bike has run " + str(self.odometer_reading) + "
kilometers on the road.")
    def updating_the_odometer(self, bmileage):
        self.odometer_reading = bmileage
        if bmileage >= self.odometer_reading:
            self.odometer_reading = bmileage
        else:
            print("You are not authorized to roll back the reading of
the odometer.")
    def incrementing_odometer(self, bmileage):
        self.odometer_reading += bmileage
class RacerBike(Bike):
    def __init__(self, bmodel, bmake, bcolor, byear):
        super().__init__(bmodel, bmake, bcolor, byear)
racer1 = RacerBike('URS: Gravel Riding', 'BMC', 'Grey', '2017')
print(racer1.fullname())
```

```
racer2 = RacerBike('Trackmachine', 'BMC', 'Blue', '2015')
print(racer2.fullname())
racer3 = RacerBike('Alpenchallenge', 'BMC', 'Red', '2012')
print(racer2.fullname())
= RESTART: C:/Users/saifia computers/Desktop/sample.py
```

We Have A Bike That Hit The Markets In 2017. The Model Is Urs: Gravel Riding. The Bike Is Manufactured By Bmc. Its Color Is Grey.

We Have A Bike That Hit The Markets In 2015. The Model Is Trackmachine. The Bike Is Manufactured By Bmc. Its Color Is Blue.

We Have A Bike That Hit The Markets In 2015. The Model Is Trackmachine. The Bike Is Manufactured By Bmc. Its Color Is Blue.

```
>>>
```

The most important thing to keep in mind while creating a child class is to keep the child class inside the parent class. The name of the child class must include parenthesis that carry the name of the parent class. I have added one additional function, the super function that aids Python in forming connections between the child class and the parent class. The child class has taken all the attributes of the parent class. I have not yet added any special attribute to the racer bike.

Child Class in Python 2.7

If you are using Python 2.7, the child class will appear to be a bit different. See the following code and note the difference.

```python
class Bike():
    """This class will build the model of a bike."""

    def __init__(self, bmodel, bmake, bcolor, byear):

        self.bmodel = bmodel
        self.bmake = bmake
        self.bcolor = bcolor
        self.byear = byear
        self.odometer_reading = 0
    def fullname(self):
        fullbikename = "We have a bike that hit the markets in " +
str(self.byear) + ". The model is " + self.bmodel + ". The bike is
manufactured by " + self.bmake + ". Its color is " + self.bcolor
+ "."
        return fullbikename.title()
    def reading_odometer(self):
        print("This bike has run " + str(self.odometer_reading) + "
kilometers on the road.")
    def updating_the_odometer(self, bmileage):
        self.odometer_reading = bmileage
        if bmileage >= self.odometer_reading:
            self.odometer_reading = bmileage
        else:
```

```
        print("You are not authorized to roll back the reading of
the odometer.")
    def incrementing_odometer(self, bmileage):
        self.odometer_reading += bmileage
class RacerBike(Bike):
    def __init__(self, bmodel, bmake, bcolor, byear):
        super(RacerBike,self).__init__(bmodel, bmake, bcolor,
byear)
racer1 = RacerBike('URS: Gravel Riding', 'BMC', 'Grey', '2017')
print(racer1.fullname())
racer2 = RacerBike('Trackmachine', 'BMC', 'Blue', '2015')
print(racer2.fullname())
racer3 = RacerBike('Alpenchallenge', 'BMC', 'Red', '2012')
print(racer2.fullname())
```

The only change I made was in the super function. I filled in the parenthesis with the name of the child class and self-parameter. An interesting thing is that this change does not affect the result of the program, no matter if you do it in Python 3 or 2.7. However, the former technique will not work in 2.7. You can see the result of the program as under:

= RESTART: C:/Users/saifia computers/Desktop/sample.py

We Have A Bike That Hit The Markets In 2017. The Model Is Urs: Gravel Riding. The Bike Is Manufactured By Bmc. Its Color Is Grey.

We Have A Bike That Hit The Markets In 2015. The Model Is Trackmachine. The Bike Is Manufactured By Bmc. Its Color Is Blue.

We Have A Bike That Hit The Markets In 2015. The Model Is Trackmachine. The Bike Is Manufactured By Bmc. Its Color Is Blue.

>>>

Child Class Attributes

Once the child class inherits the parent class's attributes, you can go on to add to it new methods and attributes. I will use the same program and add new attributes for the child class.

```
class Bike():
    """This class will build the model of a bike."""


    def __init__(self, bmodel, bmake, bcolor, byear):

        self.bmodel = bmodel
        self.bmake = bmake
        self.bcolor = bcolor
        self.byear = byear
        self.odometer_reading = 0
    def fullname(self):
        fullbikename = "We have a bike that hit the markets in " +
str(self.byear) + ". The model is " + self.bmodel + ". The bike is
```

manufactured by " + self.bmake + ". Its color is " + self.bcolor + "."

       return fullbikename.title()

  def reading_odometer(self):

    print("This bike has run " + str(self.odometer_reading) + " kilometers on the road.")

  def updating_the_odometer(self, bmileage):

    self.odometer_reading = bmileage

    if bmileage >= self.odometer_reading:

      self.odometer_reading = bmileage

    else:

      print("You are not authorized to roll back the reading of the odometer.")

  def incrementing_odometer(self, bmileage):

    self.odometer_reading += bmileage

class RacerBike(Bike):

  def __init__(self, bmodel, bmake, bcolor, byear):

    super(RacerBike,self).__init__(bmodel, bmake, bcolor, byear)

    self.performance_tire = 'three textile layered'

  def describe_tires(self):

    print("This racer bike has " + self.performance_tire + " performance tires.")

racer1 = RacerBike('URS: Gravel Riding', 'BMC', 'Grey', '2017')

print(racer1.fullname())

```
racer1.describe_tires()
racer2 = RacerBike('Trackmachine', 'BMC', 'Blue', '2015')
print(racer2.fullname())
racer2.describe_tires()
racer3 = RacerBike('Alpenchallenge', 'BMC', 'Red', '2012')
print(racer2.fullname())
racer3.describe_tires()
```

= RESTART: C:/Users/saifia computers/Desktop/sample.py

We Have A Bike That Hit The Markets In 2017. The Model Is Urs: Gravel Riding. The Bike Is Manufactured By Bmc. Its Color Is Grey.

This racer bike has three textile layered performance tires.

We Have A Bike That Hit The Markets In 2015. The Model Is Trackmachine. The Bike Is Manufactured By Bmc. Its Color Is Blue.

This racer bike has three textile layered performance tires.

We Have A Bike That Hit The Markets In 2015. The Model Is Trackmachine. The Bike Is Manufactured By Bmc. Its Color Is Blue.

This racer bike has three textile layered performance tires.

>>>

In the next code snippet, I will add another attribute to the child class. This attribute shows why a racer bike has a higher rate of aerodynamic efficiency.

```
class Bike():
```

```python
"""This class will build the model of a bike."""

def __init__(self, bmodel, bmake, bcolor, byear):

    self.bmodel = bmodel
    self.bmake = bmake
    self.bcolor = bcolor
    self.byear = byear
    self.odometer_reading = 0
def fullname(self):
    fullbikename = "We have a bike that hit the markets in " +
str(self.byear) + ". The model is " + self.bmodel + ". The bike is
manufactured by " + self.bmake + ". Its color is " + self.bcolor
+ "."
    return fullbikename.title()
def reading_odometer(self):
    print("This bike has run " + str(self.odometer_reading) + "
kilometers on the road.")
def updating_the_odometer(self, bmileage):
    self.odometer_reading = bmileage
    if bmileage >= self.odometer_reading:
        self.odometer_reading = bmileage
    else:
```

```python
        print("You are not authorized to roll back the reading of
the odometer.")
    def incrementing_odometer(self, bmileage):
        self.odometer_reading += bmileage


class RacerBike(Bike):
    def __init__(self, bmodel, bmake, bcolor, byear):
        super(RacerBike,self).__init__(bmodel, bmake, bcolor,
byear)
        self.performance_tire = 'three textile layered'
        self.aerodynamic_efficiency = 'better lift/drag ratio'
    def describe_tires(self):
        print("This racer bike has " + self.performance_tire + "
performance tires.")
    def describe_aerodynamics(self):
        print("This racer bike has " + self.aerodynamic_efficiency
+ " for improved aerodynamic efficiency.")
racer1 = RacerBike('URS: Gravel Riding', 'BMC', 'Grey', '2017')
print(racer1.fullname())
racer1.describe_tires()
racer1.describe_aerodynamics()
racer2 = RacerBike('Trackmachine', 'BMC', 'Blue', '2015')
print(racer2.fullname())
racer2.describe_tires()
```

```
racer2.describe_aerodynamics()

racer3 = RacerBike('Alpenchallenge', 'BMC', 'Red', '2012')

print(racer2.fullname())

racer3.describe_tires()

racer3.describe_aerodynamics()
```

= RESTART: C:/Users/saifia computers/Desktop/sample.py

We Have A Bike That Hit The Markets In 2017. The Model Is Urs: Gravel Riding. The Bike Is Manufactured By Bmc. Its Color Is Grey.

This racer bike has three textile layered performance tires.

This racer bike has better lift/drag ratio for improved aerodynamic efficiency.

We Have A Bike That Hit The Markets In 2015. The Model Is Trackmachine. The Bike Is Manufactured By Bmc. Its Color Is Blue.

This racer bike has three textile layered performance tires.

This racer bike has better lift/drag ratio for improved aerodynamic efficiency.

We Have A Bike That Hit The Markets In 2015. The Model Is Trackmachine. The Bike Is Manufactured By Bmc. Its Color Is Blue.

This racer bike has three textile layered performance tires.

This racer bike has better lift/drag ratio for improved aerodynamic efficiency.

>>>

Overriding Methods from Parent Class

You can override methods from the parent class by defining a method with the same name as in the parent class. Python will then block the method's execution from the parent class, allowing the child class to override the method.

```
class Bike():
    """This class will build the model of a bike."""
    def __init__(self, bmodel, bmake, bcolor, byear):
        self.bmodel = bmodel
        self.bmake = bmake
        self.bcolor = bcolor
        self.byear = byear
        self.odometer_reading = 0
    def fullname(self):
        fullbikename = "We have a bike that hit the markets in " + str(self.byear) + ". The model is " + self.bmodel + ". The bike is manufactured by " + self.bmake + ". Its color is " + self.bcolor + "."
        return fullbikename.title()
    def reading_odometer(self):
        print("This bike has run " + str(self.odometer_reading) + " kilometers on the road.")
    def updating_the_odometer(self, bmileage):
        self.odometer_reading = bmileage
```

```python
        if bmileage >= self.odometer_reading:
            self.odometer_reading = bmileage
        else:
            print("You are not authorized to roll back the reading of
the odometer.")
    def incrementing_odometer(self, bmileage):
        self.odometer_reading += bmileage
class RacerBike(Bike):
    def __init__(self, bmodel, bmake, bcolor, byear):
        super(RacerBike,self).__init__(bmodel, bmake, bcolor,
byear)
        self.performance_tire = 'three textile layered'
        self.aerodynamic_efficiency = 'better lift/drag ratio'
    def describe_tires(self):
        print("This racer bike has " + self.performance_tire + "
performance tires.")
    def describe_aerodynamics(self):
        print("This racer bike has " + self.aerodynamic_efficiency
+ " for improved aerodynamic efficiency.")
    def incrementing_odometer(self, bmileage):
        print("I cannot increment the odometer.")
racer1 = RacerBike('URS: Gravel Riding', 'BMC', 'Grey', '2017')
print(racer1.fullname())
racer1.describe_tires()
```

```
racer1.describe_aerodynamics()
racer1.reading_odometer()
racer1.incrementing_odometer(1000)
racer2 = RacerBike('Trackmachine', 'BMC', 'Blue', '2015')
print(racer2.fullname())
racer2.describe_tires()
racer2.describe_aerodynamics()
racer2.reading_odometer()
racer2.incrementing_odometer(1000)
racer3 = RacerBike('Alpenchallenge', 'BMC', 'Red', '2012')
print(racer2.fullname())
racer3.describe_tires()
racer3.describe_aerodynamics()
racer3.reading_odometer()
racer3.incrementing_odometer(5000)
= RESTART: C:/Users/saifia computers/Desktop/sample.py
>>>
```

We Have A Bike That Hit The Markets In 2017. The Model Is Urs: Gravel Riding. The Bike Is Manufactured By Bmc. Its Color Is Grey.

This racer bike has three textile layered performance tires.

This racer bike has better lift/drag ratio for improved aerodynamic efficiency.

This bike has run 0 kilometers on the road.

I cannot increment the odometer.

We Have A Bike That Hit The Markets In 2015. The Model Is Trackmachine. The Bike Is Manufactured By Bmc. Its Color Is Blue.

This racer bike has three textile layered performance tires.

This racer bike has better lift/drag ratio for improved aerodynamic efficiency.

This bike has run 0 kilometers on the road.

I cannot increment the odometer.

We Have A Bike That Hit The Markets In 2015. The Model Is Trackmachine. The Bike Is Manufactured By Bmc. Its Color Is Blue.

This racer bike has three textile layered performance tires.

This racer bike has better lift/drag ratio for improved aerodynamic efficiency.

This bike has run 0 kilometers on the road.

I cannot increment the odometer.

>>>

An interesting about classes is the flexibility they have to offer. For example, instead of making the performance tires an attribute, we can

189

turn it into a separate class. After that we can add as many instances to this new class as we want to.

```python
class Bike():
    """This class will build the model of a bike."""

    def __init__(self, bmodel, bmake, bcolor, byear):

        self.bmodel = bmodel
        self.bmake = bmake
        self.bcolor = bcolor
        self.byear = byear
        self.odometer_reading = 0
    def fullname(self):
        fullbikename = "We have a bike that hit the markets in " + str(self.byear) + ". The model is " + self.bmodel + ". The bike is manufactured by " + self.bmake + ". Its color is " + self.bcolor + "."
        return fullbikename.title()
    def reading_odometer(self):
        print("This bike has run " + str(self.odometer_reading) + " kilometers on the road.")
    def updating_the_odometer(self, bmileage):
        self.odometer_reading = bmileage
        if bmileage >= self.odometer_reading:
```

```python
            self.odometer_reading = bmileage
        else:
            print("You are not authorized to roll back the reading of
the odometer.")
    def incrementing_odometer(self, bmileage):
        self.odometer_reading += bmileage
class Performancetires():
    def __init__(self, performance_tire= 'three textile layered'):
        self.performance_tire = performance_tire
    def describe_performancetires(self):
        print("This racer bike has " + self.performance_tire + "
performance tires.")


class RacerBike(Bike):
    def __init__(self, bmodel, bmake, bcolor, byear):
        super(RacerBike,self).__init__(bmodel, bmake, bcolor,
byear)
        self.performancetires = Performancetires()
        self.aerodynamic_efficiency = 'better lift/drag ratio'
    def describe_aerodynamics(self):
        print("This racer bike has " + self.aerodynamic_efficiency
+ " for improved aerodynamic efficiency.")
    def incrementing_odometer(self, bmileage):
        print("I cannot increment the odometer.")
```

```python
racer1 = RacerBike('URS: Gravel Riding', 'BMC', 'Grey', '2017')
print(racer1.fullname())
racer1.describe_aerodynamics()
racer1.reading_odometer()
racer1.incrementing_odometer(1000)
racer1.performancetires.describe_performancetires()
racer2 = RacerBike('Trackmachine', 'BMC', 'Blue', '2015')
print(racer2.fullname())
racer2.describe_aerodynamics()
racer2.reading_odometer()
racer2.incrementing_odometer(1000)
racer2.performancetires.describe_performancetires()
racer3 = RacerBike('Alpenchallenge', 'BMC', 'Red', '2012')
print(racer2.fullname())
racer3.describe_aerodynamics()
racer3.reading_odometer()
racer3.incrementing_odometer(5000)
racer3.performancetires.describe_performancetires()
= RESTART: C:/Users/saifia computers/Desktop/sample.py
```

We Have A Bike That Hit The Markets In 2017. The Model Is Urs: Gravel Riding. The Bike Is Manufactured By Bmc. Its Color Is Grey.

This racer bike has better lift/drag ratio for improved aerodynamic efficiency.

This bike has run 0 kilometers on the road.

I cannot increment the odometer.

This racer bike has three textile layered performance tires.

We Have A Bike That Hit The Markets In 2015. The Model Is Trackmachine. The Bike Is Manufactured By Bmc. Its Color Is Blue.

This racer bike has better lift/drag ratio for improved aerodynamic efficiency.

This bike has run 0 kilometers on the road.

I cannot increment the odometer.

This racer bike has three textile layered performance tires.

We Have A Bike That Hit The Markets In 2015. The Model Is Trackmachine. The Bike Is Manufactured By Bmc. Its Color Is Blue.

This racer bike has better lift/drag ratio for improved aerodynamic efficiency.

This bike has run 0 kilometers on the road.

I cannot increment the odometer.

This racer bike has three textile layered performance tires.

>>>

Chapter Ten

Importing Classes

You can create a module of Python classes and use it later on to create different programs. When you save a Python program with the extension .py, it becomes a Python module. I have saved it with a proper file name. I will now open a new file, name it as bike.py and save the following code.

```python
class Bike():
    """This class will build the model of a bike."""
    def __init__(self, bmodel, bmake, bcolor, byear):
        self.bmodel = bmodel
        self.bmake = bmake
        self.bcolor = bcolor
        self.byear = byear
        self.odometer_reading = 0
    def fullname(self):
        fullbikename = "We have a bike that hit the markets in " + str(self.byear) + ". The model is " + self.bmodel + ". The bike is manufactured by " + self.bmake + ". Its color is " + self.bcolor + "."

        return fullbikename.title()
```

```python
    def reading_odometer(self):
        print("This bike has run " + str(self.odometer_reading) + " kilometers on the road.")
    def updating_the_odometer(self, bmileage):
        self.odometer_reading = bmileage
        if bmileage >= self.odometer_reading:
            self.odometer_reading = bmileage
        else:
            print("You are not authorized to roll back the reading of the odometer.")
    def incrementing_odometer(self, bmileage):
        self.odometer_reading += bmileage
class Performancetires():
    def __init__(self, performance_tire= 'three textile layered'):
        self.performance_tire = performance_tire
    def describe_performancetires(self):
        print("This racer bike has " + self.performance_tire + " performance tires.")
class RacerBike(Bike):
    def __init__(self, bmodel, bmake, bcolor, byear):
        super(RacerBike,self).__init__(bmodel, bmake, bcolor, byear)
        self.performancetires = Performancetires()
        self.aerodynamic_efficiency = 'better lift/drag ratio'
```

```python
def describe_aerodynamics(self):
    print("This racer bike has " + self.aerodynamic_efficiency + " for improved aerodynamic efficiency.")
def incrementing_odometer(self, bmileage):
    print("I cannot increment the odometer.")
```

Importing Multiple Classes

I have saved the file and closed it. Now I will open a new file and name it my_bike.py. I'll save it in the same location where I have saved bike.py. For example, in my case I have saved both on my desktop to access them easily. Whatever the location is, it should be the same for the two files or the code will not work in the way you have foreseen it. Now that the file my_bike has been saved. I will now write the code in it to import the code from the file bike.py.

```python
from bike import Bike
from bike import Performancetires
from bike import RacerBike
racer1 = RacerBike('URS: Gravel Riding', 'BMC', 'Grey', '2017')
print(racer1.fullname())
racer1.describe_aerodynamics()
racer1.reading_odometer()
racer1.incrementing_odometer(1000)
racer1.performancetires.describe_performancetires()
racer2 = RacerBike('Trackmachine', 'BMC', 'Blue', '2015')
```

```python
print(racer2.fullname())
racer2.describe_aerodynamics()
racer2.reading_odometer()
racer2.incrementing_odometer(1000)
racer2.performancetires.describe_performancetires()
racer3 = RacerBike('Alpenchallenge', 'BMC', 'Red', '2012')
print(racer2.fullname())
racer3.describe_aerodynamics()
racer3.reading_odometer()
racer3.incrementing_odometer(5000)
racer3.performancetires.describe_performancetires()
```

>>>= RESTART: C:/Users/saifia computers/Desktop/my_bike.py

We Have A Bike That Hit The Markets In 2017. The Model Is Urs: Gravel Riding. The Bike Is Manufactured By Bmc. Its Color Is Grey.

This racer bike has better lift/drag ratio for improved aerodynamic efficiency.

This bike has run 0 kilometers on the road.

I cannot increment the odometer.

This racer bike has three textile layered performance tires.

We Have A Bike That Hit The Markets In 2015. The Model Is Trackmachine. The Bike Is Manufactured By Bmc. Its Color Is Blue.

This racer bike has better lift/drag ratio for improved aerodynamic efficiency.

This bike has run 0 kilometers on the road.

I cannot increment the odometer.

This racer bike has three textile layered performance tires.

We Have A Bike That Hit The Markets In 2015. The Model Is Trackmachine. The Bike Is Manufactured By Bmc. Its Color Is Blue.

This racer bike has better lift/drag ratio for improved aerodynamic efficiency.

This bike has run 0 kilometers on the road.

I cannot increment the odometer.

This racer bike has three textile layered performance tires.

>>>

As all the three classes were written in the file bike.py, I have imported all of them in a sequence. As there are three classes stored in a single module, if you try to import only one of them, you will see an error in the interpreter. The error will be like this.

```
from bike import Bike
racer1 = RacerBike('URS: Gravel Riding', 'BMC', 'Grey', '2017')
print(racer1.fullname())
racer1.describe_aerodynamics()
racer1.reading_odometer()
racer1.incrementing_odometer(1000)
```

```
racer1.performancetires.describe_performancetires()
racer2 = RacerBike('Trackmachine', 'BMC', 'Blue', '2015')
print(racer2.fullname())
racer2.describe_aerodynamics()
racer2.reading_odometer()
racer2.incrementing_odometer(1000)
racer2.performancetires.describe_performancetires()
racer3 = RacerBike('Alpenchallenge', 'BMC', 'Red', '2012')
print(racer2.fullname())
racer3.describe_aerodynamics()
racer3.reading_odometer()
racer3.incrementing_odometer(5000)
racer3.performancetires.describe_performancetires()
= RESTART: C:/Users/saifia computers/Desktop/my_bike.py
Traceback (most recent call last):
  File "C:/Users/saifia computers/Desktop/my_bike.py", line 3,
in <module>
    racer1 = RacerBike('URS: Gravel Riding', 'BMC', 'Grey',
'2017')
NameError: name 'RacerBike' is not defined
>>>
```

However, if you save a single class in one module, you can correct this error.

from bike import Bike

```
racer1 = Bike('URS: Gravel Riding', 'BMC', 'Grey', '2017')
print(racer1.fullname())
racer2 = Bike('Trackmachine', 'BMC', 'Blue', '2015')
print(racer2.fullname())
racer3 = Bike('Alpenchallenge', 'BMC', 'Red', '2012')
print(racer2.fullname())
```

= RESTART: C:/Users/saifia computers/Desktop/my_bike.py

We Have A Bike That Hit The Markets In 2017. The Model Is Urs: Gravel Riding. The Bike Is Manufactured By Bmc. Its Color Is Grey.

We Have A Bike That Hit The Markets In 2015. The Model Is Trackmachine. The Bike Is Manufactured By Bmc. Its Color Is Blue.

We Have A Bike That Hit The Markets In 2015. The Model Is Trackmachine. The Bike Is Manufactured By Bmc. Its Color Is Blue.

>>>

Importing Module

You also have an option to import a complete module and then access all the classes in it. This is the simplest and the easiest of the methods to execute a program.

```
import bike
racer1 = bike.RacerBike('URS: Gravel Riding', 'BMC', 'Grey', '2017')
```

```
print(racer1.fullname())

racer1.describe_aerodynamics()

racer1.reading_odometer()

racer1.incrementing_odometer(1000)

racer1.performancetires.describe_performancetires()

racer2 = bike.RacerBike('Trackmachine', 'BMC', 'Blue', '2015')

print(racer2.fullname())

racer2.describe_aerodynamics()

racer2.reading_odometer()

racer2.incrementing_odometer(1000)

racer2.performancetires.describe_performancetires()

racer3 = bike.RacerBike('Alpenchallenge', 'BMC', 'Red', '2012')

print(racer2.fullname())

racer3.describe_aerodynamics()

racer3.reading_odometer()

racer3.incrementing_odometer(5000)

racer3.performancetires.describe_performancetires()
```

= RESTART: C:/Users/saifia computers/Desktop/my_bike.py

We Have A Bike That Hit The Markets In 2017. The Model Is Urs: Gravel Riding. The Bike Is Manufactured By Bmc. Its Color Is Grey.

This racer bike has better lift/drag ratio for improved aerodynamic efficiency.

This bike has run 0 kilometers on the road.

I cannot increment the odometer.

This racer bike has three textile layered performance tires.

We Have A Bike That Hit The Markets In 2015. The Model Is Trackmachine. The Bike Is Manufactured By Bmc. Its Color Is Blue.

This racer bike has better lift/drag ratio for improved aerodynamic efficiency.

This bike has run 0 kilometers on the road.

I cannot increment the odometer.

This racer bike has three textile layered performance tires.

We Have A Bike That Hit The Markets In 2015. The Model Is Trackmachine. The Bike Is Manufactured By Bmc. Its Color Is Blue.

This racer bike has better lift/drag ratio for improved aerodynamic efficiency.

This bike has run 0 kilometers on the road.

I cannot increment the odometer.

This racer bike has three textile layered performance tires.

>>>

Importing All Classes

There is a trick to import all classes at once.

```
from bike import *
racer1 = RacerBike('URS: Gravel Riding', 'BMC', 'Grey', '2017')
```

```
print(racer1.fullname())

racer1.describe_aerodynamics()

racer1.reading_odometer()

racer1.incrementing_odometer(1000)

racer1.performancetires.describe_performancetires()

racer2 = RacerBike('Trackmachine', 'BMC', 'Blue', '2015')

print(racer2.fullname())

racer2.describe_aerodynamics()

racer2.reading_odometer()

racer2.incrementing_odometer(1000)

racer2.performancetires.describe_performancetires()

racer3 = RacerBike('Alpenchallenge', 'BMC', 'Red', '2012')

print(racer2.fullname())

racer3.describe_aerodynamics()

racer3.reading_odometer()

racer3.incrementing_odometer(5000)

racer3.performancetires.describe_performancetires()

= RESTART: C:/Users/saifia computers/Desktop/my_bike.py
```

We Have A Bike That Hit The Markets In 2017. The Model Is Urs: Gravel Riding. The Bike Is Manufactured By Bmc. Its Color Is Grey.

This racer bike has better lift/drag ratio for improved aerodynamic efficiency.

This bike has run 0 kilometers on the road.

I cannot increment the odometer.

This racer bike has three textile layered performance tires.

We Have A Bike That Hit The Markets In 2015. The Model Is Trackmachine. The Bike Is Manufactured By Bmc. Its Color Is Blue.

This racer bike has better lift/drag ratio for improved aerodynamic efficiency.

This bike has run 0 kilometers on the road.

I cannot increment the odometer.

This racer bike has three textile layered performance tires.

We Have A Bike That Hit The Markets In 2015. The Model Is Trackmachine. The Bike Is Manufactured By Bmc. Its Color Is Blue.

This racer bike has better lift/drag ratio for improved aerodynamic efficiency.

This bike has run 0 kilometers on the road.

I cannot increment the odometer.

This racer bike has three textile layered performance tires.

>>>

Conclusion

Now that you have made it to the end of the book, I hope you have understood each concept of Python coding to the hilt. I hope that you have practiced each code very well and have also digested it well.

The next step is to keep practicing the codes that I have given and explained the book. Python coding is easier compared to other programming languages. The editor is quite helpful as the multiple colors in it guide you through the codes. The most interesting feature of Python is the display of errors. Each error carries in it its solution as well as it indicates you where the problem lies. You can track the error, rectify it, and run the program again.

You have learned from the basics like datatypes to the advanced stages like object-oriented programming. All the concepts were explained with due depth so that when you have gone through them, you are well-versed in executing them yourself.

Coding knowledge is likely to slip off your mind right after you finish the book. Therefore, the best method to retain this knowledge is to keep practicing, creating new programs. You will start enjoying it finally. Python is the best language if you are interested in automation, machine learning, and deep learning models. You can use it to be a master of artificial intelligence systems and data mining systems.

References

https://phoenixnap.com/kb/how-to-install-python-3-windows

CODING
IN PYTHON

*TIPS AND TRICKS TO CODING WITH
PYTHON USING THE PRINCIPLES AND
THEORIES OF PYTHON PROGRAMMING*

ROBERT C. MATTHEWS

209

Introduction

This book contains proven steps and strategies on how to be a master of programming in Python. I have explained each topic in detail to give you a good grasp of the topics and easily understand different concepts. Instead of hopping on from one concept to another, I have focused on filling in the book with details.

If you ask me to pick one thing that is the best about this book, it is the amount of practicality that I have tried to pack up in this book. I have written all the codes myself easily and clearly so that you can understand them, learn them, and practice them. I expect you to carry a pen and paper with you when you read the book to jot down important book concepts. I also expect you to have your laptop or personal computer ready to pick the codes and practice them. You can copy them from the book and paste them into Python text editor to see the results. When you have confirmed that the results are the same as yours, you can then alter the code to customize it as per your liking so that you can be able to learn the code by heart. Once you have customized the code, the next step is to run it and see the result. If you get the desired result, you will never forget the code.

This is how you can learn all the subjects in this book. This is a simple handbook of Python that will enable you to create models of real-life objects. This is where you can start animation and robotics. You will be able to create an object and make it move as per your requirements.

This book is for everyone who has an interest in Python. Regardless of your background in information technology (IT), you can jump into the world of Python and succeed as well. Even if you have no prior background knowledge of computer programming, you can use this book to learn the tips and tricks of coding in Python.

I recommend that everyone aspiring to build a career in Python should buy this book and read it through to the last leaf to understand Python's concepts. Python is easy but if you take it casually, it can prove to be tough for you. Simple whitespace can destroy your code and leave you wondering for hours what happened.

Chapter One

Python Basics - Variables and Data Types

Python is a language that your computer understands. Before you delve deeper into the world of programming, you need appropriate software on your computer system that allows you to code in Python. Python is the package that needs to be installed on a computer system before you start programming.

As most of the computer users use Windows operating system, I will explain in detail how you can download and install Python on the same. There are a few steps that you have to follow for the windows operating system.

- The first step is to open an internet browser and type in the following address: http://www.python.org.

- The second step is to sift through multiple links that will have different names such as Python 2.5, Python 2.6, and Python 3.7, and click on the one that you desire to install on your computer system. I have Python 3.7 installed on my computer system. Once you have selected the version, you can download the installer file on your computer. You can store the file on any drive or place on your computer system. You can select a destination or create a fresh directory.

- Now run the installer by double-clicking the same. The python installation wizard will pop up on your computer screen. You can accept the default settings and the installation will flow smoothly. Once the installation is over, you are all set to roll.

If all goes well, you can see the Python folder in the Start menu of Windows. You can open Python IDLE to practice the following codes of this chapter.

Variables

I will now open Python IDLE and check how you can create variables and use them in programs. The Python IDLE will as follows:

Python 3.8.5 (tags/v3.8.5:580fbb0, Jul 20 2020, 15:57:54) [MSC v.1924 64 bit (AMD64)] on win32

Type "help", "copyright", "credits" or "license()" for more information.

>>>

Now I will create a variable.

>>> var = "I want to become a Python programmer."

>>> print(var)

I want to become a Python programmer.

>>>

In the above code, I have stored the sentence inside a variable. This can be done differently. You can directly display the statement by using the print statement.

>>> print("I want to become a Python programmer.")

I want to become a Python programmer.

>>>

The same variable can hold a different value. See the following example:

>>> var = "Python is a very interesting language."

>>> print(var)

Python is a very interesting language.

>>>

Variables are very important in Python as each one of them holds a specific value that can be used in different ways. Creating and adding a variable in a program makes things easier for a programmer.

The Naming Tradition

When you are using variables in Python, you ought to adhere to specific rules and traditions. If you break any one of them, it will trigger errors in the code. Even if it does not cause errors, it will make the code hard to write. So naming the variables in the right manner will make the code comprehensible. You ought to make sure that you follow the below-mentioned rules when you are creating a program.

- The names of the variables must contain only numbers, underscores, and alphabets. The variable must start with a letter and not with a number.

- You cannot add spaces to the name of a variable. Instead, you can insert spaces between the names of variables to avoid errors.

- Python keywords cannot be used as names of variables. For example, print is a Python keyword so you cannot use it in a program.

- The names of the variable must be sort but descriptive, so that when you return to reading the code, you can easily understand your own words.

As you move further into the world of programming, you will learn how to create and use the names of variables in your programs. Names of variables will become significant when you build lengthy and complex programs. Just reading the name will be enough to understand the code. Use lowercase to name the variables. Uppercase names don't trigger errors, but they are not in practice and also they are not a part of the naming tradition.

When you are writing complex Python programs, it is normal to trigger errors. Take a look at the following spelling error in the name of the variable.

```
>>> var = "Python is a very interesting language."
```

```
>>> print(var)
```

Python is a very interesting language.

```
>>> print(varr)
```

Traceback (most recent call last):

```
File "<pyshell#5>", line 1, in <module>
    print(varr)
NameError: name 'varr' is not defined
>>>
```

Python interpreter or IDLE displays clear errors that help you understand the root cause of the problem. The interpreter provides a Traceback message and tells the programmer why it failed to execute the code. If you read the error message carefully, you can understand it well and remove the cause of the error.

Python Strings

Most programs are aimed at defining, creating, and gathering different types of data. They use the same data to create or do something useful with the same. There are different types of data that Python allows you to use. The most common and most used type of data is strings. Strings are simple if you take a simple glance at them but they offer complex ways of creating programs. A string is composed of multiple characters. Anything that is packed inside quotes is named as Python string. As for the quotes, you can either use single or double quotes around the same.

Note: From here on I will switch from Python IDLE to Python text editor. To do this, you should go to the File tab in Python interpreter. A list will dropdown. Click on New. A new window will pop up on your computer screen. This is a Python text editor. You can write your code in the editor and see its display on the Python IDLE. To run it effectively, save the file and click on Run on the top menu. See the following example.

```
var = "Python is a very interesting language."
print(var)
var = 'Python is a very interesting language.'
print(var)
==== RESTART: C:/Users/saifia
computers/Desktop/sample1.py ===
Python is a very interesting language.
Python is a very interesting language.
>>>
```

The code right after Restart is the display from Python IDLE. Everything above is written in the text editor. There is a problem with the use of single quotes if the string you are using contains an apostrophe.

```
var1 = "You must delve deeper into Python's datatypes to understand them well so that you can use them later."
var = "Python is a very interesting language but it is not the 'Python' that you find in a jungle."
```

```
print(var1)

print(var)

==== RESTART: C:/Users/saifia
computers/Desktop/sample1.py ===
```

You must delve deeper into Python's datatypes to understand them well so that you can use them later.

Python is a very interesting language but it is not the 'Python' that you find in a jungle.

```
>>>
```

When you put the apostrophe inside single quotes, you will get an invalid syntax error. Python strings offer you a lot of flexibility. You can change the string into upper and lower cases.

```
var1 = "You must delve deeper into Python's datatypes to understand them well so that you can use them later."
var = "Python is a very interesting language but it is not the 'Python' that you find in a jungle."
print(var1.title())

print(var.upper())

print(var1.lower())

==== RESTART: C:/Users/saifia
computers/Desktop/sample1.py ===
```

You Must Delve Deeper Into Python'S Datatypes To Understand Them Well So That You Can Use Them Later.

PYTHON IS A VERY INTERESTING LANGUAGE BUT IT IS NOT THE 'PYTHON' THAT YOU FIND IN A JUNGLE.

you must delve deeper into python's datatypes to understand them well so that you can use them later.

>>>

In the above example, I have changed the strings into a title, lower and upper cases. I have deployed the title() method after the variable when I wrote the print() statement. A Python method is defined as an action that Python performs on a certain piece of information. The dot that I have inserted after the variable's name instructs Python to take action as defined in the method. So, I have used three methods that defined three different types of actions. The parenthesis that you can use with each method is used to fill in the method with additional information.

Note: Most of the data is stored in lower() cases.

String Concatenation

Combining strings is most often quite useful. Let us see how to do that.

```
var1 = "You must delve deeper into Python's datatypes to
understand them well so that you can use them later."
var = "Python is a very interesting language but it is not the
'Python' that you find in a jungle."
combo_info = var + " " + var1
```

```
print(combo_info)
```

==== RESTART: C:/Users/saifia computers/Desktop/sample1.py ===

Python is a very interesting language but it is not the 'Python' that you find in a jungle. You must delve deeper into Python's datatypes to understand them well so that you can use them later.

>>>

The + operator is very important in string concatenation. You miss out on it, you will see an invalid syntax error. You can use string concatenation to display messages.

```
var1 = "you must delve deeper into Python's datatypes to understand them well so that you can use them later."
var = "Python is a very interesting language but it is not the 'Python' that you find in a jungle."
combo_info = var1 + " " + var
```

```
print(" I have learned from my coding experience that to learn Python effectively, " + combo_info)
```

==== RESTART: C:/Users/saifia computers/Desktop/sample1.py ===

I have learned from my coding experience that to learn Python effectively, you must delve deeper into Python's datatypes to understand them well so that you can use them later. Python is a very interesting language but it is not the 'Python' that you find in a jungle.

>>>

You can make the code a bit more complex by storing the concatenated information inside another variable to use it later.

```
var1 = "you must delve deeper into Python's datatypes to
understand them well so that you can use them later."
var = "Python is a very interesting language but it is not the
'Python' that you find in a jungle."
combo_info = var1 + " " + var


combo_info1 = " I have learned from my coding experience that
to learn Python effectively, " + combo_info
print(combo_info1)
==== RESTART: C:/Users/saifia
computers/Desktop/sample1.py ===
```

I have learned from my coding experience that to learn Python effectively, you must delve deeper into Python's datatypes to understand them well so that you can use them later. Python is a very interesting language but it is not the 'Python' that you find in a jungle.

>>>

All it took is another line of code.

TypeErrors

Sometimes strings functions do not go well. More often you will need to use the value of a variable inside a message that includes a digit.

date = 21

notification = "I will see you on the " + date + "st of January."

print(notification)

==== RESTART: C:/Users/saifia computers/Desktop/sample1.py ===

Traceback (most recent call last):

  File "C:/Users/saifia computers/Desktop/sample1.py", line 2, in <module>

  notification = "I will see you on the " + date + "st of January."

TypeError: can only concatenate str (not "int") to str

>>>

As you can see in the message, the error is known as TypeError. You cannot add an integer to a string simply by using the plus operator. Python has failed to recognize the type of information you have added to the code. The variable date carries an integer. If you want to pair up an integer with a string, you must first convert the integer into a string and then run the code. The conversion is quite easy to do. I will convert the same integer into a string and then use it in the code.

date = 21

notification = "I will see you on the " + str(date) + "st of January."

print(notification)

==== RESTART: C:/Users/saifia computers/Desktop/sample1.py ===

I will see you on the 21st of January.

>>>

Whitespaces

Whitespace, in the world of programming, refers to the characters that usually are not printed. These include tabs, spaces, and symbols that are placed at the end of the line. You can manage whitespaces to organize the input that is easier for you to read. If you want to add a tab to a line of code, you can use the\t combination.

var1 = "You must delve deeper into Python's datatypes to understand them well so that you can use them later."

print(var1)

var1 = "\tYou must delve deeper into Python's datatypes to understand them well so that you can use them later."

print(var1)

==== RESTART: C:/Users/saifia computers/Desktop/sample1.py ===

You must delve deeper into Python's datatypes to understand them well so that you can use them later.

You must delve deeper into Python's datatypes to understand them well so that you can use them later.

>>>

You can add the combination \n to start a newline inside a string.

```
var1 = "You must \ndelve deeper into \nPython's datatypes \nto understand them well."
print(var1)
==== RESTART: C:/Users/saifia computers/Desktop/sample1.py ===
You must
delve deeper into
Python's datatypes
to understand them well.
```

>>>

Python Numbers

Programming is all about doing the right calculation. You can use numbers to maintain scores in games, data visualization, and storing information inside different web applications. Python treats different types of numbers such as integers and decimals in different ways. Here are the basic mathematical functions with numbers.

```
>>> 55 + 67
122
>>> 1567 - 56
```

1511

>>> 55 * 55

3025

>>> 100 / 2

50.0

>>>

Mathematics revolves around the order of mathematical operations. Python can discriminate in regard to the order. It can identify which symbol should be used first and which should be used later.

>>> 55 * 55 + 500

3525

>>> 5 * 5 - 10

15

>>> 5 * 5 * 5

125

>>> 50 + 5 * 2

60

>>> 100 / 2 + 5

55.0

>>> 100 / 2 + 50 - 45

55.0

>>>

I will enclose a few operations in parentheses to modify the result.

```
>>> (55 * 55) + 5
3030
>>> 55 * (55 + 5)
3300
>>> 100 - (50 * 5)
-150
>>> (100 - 50) * 5
250
>>>
```

Chapter Two

Python Lists

This chapter will walk you through the concepts of Python lists and the related methods and functions. You will learn how to create a list in Python, how to fill it up with different types of elements, how to maintain it, how to use it, and how to work with it. Python lists are remarkable because they have the capacity to store one element to a million elements. Python lists are very powerful as they help to bind together a number of concepts in the world of programming.

A list in Python is a collection of different items that are packed in a certain order. You can create a list that includes digits, letters of alphabets, and names of people. A list can have anything such as credit card information, items information for a game, and grocery items in a grocery store. As a list contains more than one item, you should name the list in the plural. Python lists can be identified with the help of square brackets. You have to insert commas to separate different elements in a list.

In the next example, I will start creating a game now. In the game, there is a player who has to conduct a counter-terrorism operation in Agham. As a developer, you have to create a list of guns that the player will use during his ventures. Let us create a list first.

```
guns = ['rifle', 'shotgun', 'submachine gun', 'assault rifle',
'revolver']
print(guns)
= RESTART: C:/Users/saifia computers/Desktop/strike
game.py
['rifle', 'shotgun', 'submachine gun', 'assault rifle', 'revolver']
>>>
```

A list should be enclosed inside square brackets. The result is also displayed enclosed inside square brackets. When the player wants you to see the kind of guns he has on the list, he can simply use the access method. As a developer, you can add a method to your code and allow the player to see the list of guns.

```
guns = ['rifle', 'shotgun', 'submachine gun', 'assault rifle',
'revolver']
print(guns[0])
print(guns[1])
print(guns[2])
print(guns[3])
print(guns[4])
print(guns[5])
= RESTART: C:/Users/saifia computers/Desktop/strike
game.py
rifle
shotgun
```

submachine gun

assault rifle

revolver

Traceback (most recent call last):

File "C:/Users/saifia computers/Desktop/strike game.py", line 7, in <module>

print(guns[5])

IndexError: list index out of range

>>>

The index error at the end shows that the list has reached its end. The player may see a customized message that tells him or her that he has reached the limit of guns. You can customize the result as per your needs. You can display the result in the title, upper or lower cases. It does not affect the function of the game but it will affect the formatting of your game.

```
guns = ['rifle', 'shotgun', 'submachine gun', 'assault rifle', 'revolver']
print(guns[0].title())
print(guns[1].upper())
print(guns[2].lower())
print(guns[3].title())
print(guns[4].title())
= RESTART: C:/Users/saifia computers/Desktop/strike game.py
```

Rifle

SHOTGUN

submachine gun

Assault Rifle

Revolver

>>>

Python Indexing

Python recognizes the start of the index from position 0 and not at 1. This is a standard indexing method with all programming languages. This type of indexing helps in negative indexing. You can start negative indexing by -1. While index 0 starts from the first item in the list, index -1 will be placed at the end of the list. When you add negative indexing to your code, you allow the player to view the guns from his stock from the opposite end of the list.

```
guns = ['rifle', 'shotgun', 'submachine gun', 'assault rifle', 'revolver']
print(guns[0].title())
print(guns[-1].upper())
print(guns[-2].lower())
print(guns[-3].title())
print(guns[-4].title())
= RESTART: C:/Users/saifia computers/Desktop/strike game.py
Rifle
```

REVOLVER

assault rifle

Submachine Gun

Shotgun

>>>

Displaying a Message to the Player

To make your game more interactive, you can use individual values from the gun list and add them to a message. I will be deploying the concatenation method to develop a message that will be displayed on the screen for the user of the game. See the following example.

guns = ['rifle', 'shotgun', 'submachine gun', 'assault rifle', 'revolver']

note = "You are now using a " + guns[0].title() + " to kill the enemy."

print(note)

note1 = "You are now using a " + guns[3].title() + " to kill the enemy."

print(note1)

= RESTART: C:/Users/saifia computers/Desktop/strike game.py

You are now using a Rifle to kill the enemy.

You are now using an Assault Rifle to kill the enemy.

>>>

List Modification

Python lists are amazing in the sense that you can easily modify them by adding, removing, and changing items in the list. Lists are dynamic. You can build them from scratch. You can add new items to the list. You can remove the existing ones and you also can replace items on the list. You can allow the game players to pick different weapons from the ground or snatch them from the enemies to build his stock. You also can allow the player to add new guns to the stock, remove the ones that are empty of bullets, and replace the guns you do not like with new guns of your choice. Simple methods in the list will allow you to develop an interactive game. In the following example, I will add small code lines to the program and get the desired results.

```
guns = ['rifle', 'shotgun', 'submachine gun', 'assault rifle',
'revolver']
print(guns)
# this line will replace elements in the list.
guns[0] = 'bazooka'
print(guns)
= RESTART: C:/Users/saifia computers/Desktop/strike
game.py
['rifle', 'shotgun', 'submachine gun', 'assault rifle', 'revolver']
['bazooka', 'shotgun', 'submachine gun', 'assault rifle', 'revolver']
>>>
```

You can replace more than one item in the list.

233

```
guns = ['rifle', 'shotgun', 'submachine gun', 'assault rifle',
'revolver']
print(guns)
# this line will replace elements in the list.
guns[0] = 'bazooka'
print(guns)

guns[1] = 'bazooka'
print(guns)

guns[2] = 'pistol'
print(guns)
```

= RESTART: C:/Users/saifia computers/Desktop/strike game.py

['rifle', 'shotgun', 'submachine gun', 'assault rifle', 'revolver']

['bazooka', 'shotgun', 'submachine gun', 'assault rifle', 'revolver']

['bazooka', 'bazooka', 'submachine gun', 'assault rifle', 'revolver']

['bazooka', 'bazooka', 'pistol', 'assault rifle', 'revolver']

>>>

Adding Items

You can add as many items to the list as you want. You may allow the player to collect and add as many guns to the list as you want. The simplest method to add a new item is by using the append()

method. When you apply the append() method, you get to add a new item to the list.

```
guns = ['rifle', 'shotgun', 'submachine gun', 'assault rifle',
'revolver']
print(guns)
# this line will append items to the list.
guns.append('bazooka')
print(guns)

guns.append('Ak-47')
print(guns)
```

```
= RESTART: C:/Users/saifia computers/Desktop/strike
game.py
['rifle', 'shotgun', 'submachine gun', 'assault rifle', 'revolver']
['rifle', 'shotgun', 'submachine gun', 'assault rifle', 'revolver',
'bazooka']
['rifle', 'shotgun', 'submachine gun', 'assault rifle', 'revolver',
'bazooka', 'Ak-47']
>>>
```

The items that I have added through the append() method have been added to the end of the list. This is how you can add as many items to the list as you can or want to. When you are building a random list from scratch, you can use the append() method and fill in the list.

```
guns = []
print(guns)
# these lines will append items to the list.
guns.append('rifle')
print(guns)
guns.append('shotgun')
print(guns)
guns.append('submachine gun')
print(guns)
guns.append('assault rifle')
print(guns)
guns.append('revolver')
print(guns)
= RESTART: C:/Users/saifia computers/Desktop/strike
game.py
[]
['rifle']
['rifle', 'shotgun']
['rifle', 'shotgun', 'submachine gun']
['rifle', 'shotgun', 'submachine gun', 'assault rifle']
['rifle', 'shotgun', 'submachine gun', 'assault rifle', 'revolver']
>>>
```

This is the most brilliant method to build lists and highly interactive as well. You can allow the players to start from an empty list and fill up the stocks with the guns they pick up along the way. This also puts the users in control of the game. You can allow them to define a list and move on with the fill up as they proceed into the game. The append method allows you to add elements to the end of the list and the insert method allows you to add items at the place of your choice. The insert() method needs to specify the index for the item you like to add to the list.

```
guns = ['rifle', 'shotgun', 'submachine gun', 'assault rifle', 'revolver']
print(guns)
# these lines will insert items to the list.
guns.insert(0, 'machine gun')
print(guns)

guns.insert(3, 'bazooka')
print(guns)
= RESTART: C:/Users/saifia computers/Desktop/strike game.py
['rifle', 'shotgun', 'submachine gun', 'assault rifle', 'revolver']
['machine gun', 'rifle', 'shotgun', 'submachine gun', 'assault rifle', 'revolver']
['machine gun', 'rifle', 'shotgun', 'bazooka', 'submachine gun', 'assault rifle', 'revolver']
>>>
```

Removing Items

In a game that is based on counter-terrorism operations, players have to use lots of guns and bullets. Off and on, a gun will be empty of the bullets. To make the game more realistic, you may allow the player to throw away the empty guns as soon as they are void of bullets. There are different methods to remove items from the list. One of the most common methods to remove items is using the del statement.

```
guns = ['rifle', 'shotgun', 'submachine gun', 'assault rifle', 'revolver']
print(guns)
# this code will delete items from the list.
del guns[0]
print(guns)

del guns[1]
print(guns)

del guns[2]
print(guns)
= RESTART: C:/Users/saifia computers/Desktop/strike game.py
['rifle', 'shotgun', 'submachine gun', 'assault rifle', 'revolver']
['shotgun', 'submachine gun', 'assault rifle', 'revolver']
['shotgun', 'assault rifle', 'revolver']
```

['shotgun', 'assault rifle']

>>>

There is another method to remove items. This one is known as the pop() method. Sometimes you need to use the value of the removed item in the code after its removal. You want the player to keep track of the thrown guns so that he may realize how much ammunition has consumed to strike down a specific number of enemy soldiers. The pop() method tends to remove the last item in your list but you can work with the item later. As the method's name suggests, the pop() method ejects the top item on the list. Here the top denotes the end of the list.

```
guns = ['rifle', 'shotgun', 'submachine gun', 'assault rifle', 'revolver']
print(guns)
# this code will delete items from the list.
popped_guns = guns.pop()
print(guns)
print(popped_guns)


popped_guns = guns.pop()
print(guns)
print(popped_guns)


popped_guns = guns.pop()
```

```
print(guns)
print(popped_guns)

popped_guns = guns.pop()
print(guns)
print(popped_guns)

popped_guns = guns.pop()
print(guns)
print(popped_guns)
= RESTART: C:/Users/saifia computers/Desktop/strike
game.py
['rifle', 'shotgun', 'submachine gun', 'assault rifle', 'revolver']
['rifle', 'shotgun', 'submachine gun', 'assault rifle']
revolver
['rifle', 'shotgun', 'submachine gun']
assault rifle
['rifle', 'shotgun']
submachine gun
['rifle']
shotgun
[]
rifle
>>>
```

I have popped out all items from the list one by one until I am left with an empty list. I will store the popped items in a separate variable and then use them later. In the following, I will pair up a print statement with the popped() method to get the desired result.

```
guns = ['rifle', 'shotgun', 'submachine gun', 'assault rifle',
'revolver']
print(guns)
# this code will delete items from the list.
empty_guns = guns.pop()
print("You have consumed all the bullets in the " +
empty_guns.title() + " and have discarded the weapon.")


empty_guns = guns.pop()
print("You have consumed all the bullets in the " +
empty_guns.title() + " and have discarded the weapon.")


empty_guns = guns.pop()
print("You have consumed all the bullets in the " +
empty_guns.title() + " and have discarded the weapon.")


empty_guns = guns.pop()
print("You have consumed all the bullets in the " +
empty_guns.title() + " and have discarded the weapon.")
```

```
['rifle', 'shotgun', 'submachine gun', 'assault rifle', 'revolver']
```

You have consumed all the bullets in the Revolver and have discarded the weapon.

You have consumed all the bullets in the Assault Rifle and have discarded the weapon.

You have consumed all the bullets in the Submachine Gun and have discarded the weapon.

You have consumed all the bullets in the Shotgun and have discarded the weapon.

>>>

The pop() method can also be used with the index numbers to remove items at a specific position in the list. I will alter the latest code in the next example to fill it in with index numbers.

```
guns = ['rifle', 'shotgun', 'submachine gun', 'assault rifle', 'revolver']
print(guns)
# this code will delete items from the list.
empty_guns = guns.pop(0)
print("You have consumed all the bullets in the " +
empty_guns.title() + " and have discarded the weapon.")


empty_guns = guns.pop(1)
```

```
print("You have consumed all the bullets in the " +
empty_guns.title() + " and have discarded the weapon.")


empty_guns = guns.pop(2)
print("You have consumed all the bullets in the " +
empty_guns.title() + " and have discarded the weapon.")
```

= RESTART: C:/Users/saifia computers/Desktop/strike game.py

['rifle', 'shotgun', 'submachine gun', 'assault rifle', 'revolver']

You have consumed all the bullets in the Rifle and have discarded the weapon.

You have consumed all the bullets in the Submachine Gun and have discarded the weapon.

You have consumed all the bullets in the Revolver and have discarded the weapon.

>>>

You can make your game more complex by using the remove() method that you have to fill up with the value of the item in the list. This is more specific.

```
guns = ['rifle', 'shotgun', 'submachine gun', 'assault rifle',
'revolver']
print(guns)
# this code will remove items from the list.
empty_guns = guns.remove('rifle')
```

```
print(guns)

empty_guns = guns.remove('shotgun')
print(guns)

empty_guns = guns.remove('revolver')
print(guns)
```

= RESTART: C:/Users/saifia computers/Desktop/strike game.py

['rifle', 'shotgun', 'submachine gun', 'assault rifle', 'revolver']

['shotgun', 'submachine gun', 'assault rifle', 'revolver']

['submachine gun', 'assault rifle', 'revolver']

['submachine gun', 'assault rifle']

If the item you want to remove from the list does not exist in the list, an error will pop up on your screen. It will look like the following text.

```
guns = ['rifle', 'shotgun', 'submachine gun', 'assault rifle', 'revolver']
print(guns)

empty_guns = guns.remove('bazooka')
print(guns)
```

= RESTART: C:/Users/saifia computers/Desktop/strike game.py

['rifle', 'shotgun', 'submachine gun', 'assault rifle', 'revolver']
Traceback (most recent call last):
  File "C:/Users/saifia computers/Desktop/strike game.py", line 4, in <module>
    empty_guns = guns.remove('bazooka')
ValueError: list.remove(x): x not in list
>>>

The error message is properly customized as it tells you that you have fill in the code with the wrong value.

An interesting thing about using the remove function is that you can also explain the reason behind the removal of an item. Just like I did with the pop() method, I will add a print statement to the code to do the job.

```
guns = ['rifle', 'shotgun', 'submachine gun', 'assault rifle', 'revolver']
print(guns)

empty_guns = 'rifle'
guns.remove(empty_guns)
print(guns)
print("\nYou have used the " + empty_guns.title() + " and it has been discarded.")

empty_guns = 'assault rifle'
```

245

```
guns.remove(empty_guns)

print(guns)

print("\nYou have used the " + empty_guns.title() + " and it has
been discarded.")
```

= RESTART: C:/Users/saifia computers/Desktop/strike
game.py

['rifle', 'shotgun', 'submachine gun', 'assault rifle', 'revolver']

['shotgun', 'submachine gun', 'assault rifle', 'revolver']

You have used the Rifle, and it has been discarded.

['shotgun', 'submachine gun', 'revolver']

You have used the Assault Rifle, and it has been discarded.

>>>

List Organization

Python lists are amazing in that they allow you to organize them.
When you create a list, it usually is in an unpredictable order. You
cannot always control the order if you have built a list filled with user
data. The data you receive can be different in style that you are
looking forward to storing in the database. For example, you might
want to store data in lower case and the users are filling up the
database with data in upper case. Python gives you multiple ways to
organize your lists according to your custom needs.

You can use the sort() method to sort out a list into alphabetical order. If you do this for the game, you will help your players to review the guns in a predictable order.

```
guns = ['rifle', 'shotgun', 'submachine gun', 'assault rifle',
'revolver']
print(guns)


guns.sort()
print(guns)
= RESTART: C:/Users/saifia computers/Desktop/strike
game.py
['rifle', 'shotgun', 'submachine gun', 'assault rifle', 'revolver']
['assault rifle', 'revolver', 'rifle', 'shotgun', 'submachine gun']
>>>
```

You also can store the list in a reverse alphabetical order by the following method.

```
guns = ['rifle', 'shotgun', 'submachine gun', 'assault rifle',
'revolver']
print(guns)


guns.sort(reverse=True)
print(guns)
= RESTART: C:/Users/saifia computers/Desktop/strike
game.py
```

['rifle', 'shotgun', 'submachine gun', 'assault rifle', 'revolver']

['submachine gun', 'shotgun', 'rifle', 'revolver', 'assault rifle']

>>>

There is a temporary list method that sorts a list temporarily. The sorted() function changes the list for the time being. It will be reverted back to the original order after the temporary display. I will use the same list and apply the sorted() function.

```
guns = ['rifle', 'shotgun', 'submachine gun', 'assault rifle',
'revolver']
#I will print here the original list
print(guns)


#The following is the sorted list
print(sorted(guns))


#Now I will print guns and you will see the original list
print(guns)
```

= RESTART: C:/Users/saifia computers/Desktop/strike game.py

['rifle', 'shotgun', 'submachine gun', 'assault rifle', 'revolver']

['assault rifle', 'revolver', 'rifle', 'shotgun', 'submachine gun']

['rifle', 'shotgun', 'submachine gun', 'assault rifle', 'revolver']

>>>

You can reverse the order of the list by using the reverse() method.

```
guns = ['rifle', 'shotgun', 'submachine gun', 'assault rifle',
'revolver']
print(guns)


guns.reverse()
print(guns)
= RESTART: C:/Users/saifia computers/Desktop/strike
game.py
['rifle', 'shotgun', 'submachine gun', 'assault rifle', 'revolver']
['revolver', 'assault rifle', 'submachine gun', 'shotgun', 'rifle']
>>>
```

With a simple method, you can find out the length of the list by using the len() function.

```
guns = ['rifle', 'shotgun', 'submachine gun', 'assault rifle',
'revolver']
print(guns)
print(len(guns))
= RESTART: C:/Users/saifia computers/Desktop/strike
game.py
['rifle', 'shotgun', 'submachine gun', 'assault rifle', 'revolver']
5
>>>
```

Creating a Loop Through a List

Sometimes you need to create a loop through your lists. You may allow your player to view all the guns in his stock when he is in the midst of the operation to be sure of himself. A simple loop will allow you to give your player this privilege. The loop will display all the items on the screen one by one. I will use the *for* loop to do the job for me.

The following code will display all the items in the list in a neat and clean way. The loop will retrieve each name from the list and display it on the screen.

```
guns = ['rifle', 'shotgun', 'submachine gun', 'assault rifle', 'revolver']
for gun in guns:
    print(gun)
= RESTART: C:/Users/saifia computers/Desktop/strike game.py
rifle
shotgun
submachine gun
assault rifle
revolver
>>>
```

You also can add a statement to the loop. The statement will be added to each item and repeated on the screen in a neatly formatted way.

```
guns = ['rifle', 'shotgun', 'submachine gun', 'assault rifle',
'revolver']
for gun in guns:
    print("You can use the " + gun.title() + " to subdue the
enemy.")
```

= RESTART: C:/Users/saifia computers/Desktop/strike game.py

You can use the Rifle to subdue the enemy.

You can use the Shotgun to subdue the enemy.

You can use the Submachine Gun to subdue the enemy.

You can use the Assault Rifle to subdue the enemy.

You can use the Revolver to subdue the enemy

>>>

The biggest benefit of pairing up loops and lists is that you do not have to repeat the code for each item in the list. All the items are looped through by Python and added to the statement. You can write multiple print statements and each of them will take items from the list one by one and properly display the messages.

```
guns = ['rifle', 'shotgun', 'submachine gun', 'assault rifle',
'revolver']
for gun in guns:
    print("You can use the " + gun.title() + " to subdue the
enemy.")
```

```
print("You should keep the " + gun.title() + " in a locked
mode to avoid any misadventure.")
```

= RESTART: C:/Users/saifia computers/Desktop/strike
game.py

You can use the Rifle to subdue the enemy.

You should keep the Rifle in a locked mode to avoid any
misadventure.

You can use the Shotgun to subdue the enemy.

You should keep the Shotgun in a locked mode to avoid any
misadventure.

You can use the Submachine Gun to subdue the enemy.

You should keep the Submachine Gun in a locked mode to
avoid any misadventure.

You can use the Assault Rifle to subdue the enemy.

You should keep the Assault Rifle in a locked mode to avoid
any misadventure.

You can use the Revolver to subdue the enemy.

You should keep the Revolver in a locked mode to avoid any
misadventure.

>>>

You can add more than two statements to improve the quality of
communications in the game. You can notice that there is no space
between the statements hence they do not look quite clean. I will add
\n at the end of the last print statement to maintain proper space
between multiple blocks of statements.

```
guns = ['rifle', 'shotgun', 'submachine gun', 'assault rifle',
'revolver']
for gun in guns:
    print("You can use the " + gun.title() + " to subdue the
enemy.")
    print("You should keep the " + gun.title() + " in a locked
mode to avoid any misadventure.")
    print("Do you want to keep the " + gun.title() + " in the
stock?\n")
```

= RESTART: C:/Users/saifia computers/Desktop/strike game.py

You can use the Rifle to subdue the enemy.

You should keep the Rifle in a locked mode to avoid any misadventure.

Do you want to keep the Rifle in the stock?

You can use the Shotgun to subdue the enemy.

You should keep the Shotgun in a locked mode to avoid any misadventure.

Do you want to keep the Shotgun in the stock?

You can use the Submachine Gun to subdue the enemy.

You should keep the Submachine Gun in a locked mode to avoid any misadventure.

Do you want to keep the Submachine Gun in the stock?

You can use the Assault Rifle to subdue the enemy.

You should keep the Assault Rifle in a locked mode to avoid any misadventure.

Do you want to keep the Assault Rifle in the stock?

You can use the Revolver to subdue the enemy.

You should keep the Revolver in a locked mode to avoid any misadventure.

Do you want to keep the Revolver in the stock?

>>>

You can add a final message at the end of the loop. Your player can speak about how much he likes the guns and that he is ready to start the mission and kill enemies. See the changes in the code.

```
guns = ['rifle', 'shotgun', 'submachine gun', 'assault rifle', 'revolver']
for gun in guns:
    print("You can use the " + gun.title() + " to subdue the enemy.")
    print("You should keep the " + gun.title() + " in a locked mode to avoid any misadventure.")
    print("Do you want to keep the " + gun.title() + " in the stock?\n")
```

print("Thanks for the information! I want to keep these weapons.")

= RESTART: C:/Users/saifia computers/Desktop/strike game.py

You can use the Rifle to subdue the enemy.

You should keep the Rifle in a locked mode to avoid any misadventure.

Do you want to keep the Rifle in the stock?

You can use the Shotgun to subdue the enemy.

You should keep the Shotgun in a locked mode to avoid any misadventure.

Do you want to keep the Shotgun in the stock?

You can use the Submachine Gun to subdue the enemy.

You should keep the Submachine Gun in a locked mode to avoid any misadventure.

Do you want to keep the Submachine Gun in the stock?

You can use the Assault Rifle to subdue the enemy.

You should keep the Assault Rifle in a locked mode to avoid any misadventure.

Do you want to keep the Assault Rifle in the stock?

You can use the Revolver to subdue the enemy.

You should keep the Revolver in a locked mode to avoid any misadventure.

Do you want to keep the Revolver in the stock?

Thanks for the information! I want to keep these weapons.

>>>

You will find this option highly useful when you have to process a large amount of data and then display a final result. You also can add this method to the start of your game to display different characters that a user must choose from to play the game.

Numerical Lists

You can build numerical lists quite easily. There is more than one reason to store a set of numbers. You ought to keep track of the number of enemies dead and the number of guns used in a single gaming session. When you do data visualization, you have to work with numbers and sizes of different items. Lists offer you a perfect medium for storing numbers and working with them efficiently. When you have learned to use numbers effectively, your code is likely to work fine even if you have packed up the lists with millions of items.

The range() function

The range() function in Python makes it fun to generate lots of numbers without writing them in the program. If you need 30 numbers, you can generate them by the range() function.

```
for number in range(0,30):
    print(number)
```

= RESTART: C:/Users/saifia computers/Desktop/strike game.py

```
0
1
2
3
4
5
6
7
8
9
10
11
12
13
14
```

15

16

17

18

19

20

21

22

23

24

25

26

27

28

29

>>>

The values can change if you change the input in the code.

```
for number in range(5000,5030):
    print(number)
```
= RESTART: C:/Users/saifia computers/Desktop/strike game.py

5000

5001

5002

5003

5004

5005

5006

5007

5008

5009

5010

5011

5012

5013

5014

5015

5016

5017

5018

5019

5020

5021

5022

5023

5024

5025

5026

5027

5028

5029

>>>

You can use the range() function to create a list of numbers. By this method, you will be able to convert the numbers into a list without working separately on the creation of the list. I will use the range() function that will do the job.

numbers = list(range(5000,5030))

print(numbers)

= RESTART: C:/Users/saifia computers/Desktop/strike game.py

[5000, 5001, 5002, 5003, 5004, 5005, 5006, 5007, 5008, 5009, 5010, 5011, 5012, 5013, 5014, 5015, 5016, 5017, 5018, 5019, 5020, 5021, 5022, 5023, 5024, 5025, 5026, 5027, 5028, 5029]

>>>

You can use the range() function to instruct Python on skipping numbers that fall into a given range. I will list even numbers that fall in between 1 and 10.

e_numbers = list(range(2,20,2))

print(e_numbers)

= RESTART: C:/Users/saifia computers/Desktop/strike game.py

[2, 4, 6, 8, 10, 12, 14, 16, 18]

>>>

You can edit the range and increase the skipping difference even numbers.

e_numbers = list(range(4,50,4))

print(e_numbers)

= RESTART: C:/Users/saifia computers/Desktop/strike game.py

[4, 8, 12, 16, 20, 24, 28, 32, 36, 40, 44, 48]

>>>

The range() function starts at numbers 2 and 4 respectively in the two examples. Numbers 2 and 4 are respectively added to the numbers to derive the requisite result. With the help of the range() function, you can create different sets of numbers. Let us move forward to other amazing things that you can do with numbers.

e_numbers = [1, 2, 3 , 4, 5, 6, 7, 8, 9, 10, 11, 12, 13]

print(e_numbers)

print(min(e_numbers))

print(max(e_numbers))

```
print(sum(e_numbers))
```

= RESTART: C:/Users/saifia computers/Desktop/strike
game.py

[1, 2, 3, 4, 5, 6, 7, 8, 9, 10, 11, 12, 13]

1

13

91

>>>

List Slicing

You can slice a list in half or into multiple pieces as per your requirements. You must remember the index numbers to produce the slices of your choice. The first and last items of the chunk of the list are needed to fill in the slice method. As is the case with the range() function, Python stops at one item before the last index item you mention in the code. The following example will help clear your mind about the slicing method.

```
guns = ['rifle', 'shotgun', 'submachine gun', 'assault rifle',
'revolver']
print(guns)
```

```
#This is the code for producing a perfect slice
print(guns[0:3])
```

= RESTART: C:/Users/saifia computers/Desktop/strike
game.py

['rifle', 'shotgun', 'submachine gun', 'assault rifle', 'revolver']

['rifle', 'shotgun', 'submachine gun']

>>>

You can see that the result does not include the index number 3. The code stopped one item before the requisite index number. The slicing method offers you an opportunity to produces different slices.

```
guns = ['rifle', 'shotgun', 'submachine gun', 'assault rifle',
'revolver']
print(guns)


#This is the code for producing a perfect slice
print(guns[0:3])
print(guns[1:3])
print(guns[1:4])
= RESTART: C:/Users/saifia computers/Desktop/strike
game.py
```

['rifle', 'shotgun', 'submachine gun', 'assault rifle', 'revolver']

['rifle', 'shotgun', 'submachine gun']

['shotgun', 'submachine gun']

['shotgun', 'submachine gun', 'assault rifle']

>>>

You also can leave out the first part of the index. It will start the slice from the first item in the list.

```
guns = ['rifle', 'shotgun', 'submachine gun', 'assault rifle',
'revolver']
print(guns)


#This is the code for producing a perfect slice
print(guns[:3])
print(guns[:3])
print(guns[:4])
```

= RESTART: C:/Users/saifia computers/Desktop/strike game.py

['rifle', 'shotgun', 'submachine gun', 'assault rifle', 'revolver']

['rifle', 'shotgun', 'submachine gun']

['rifle', 'shotgun', 'submachine gun']

['rifle', 'shotgun', 'submachine gun', 'assault rifle']

>>>

Similarly, you can leave out the second part of the index. It will let the slice reach the last item of the index.

```
guns = ['rifle', 'shotgun', 'submachine gun', 'assault rifle',
'revolver']
print(guns)


#This is the code for producing a perfect slice
print(guns[0:])
print(guns[1:])
```

```
print(guns[2:])
```

```
= RESTART: C:/Users/saifia computers/Desktop/strike
game.py
['rifle', 'shotgun', 'submachine gun', 'assault rifle', 'revolver']
['rifle', 'shotgun', 'submachine gun', 'assault rifle', 'revolver']
['shotgun', 'submachine gun', 'assault rifle', 'revolver']
['submachine gun', 'assault rifle', 'revolver']
>>>
```

The slicing method gives you the freedom to produce slices through negative indexing.

```
guns = ['rifle', 'shotgun', 'submachine gun', 'assault rifle',
'revolver']
print(guns)
```

```
#This is the code for producing a perfect slice
print(guns[-1:])
print(guns[:-1])
print(guns[-2:])
```

```
= RESTART: C:/Users/saifia computers/Desktop/strike
game.py
['rifle', 'shotgun', 'submachine gun', 'assault rifle', 'revolver']
['revolver']
['rifle', 'shotgun', 'submachine gun', 'assault rifle']
['assault rifle', 'revolver']
>>>
```

Just like we have looped through the lists, we also can create and run loops through slices. In the next code snippet, I will build and run a loop through the list slice. Your player may feel the need to display the list of guns that he has consumed in your game. You can add a line of code to the game that tells the player the names of the guns he has already consumed.

```
guns = ['rifle', 'shotgun', 'submachine gun', 'assault rifle',
'revolver']
```

```
print("Here is the list of guns that you have used up till now:")
for gun in guns[:4]:
    print(gun.title())
= RESTART: C:/Users/saifia computers/Desktop/strike
game.py
Here is the list of guns that you have used up till now:
Rifle
Shotgun
Submachine Gun
Assault Rifle
>>>
```

The loop has not displayed all the items but only those that we have specified in the slice method. Slices can help you in different situations. You can compile a player's score but add a slice of it to the final score each time a player concludes playing the game.

Copying Lists

You might want to start with a list first and create an entirely new one based on the original. I will use the [:] operator that tells Python to create a slice from the first to the last item. So, the copy of a list is a big slice that encompasses the original list from the start to the end.

guns = ['rifle', 'shotgun', 'submachine gun', 'assault rifle', 'revolver']

my_guns = guns[:]

print("These are the guns you were given at the start of the game:")

print(guns)

print("\nThese are the guns that you have consumed so far:")

print(my_guns)

= RESTART: C:/Users/saifia computers/Desktop/strike game.py

These are the guns you were given at the start of the game:

['rifle', 'shotgun', 'submachine gun', 'assault rifle', 'revolver']

These are the guns that you have consumed so far:

['rifle', 'shotgun', 'submachine gun', 'assault rifle', 'revolver']

>>>

You can check if you have really produced a copy of the original list by adding new items to the original list.

```
guns = ['rifle', 'shotgun', 'submachine gun', 'assault rifle',
'revolver']
my_guns = guns[:]

guns.append('bazooka')
my_guns.append('AK-47')
print("These are the guns you were given at the start of the
game:")
print(guns)

print("\nThese are the guns that you have consumed so far:")
print(my_guns)
= RESTART: C:/Users/saifia computers/Desktop/strike
game.py
These are the guns you were given at the start of the game:
['rifle', 'shotgun', 'submachine gun', 'assault rifle', 'revolver',
'bazooka']

These are the guns that you have consumed so far:
['rifle', 'shotgun', 'submachine gun', 'assault rifle', 'revolver',
'AK-47']
>>>
```

You can see that the items are separately added to the two lists. This proves that you now have two lists. Now I will remove the slice method from the code and see what happens when I try to add the same items to the two lists with different names.

```
guns = ['rifle', 'shotgun', 'submachine gun', 'assault rifle', 'revolver']
my_guns = guns

guns.append('bazooka')
my_guns.append('AK-47')
print("These are the guns you were given at the start of the game:")
print(guns)

print("\nThese are the guns that you have consumed so far:")
print(my_guns)
= RESTART: C:/Users/saifia computers/Desktop/strike game.py
These are the guns you were given at the start of the game:
['rifle', 'shotgun', 'submachine gun', 'assault rifle', 'revolver', 'bazooka', 'AK-47']
```

These are the guns that you have consumed so far:

['rifle', 'shotgun', 'submachine gun', 'assault rifle', 'revolver', 'bazooka', 'AK-47']

>>>

The output shows that the result is not what we had intended in the first place. The two lists now contain the same two items that we had intended to add to two different lists.

Tuples

Python tuples appear like lists as programmers use them to pack up different items but they are different in nature. Python lists work very well to store items that tend to change throughout a program. Lists offer the best programming practice because you can easily modify them. But sometimes you need to create a list that you do not want to change. Here tuples come to the rescue. Python names the values that you cannot change as immutable. In this way, a tuple is an immutable list.

A tuple looks just like a list except for the fact that you have to use parenthesis for tuples instead of square brackets. Once you have defined a tuple, you can go on to access all items in the list by the index number. It is the same as it is for a list.

I will convert the same list of items into a tuple but including it in a game is a bit odd. If you are running a financial institution and you have to store information that you want to remain unchangeable, you can load it up in a tuple.

```
guns = ('rifle', 'shotgun', 'submachine gun', 'assault rifle',
'revolver')
print(guns)
```

= RESTART: C:/Users/saifia computers/Desktop/strike
game.py

('rifle', 'shotgun', 'submachine gun', 'assault rifle', 'revolver')

>>>

In the following example, I will attempt to change the values of a tuple. The code is expected to display an error.

```
guns = ('rifle', 'shotgun', 'submachine gun', 'assault rifle',
'revolver')
print(guns)


# I will now attempt to change a couple of values in the tuple.
guns[0] = 'bazooka'
guns[2] = 'AK-47'
```

= RESTART: C:/Users/saifia computers/Desktop/strike
game.py

('rifle', 'shotgun', 'submachine gun', 'assault rifle', 'revolver')

Traceback (most recent call last):

  File "C:/Users/saifia computers/Desktop/strike game.py", line
5, in <module>

    guns[0] = 'bazooka'

TypeError: 'tuple' object does not support item assignment

>>>

271

Creating a Loop Through a Tuple

You can create and run a loop through a tuple by using the *for* loop.

```
guns = ('rifle', 'shotgun', 'submachine gun', 'assault rifle',
'revolver')
print(guns)


for gun in guns:
    print(gun)
= RESTART: C:/Users/saifia computers/Desktop/strike
game.py
('rifle', 'shotgun', 'submachine gun', 'assault rifle', 'revolver')
rifle
shotgun
submachine gun
assault rifle
revolver
>>>
```

Python returns almost all the items of the tuple. You cannot change individual values in a tuple but you can modify an entire tuple.

```
guns = ('rifle', 'shotgun', 'submachine gun', 'assault rifle',
'revolver')
print(guns)
```

```
for gun in guns:
    print(gun)
```

```
guns = ('AK-47', 'bazooka')
print("\nThis is a modified tuple:")
for gun in guns:
    print(gun)
= RESTART: C:/Users/saifia computers/Desktop/strike
game.py
('rifle', 'shotgun', 'submachine gun', 'assault rifle', 'revolver')
rifle
shotgun
submachine gun
assault rifle
revolver

This is a modified tuple:
AK-47
bazooka
>>>
```

Python did not raise errors because I have overwritten the tuple. Tuples are simple data structures as compared to lists. You can use them when you want to store different values that you do not like to be changed throughout the program's entire life.

Chapter Three

Python Conditionals

Programming may land you in a position where you have to examine a set of conditions. You also have to decide upon which action you have to take after the conditions have been tested. Python allows you to examine the program and then respond accordingly. In this chapter, I will explain how you can write the conditional tests that allow you to check a certain condition of interest. This chapter will walk you through the process of writing the *if* statements. I will also explain how you can write complex conditional statements.

In the next code snippet, I will give you a short example of how the *if* statements work. I will use the same list of guns to integrate the if statement.

```
guns = ['rifle', 'shotgun', 'submachine gun', 'assault rifle',
'revolver']

for gun in guns:
    if gun == 'rifle':
        print(gun.upper())
    else:
        print(gun.lower())
```

= RESTART: C:/Users/saifia computers/Desktop/strike game.py

RIFLE

shotgun

submachine gun

assault rifle

revolver

>>>

I will determine in the next code snippet if the conditions are not equal.

```
guns = ('rifle', 'shotgun', 'submachine gun', 'assault rifle', 'revolver')


if guns != 'Ak-47':
    print("You must find and use an AK-47.")


if guns != 'bazooka':
    print("You must find and use a bazooka.")
```

= RESTART: C:/Users/saifia computers/Desktop/strike game.py

You must find and use an AK-47.

You must find and use a bazooka.

>>>

Now I will go back to IDLE to test different conditions.

```
>>> players_age = 20
>>> players_age < 22
True
>>> players_age < 18
False
>>> players_age > 22
False
>>> players_age <= 22
True
>>>
```

See more conditional tests. I will now test multiple conditions in the code. To check if two conditions appear to be True, you can use *and* keyword and combine the conditional tests. If a certain passes, the expression can evaluate to be true. If both tests fail, the expression will be evaluated to be False.

```
>>> players_age = 22
>>> players1_age = 20
>>> players_age >= 22 and players1_age >= 22
False
>>> players1_age = 22
>>> players_age >= 22 and players1_age >= 22
True
>>>
```

With the help of conditional tests, you can check if a list contains a specific value before you take an action. Sometimes, you might need to check if a weapon exists in the player's stock before he jumps into the valley to conduct the counter-terrorism operation. I will add the keyword *in*to the code and see how it works.

> guns = ('rifle', 'shotgun', 'submachine gun', 'assault rifle', 'revolver')
>
> 'revolver' in guns

You can add *if* statements to the code to write many if statements. Multiple if statements can co-exist in the code. You can test a player's eligibility for an operation based on the number of guns he has collected from the magazine or snatched from the enemies. See the following example that tests this condition and allows or rejects the eligibility of a player.

> guns = 6

> if guns >= 5:
>
>   print("Player: You can now proceed to the field operation.")
>
> = RESTART: C:/Users/saifia computers/Desktop/strike game.py
>
> Player: You can now proceed to the field operation.
>
> >>>

Python tests the condition to check if the value in the guns variable is greater than that in the condition. If it finds the condition to be true,

277

it runs the condition and executes the statement. You can add as many messages to the code as you want to.

```
guns = 6


if guns >= 5:
    print("Player: You can now proceed to the field operation.")
    print("Are you ready to strike?")
    print("Check your weapons and tie up the parachute. We will
drop you over the hills.")
= RESTART: C:/Users/saifia computers/Desktop/strike
game.py
Player: You can now proceed to the field operation.
Are you ready to strike?
Check your weapons and tie up the parachute. We will drop you
over the hills.
>>>
```

The if-else Statement

You might feel that what happens if the players say that he has a lesser number of guns hence he is not eligible. Here comes to play the else statement. The if-else block makes it possible for the player to take appropriate action. The else statement navigates the code otherwise if the condition stands false. I have changed the code but I have not yet changed the number of guns.

```
guns = 6
```

```
if guns >= 5:
    print("Player: You can now proceed to the field operation.")
    print("Are you ready to strike?")
    print("Check your weapons and tie up the parachute. We will
drop you over the hills.")
else:
    print("Player: I am sorry! You don't have enough weapons.")
    print("Move on to the field, and collect or snatch more
weapons to proceed toward the mission.")
```

– RESTART: C:/Users/saifia computers/Desktop/strike
game.py

Player: You can now proceed to the field operation.

Are you ready to strike?

Check your weapons and tie up the parachute. We will drop you
over the hills.

>>>

In the following example, I will change the number of guns so that
the else block gets to work.

```
guns = 4
```

```
if guns >= 5:
    print("Player: You can now proceed to the field operation.")
```

print("Are you ready to strike?")

print("Check your weapons and tie up the parachute. We will drop you over the hills.")

else:

print("Player: I am sorry! You don't have enough weapons.")

print("Move on to the field, and collect or snatch more weapons to proceed toward the mission.")

= RESTART: C:/Users/saifia computers/Desktop/strike game.py

Player: I am sorry! You don't have enough weapons.

Move on to the field, and collect or snatch more weapons to proceed toward the mission.

>>>

When the conditional test passes, the first block of code gets to work. When the conditional test fails, the second block of code gets to work.

The if-elif-else Chain

More often, you need to test multiple situations. You can use Python's if-elif-else chain to evaluate these. Python executes one statement at a time. It runs each conditional test and stops at the one that passes.

guns = 2

if guns > 5:

```python
    print("Player: You can now proceed to the field operation.")
    print("Are you ready to strike?")
    print("Check your weapons and tie up the parachute. We will
drop you over the hills.")
elif guns > 10:
    print("You are super ready for the operation. Gear up asap!")
else:
    print("Player: I am sorry! You don't have enough weapons.")
    print("Move on to the field, and collect or snatch more
weapons to proceed toward the mission.")
```

>>> = RESTART: C:/Users/saifia computers/Desktop/strike game.py

Player: I am sorry! You don't have enough weapons.

Move on to the field, and collect or snatch more weapons to proceed toward the mission.

>>>

You can test multiple conditions with the help of if-elif-else chains. When Python finds one test that can pass, it runs it, skipping the rest of the tests.

```python
guns = ['rifle', 'shotgun', 'submachine gun', 'assault rifle',
'revolver']

if 'rifle' in guns:
    print("You can use rifle to kill the enemy.")
```

```python
if 'shotgun' in guns:
    print("You can use shotgun to kill the enemy.")
if 'submachine gun' in guns:
    print("You can use submachine gun to kill the enemy.")
if 'assault rifle' in guns:
    print("You can use assault rifle to kill the enemy.")
if 'revolver' in guns:
    print("You can use revolver to kill the enemy.")
if 'AK-47' in guns:
    print("You can use AK-47 to kill the enemy.")


print("\nYou are equipped with all the weapons you need for the mission.")
```

= RESTART: C:/Users/saifia computers/Desktop/strike game.py

You can use rifle to kill the enemy.

You can use shotgun to kill the enemy.

You can use submachine gun to kill the enemy.

You can use assault rifle to kill the enemy.

You can use revolver to kill the enemy.

You are equipped with all the weapons you need for the mission.

>>>

The same code will not work if you use an if-elif-else block because it will cease operations after one test runs its course.

```python
guns = ['rifle', 'shotgun', 'submachine gun', 'assault rifle', 'revolver']

if 'rifle' in guns:
    print("You can use rifle to kill the enemy.")
elif 'shotgun' in guns:
    print("You can use shotgun to kill the enemy.")
elif 'submachine gun' in guns:
    print("You can use submachine gun to kill the enemy.")
elif 'assault rifle' in guns:
    print("You can use assault rifle to kill the enemy.")
elif 'revolver' in guns:
    print("You can use revolver to kill the enemy.")
elif 'AK-47' in guns:
    print("You can use AK-47 to kill the enemy.")

print("\nYou are equipped with all the weapons you need for the mission.")
```

```
= RESTART: C:/Users/saifia computers/Desktop/strike game.py
You can use rifle to kill the enemy.
```

You are equipped with all the weapons you need for the mission.

>>>

Combining if Statements and Lists

You can combine Python if statements with Python lists. You can manage the change of conditions like the availability of guns for the player during a gaming session.

```
guns = ['rifle', 'shotgun', 'submachine gun', 'assault rifle', 'revolver']


for gun in guns:
    print("You can use " + gun + " to shoot the enemy soldiers.")


print("\nYou are equipped with all the weapons you need for the mission.")
```

= RESTART: C:/Users/saifia computers/Desktop/strike game.py

You can use rifle to shoot the enemy soldiers.

You can use shotgun to shoot the enemy soldiers.

You can use submachine gun to shoot the enemy soldiers.

You can use assault rifle to shoot the enemy soldiers.

You can use revolver to shoot the enemy soldiers.

You are equipped with all the weapons you need for the mission.

>>>

There might be a situation when a player runs out of a particular weapon in the middle of the game. If you pack up an if statement into the for loop, you will be able to handle the situation quite well. I will pack up the if statement in a for loop.

```
guns = ['rifle', 'shotgun', 'submachine gun', 'assault rifle',
'revolver']

for gun in guns:
    if gun == 'shotgun':
        print("Sorry, shotgun is empty of bullets.")
    else:
        print("You can use " + gun + " to shoot the enemy
soldiers.")

print("\nYou are equipped with all the weapons you need for the
mission.")
```

>>>= RESTART: C:/Users/saifia computers/Desktop/strike game.py

You can use rifle to shoot the enemy soldiers.

Sorry, shotgun is empty of bullets.

You can use submachine gun to shoot the enemy soldiers.

285

You can use assault rifle to shoot the enemy soldiers.

You can use revolver to shoot the enemy soldiers.

You are equipped with all the weapons you need for the mission.

>>>

I will add to the code so that the player can get the same message for more than one gun if those guns run out of bullets in a gaming session.

```
guns = ['rifle', 'shotgun', 'submachine gun', 'assault rifle', 'revolver']


for gun in guns:
    if gun == 'shotgun':
        print("Sorry, shotgun is empty of bullets.")
    elif gun == 'rifle':
        print("Sorry, rifle is empty of bullets.")
    elif gun == 'revolver':
        print("Sorry, revolver is empty of bullets.")
    else:
        print("You can use " + gun + " to shoot the enemy soldiers.")
```

```
print("\nYou are equipped with all the weapons you need for the
mission.")
```

= RESTART: C:/Users/saifia computers/Desktop/strike
game.py

Sorry, rifle is empty of bullets.

Sorry, shotgun is empty of bullets.

You can use submachine gun to shoot the enemy soldiers.

You can use assault rifle to shoot the enemy soldiers.

Sorry, revolver is empty of bullets.

You are equipped with all the weapons you need for the
mission.

>>>

I have two elif code blocks to display the same message for more than one gun. The code checks each gun before it hands it over to the player and displays the message accordingly. The else block ensures that all the guns are added to the player's suit before he enters the battleground. You can alter the code to see if the list of weapons is empty or not. You can check the list before the loop runs its course. If Python finds the list to be empty before adding guns to the player's suit, the player will see a different message a different strategy for the game.

```
guns = []


if guns:
```

```
for gun in guns:

    print("You can use " + gun + " to shoot the enemy
soldiers.")

    print("\nYou are equipped with all the weapons you need for
the mission.")
else:

    print("Would you like to use knives instead to finish the
job?")
```

= RESTART: C:/Users/saifia computers/Desktop/strike
game.py

Would you like to use knives instead to finish the job?

>>>

You can add more than one list to your code. In the next example, I will add two lists to the code. You can allow your player to request for a gun in the middle of a mission. For that purpose, you will have two lists. One list will be of the guns that have been added to the suit of the player the other list will contain the guns that can be provided on request. Note the changes in the code to develop this interesting feature for your game or program.

```
guns = ['rifle', 'shotgun', 'submachine gun', 'assault rifle',
'revolver']

demanded_guns = ['AK-47', 'machine gun', 'bazooka']
```

```
for demanded_gun in demanded_guns:

    if demanded_gun in demanded_guns:

        print("You can use " + demanded_gun + " to shoot the
enemy soldiers.")

    else:

        print("Sorry, you cannot access " + demanded_gun + ".")


print("\nYou are equipped with all the weapons you need for the
mission.")
```

= RESTART: C:/Users/saifia computers/Desktop/strike
game.py

You can use AK-47 to shoot the enemy soldiers.

You can use machine gun to shoot the enemy soldiers.

You can use bazooka to shoot the enemy soldiers.

You are equipped with all the weapons you need for the
mission.

>>>

I have defined the list of the guns that a player can access. Then I
created a loop that ran through the demanded guns.

Chapter Four

Python Dictionaries

This chapter will walk you through the art of creating Python dictionaries and learning how to use them in code effectively. This allows you to connect different pieces of information. I will explain how to access elements from a dictionary. You can store an unlimited amount of information inside a dictionary. I will explain how you can add a loop to the dictionary. Python dictionaries enable you to model a wide range of real-life objects to build the programs of your choice. You can create the model of a person and store as much information about him or her as you can. Dictionaries are filled up with pairs of information.

In the following example, I will create pairs of information to fill in a dictionary. I will add the color of each gun to give the player choice. See the example of the following dictionary.

guns = {'rifle': 'green', 'shotgun': 'blue', 'submachine gun': 'navy blue', 'assault rifle': 'yellow', 'revolver': 'black'}

print(guns)
= RESTART: C:/Users/saifia computers/Desktop/strike game.py

{'rifle': 'green', 'shotgun': 'blue', 'submachine gun': 'navy blue', 'assault rifle': 'yellow', 'revolver': 'black'}

\>\>\>

I will access one element from a pair and display it in the IDLE.

```
guns = {'rifle': 'green',  'shotgun': 'blue', 'submachine gun': 'navy blue', 'assault rifle': 'yellow', 'revolver': 'black'}
print(guns['rifle'])
print(guns['shotgun'])
print(guns['revolver'])
```

= RESTART: C:/Users/saifia computers/Desktop/strike game.py

green

blue

black

\>\>\>

A dictionary in Python exists in the form of key-value pairs where each key is linked to the value. You can use the key to access the value that is associated with the key. The value can be an integer, a list, or a string. It also can be another dictionary as well. You have to use braces to enclose a dictionary. A key-value pair is connected to each other. When you enter the key, Python will return the value that is associated with the key. Each key is separated from the value by a colon. You can separate the key-value pairs with the help of commas. A dictionary may contain as many pairs as you want. In the next code example, I will pick a value from the dictionary and use it to display a message for the player in your game.

```
guns = {'rifle': 'green', 'shotgun': 'blue', 'submachine gun': 'navy blue', 'assault rifle': 'yellow', 'revolver': 'black'}
game_guns = guns['rifle']
print("I will pick a rifle of " + game_guns + " color.")
= RESTART: C:/Users/saifia computers/Desktop/strike game.py
I will pick a rifle of green color.
>>>
```

Now I will add more messages to the code.

```
guns = {'rifle': 'green', 'shotgun': 'blue', 'submachine gun': 'navy blue', 'assault rifle': 'yellow', 'revolver': 'black'}
game_guns = guns['rifle']
print("I will pick a rifle of " + game_guns + " color.")


game_guns1 = guns['shotgun']
print("I will pick a shotgun of " + game_guns1 + " color.")


game_guns2 = guns['revolver']
print("I will pick a rifle of " + game_guns2 + " color.")
= RESTART: C:/Users/saifia computers/Desktop/strike game.py
I will pick a rifle of green color.
```

I will pick a shotgun of blue color.

I will pick a rifle of black color.

>>>

As you move on into the world of dictionaries, you can add as many key-value pairs to the dictionary as you want to. Dictionaries are highly dynamic. They welcome as many pairs as you can add to them.

guns = {'rifle': 'green', 'shotgun': 'blue', 'submachine gun': 'navy blue', 'assault rifle': 'yellow', 'revolver': 'black'}

print(guns)

guns['bazooka'] = 'grey'

guns['AK-47'] = 'brown'

print(guns)

= RESTART: C:/Users/saifia computers/Desktop/strike game.py

{'rifle': 'green', 'shotgun': 'blue', 'submachine gun': 'navy blue', 'assault rifle': 'yellow', 'revolver': 'black'}

{'rifle': 'green', 'shotgun': 'blue', 'submachine gun': 'navy blue', 'assault rifle': 'yellow', 'revolver': 'black', 'bazooka': 'grey', 'AK-47': 'brown'}

>>>

With the same process, you can fill in an empty dictionary. I will initiate with an empty dictionary and fill it up with key-value pairs.

```
guns = {}
print(guns)

guns['bazooka'] = 'grey'
guns['AK-47'] = 'brown'
guns['rifle']= 'green'
guns['shotgun'] = 'blue'
guns['submachine gun'] = 'navy blue'
guns['assault rifle'] = 'yellow'
guns['revolver'] = 'black'
print(guns)
= RESTART: C:/Users/saifia computers/Desktop/strike
game.py
{}
{'bazooka': 'grey', 'AK-47': 'brown', 'rifle': 'green', 'shotgun':
'blue', 'submachine gun': 'navy blue', 'assault rifle': 'yellow',
'revolver': 'black'}
>>>
```

Modifying Dictionaries

You can modify a certain dictionary in a dictionary. I will change the color of the guns that a player can use. See the following example.

```
guns = {'rifle': 'green', 'shotgun': 'blue', 'submachine gun': 'navy
blue', 'assault rifle': 'yellow', 'revolver': 'black'}
print("I will pick rifle of " + guns['rifle'] + " color.")


guns['rifle'] = 'purple'
print("Now I will pick rifle of " + guns['rifle'] + " color.")
= RESTART: C:/Users/saifia computers/Desktop/strike
game.py
I will pick rifle of green color.
Now I will pick rifle of purple color.
>>>
```

Pair Removal

When you are done using a certain key-value pair, you can remove it from the dictionary using a simple method. The del statement is used to remove the pairs. You just have to fill up the del method with the dictionary's name and the key that you ought to remove.

```
guns = {'rifle': 'green', 'shotgun': 'blue', 'submachine gun': 'navy
blue', 'assault rifle': 'yellow', 'revolver': 'black'}
print(guns)


del guns['rifle']
print(guns)
```

```python
del guns['shotgun']
print(guns)

del guns['submachine gun']
print(guns)

del guns['assault rifle']
print(guns)

del guns['revolver']
print(guns)
```
= RESTART: C:/Users/saifia computers/Desktop/strike game.py

{'rifle': 'green', 'shotgun': 'blue', 'submachine gun': 'navy blue', 'assault rifle': 'yellow', 'revolver': 'black'}

{'shotgun': 'blue', 'submachine gun': 'navy blue', 'assault rifle': 'yellow', 'revolver': 'black'}

{'submachine gun': 'navy blue', 'assault rifle': 'yellow', 'revolver': 'black'}

{'assault rifle': 'yellow', 'revolver': 'black'}

{'revolver': 'black'}

{}

>>>

You must keep in mind that the del statement permanently removes a pair from the dictionary.

Looping Through Dictionaries

I will use the same dictionary that I have created to store guns and their colors. I will build and run a loop through it.

```
guns = {'rifle': 'green', 'shotgun': 'blue', 'submachine gun': 'navy blue', 'assault rifle': 'yellow', 'revolver': 'black'}
print(guns)

for gun in guns:
    print(gun)
>>>= RESTART: C:/Users/saifia computers/Desktop/strike game.py
{'rifle': 'green', 'shotgun': 'blue', 'submachine gun': 'navy blue', 'assault rifle': 'yellow', 'revolver': 'black'}
rifle
shotgun
submachine gun
assault rifle
revolver
>>>
```

In the next code snippet, I will access different values from the dictionary and use them in the code.

```
guns = {'rifle': 'green',  'shotgun': 'blue', 'submachine gun': 'navy
blue', 'assault rifle': 'yellow', 'revolver': 'black'}
print(guns)

for key, value in guns.items():
    print("\nKey: " + key)
    print("Value: " + value)
```

= RESTART: C:/Users/saifia computers/Desktop/strike
game.py
{'rifle': 'green', 'shotgun': 'blue', 'submachine gun': 'navy blue',
'assault rifle': 'yellow', 'revolver': 'black'}

Key: rifle
Value: green

Key: shotgun
Value: blue

Key: submachine gun
Value: navy blue

Key: assault rifle
Value: yellow

Key: revolver

Value: black

>>>

Python does not care about the order in which it returns the key-value pairs of a dictionary. It only tracks the pairs and prints them in the order it deems fit. I will use the keys and the values in the same print statements to make the code a bit complex and useful. Creating loops through a dictionary work well.

```
guns = {'rifle': 'green', 'shotgun': 'blue', 'submachine gun': 'navy blue', 'assault rifle': 'yellow', 'revolver': 'black'}
print(guns)

for weapons, colors in guns.items():
    print("You can pick up the " + weapons.title() + " to fight the enemy but it is only available in " + colors.title() + ".")
```

= RESTART: C:/Users/saifia computers/Desktop/strike game.py

{'rifle': 'green', 'shotgun': 'blue', 'submachine gun': 'navy blue', 'assault rifle': 'yellow', 'revolver': 'black'}

You can pick up the Rifle to fight the enemy but it is only available in Green.

You can pick up the Shotgun to fight the enemy but it is only available in Blue.

You can pick up the Submachine Gun to fight the enemy but it is only available in Navy Blue.

You can pick up the Assault Rifle to fight the enemy but it is only available in Yellow.

You can pick up the Revolver to fight the enemy but it is only available in Black.

>>>

The code tells Python to create a loop and run it through each key-value pair of the dictionary. As the loop runs its course through the pairs, Python stores the keys in the variable named weapons and it stores the values in the variable named colors. The practice of creating descriptive names helps you to scan the code easily when you have to read it later. I do not have to work with the values, you can change the code to loop only through the keys. This is an easy and clean method to see what you have got in the dictionary's keys.

```
guns = {'rifle': 'green',  'shotgun': 'blue', 'submachine gun': 'navy blue', 'assault rifle': 'yellow', 'revolver': 'black'}
print(guns)


for weapons in guns.keys():
    print("You can pick up the " + weapons.title() + " to fight the enemy.")


= RESTART: C:/Users/saifia computers/Desktop/strike game.py
```

{'rifle': 'green', 'shotgun': 'blue', 'submachine gun': 'navy blue', 'assault rifle': 'yellow', 'revolver': 'black'}

You can pick up the Rifle to fight the enemy.

You can pick up the Shotgun to fight the enemy.

You can pick up the Submachine Gun to fight the enemy.

You can pick up the Assault Rifle to fight the enemy.

You can pick up the Revolver to fight the enemy.

>>>

Similarly, you can pull all the values from the dictionary and use them alone if you want to.

```
guns = {'rifle': 'green', 'shotgun': 'blue', 'submachine gun': 'navy blue', 'assault rifle': 'yellow', 'revolver': 'black'}
print(guns)


for colors in guns.values():
    print("This gun is only available in " + colors.title() + ".")
```

= RESTART: C:/Users/saifia computers/Desktop/strike game.py

{'rifle': 'green', 'shotgun': 'blue', 'submachine gun': 'navy blue', 'assault rifle': 'yellow', 'revolver': 'black'}

This gun is only available in Green.

This gun is only available in Blue.

This gun is only available in Navy Blue.

This gun is only available in Yellow.

This gun is only available in Black.

>>>

You also can have the option to access any value that is associated with a particular key. You can then go on to tuck it into a loop and use it. Then you can print a message to display to the player. I will now loop through particular items in a dictionary.

Dictionary Looping

A dictionary maintains a proper connection between the value and the keys of the items of the dictionary. As already mentioned, Python does not care about the order of the dictionaries when it returns them. So, you have to do something to sort the order. One method to return the items is to use the sorted function. You can add this function to the code to adjust the order.

```
guns = {'rifle': 'green', 'shotgun': 'blue', 'submachine gun': 'navy
blue', 'assault rifle': 'yellow', 'revolver': 'black'}


for weapons in sorted(guns.keys()):
    print(" You can use the " + weapons.title() + " to fight the
battle.")
```

= RESTART: C:/Users/saifia computers/Desktop/strike game.py

You can use the Assault Rifle to fight the battle.

You can use the Revolver to fight the battle.

You can use the Rifle to fight the battle.

You can use the Shotgun to fight the battle.

You can use the Submachine Gun to fight the battle.

>>>

Now I will use the sorted() method for bringing the values of the dictionary in order.

guns = {'rifle': 'green', 'shotgun': 'blue', 'submachine gun': 'navy blue', 'assault rifle': 'yellow', 'revolver': 'black'}

for colors in sorted(guns.values()):
    print(" Your weapon is of " + colors.title() + " color.")

= RESTART: C:/Users/saifia computers/Desktop/strike game.py

Your weapon is of Black color.

Your weapon is of Blue color.

Your weapon is of Green color.

Your weapon is of Navy Blue color.

Your weapon is of Yellow color.

>>>

There might be a dictionary that has repetitive values. The sorted() method does not care about the repeats. You can discourage this practice by adding the set() function to the code. A set demands that each value in the code must be unique.

There are two blue colored weapons in the code but Python will only return one unique color. See the following example.

```
guns = {'rifle': 'blue',  'shotgun': 'blue', 'submachine gun': 'navy blue', 'assault rifle': 'yellow', 'revolver': 'black'}
print("The player is using the following colors.")


for colors in set(guns.values()):
    print(" Your weapon is of " + colors.title() + " color.")
```

```
= RESTART: C:/Users/saifia computers/Desktop/strike game.py
The player is using the following colors.
 Your weapon is of Black color.
 Your weapon is of Blue color.
 Your weapon is of Navy Blue color.
 Your weapon is of Yellow color.
>>>
```

Dictionary Nesting

There may come a time when you desire to create a list of dictionaries. This requires that you pack up multiple dictionaries into a list. The process of packing up different dictionaries inside a list is called nesting. Nesting is a power that allows you to pack up a dictionary inside another dictionary.

```python
guns = {'rifle': 'blue',  'shotgun': 'blue'}
guns1 = {'submachine gun': 'navy blue', 'assault rifle': 'yellow'}
guns2 = {'revolver': 'black', 'bazooka': 'white'}


game_guns = [guns, guns1, guns2]


for game_gun in game_guns:
    print(game_gun)
```

>>>= RESTART: C:/Users/saifia computers/Desktop/strike game.py
{'rifle': 'blue', 'shotgun': 'blue'}
{'submachine gun': 'navy blue', 'assault rifle': 'yellow'}
{'revolver': 'black', 'bazooka': 'white'}
>>>

This shows how easy it is to nest multiple dictionaries into a list. See another practical example.

```python
game_guns = []


for game_guns1 in range(10):
    guns = {'rifle': 'blue',  'shotgun': 'blue', 'submachine gun':
'navy blue', 'assault rifle': 'yellow', 'revolver': 'black', 'bazooka':
'white'}
    game_guns.append(guns)
```

```
for game_gun in game_guns[:6]:
    print(game_gun)
```

= RESTART: C:/Users/saifia computers/Desktop/strike game.py

{'rifle': 'blue', 'shotgun': 'blue', 'submachine gun': 'navy blue', 'assault rifle': 'yellow', 'revolver': 'black', 'bazooka': 'white'}

{'rifle': 'blue', 'shotgun': 'blue', 'submachine gun': 'navy blue', 'assault rifle': 'yellow', 'revolver': 'black', 'bazooka': 'white'}

{'rifle': 'blue', 'shotgun': 'blue', 'submachine gun': 'navy blue', 'assault rifle': 'yellow', 'revolver': 'black', 'bazooka': 'white'}

{'rifle': 'blue', 'shotgun': 'blue', 'submachine gun': 'navy blue', 'assault rifle': 'yellow', 'revolver': 'black', 'bazooka': 'white'}

{'rifle': 'blue', 'shotgun': 'blue', 'submachine gun': 'navy blue', 'assault rifle': 'yellow', 'revolver': 'black', 'bazooka': 'white'}

{'rifle': 'blue', 'shotgun': 'blue', 'submachine gun': 'navy blue', 'assault rifle': 'yellow', 'revolver': 'black', 'bazooka': 'white'}

>>>

The range() function will return numbers that tells Python as to how many times you want to repeat the loop. Each time the loop runs, you will be able to create a new weapon.

```
game_guns = []
```

```
for game_guns1 in range(0, 10):
    guns = {'rifle': 'blue', 'shotgun': 'blue', 'submachine gun':
'navy blue', 'assault rifle': 'yellow', 'revolver': 'black', 'bazooka':
'white'}
    game_guns.append(guns)


for game_gun in game_guns[0:4]:
    if game_gun['bazooka'] == 'white':
        game_gun['AK-47'] = 'brown'
        game_gun['rocket launcher'] = 'orange'


for game_gun in game_guns[:6]:
    print(game_gun)
```

= RESTART: C:/Users/saifia computers/Desktop/strike
game.py

{'rifle': 'blue', 'shotgun': 'blue', 'submachine gun': 'navy blue',
'assault rifle': 'yellow', 'revolver': 'black', 'bazooka': 'white', 'AK-
47': 'brown', 'rocket launcher': 'orange'}

{'rifle': 'blue', 'shotgun': 'blue', 'submachine gun': 'navy blue',
'assault rifle': 'yellow', 'revolver': 'black', 'bazooka': 'white', 'AK-
47': 'brown', 'rocket launcher': 'orange'}

{'rifle': 'blue', 'shotgun': 'blue', 'submachine gun': 'navy blue',
'assault rifle': 'yellow', 'revolver': 'black', 'bazooka': 'white', 'AK-
47': 'brown', 'rocket launcher': 'orange'}

{'rifle': 'blue', 'shotgun': 'blue', 'submachine gun': 'navy blue', 'assault rifle': 'yellow', 'revolver': 'black', 'bazooka': 'white', 'AK-47': 'brown', 'rocket launcher': 'orange'}

{'rifle': 'blue', 'shotgun': 'blue', 'submachine gun': 'navy blue', 'assault rifle': 'yellow', 'revolver': 'black', 'bazooka': 'white'}

{'rifle': 'blue', 'shotgun': 'blue', 'submachine gun': 'navy blue', 'assault rifle': 'yellow', 'revolver': 'black', 'bazooka': 'white'}

>>>

I will now add an elif block that changes the color of the guns. The code will appear like the following when I will add the elif block to the same.

```
game_guns = []

for game_guns1 in range(0, 10):
    guns = {'rifle': 'blue',  'shotgun': 'blue', 'submachine gun': 'navy blue', 'assault rifle': 'yellow', 'revolver': 'black', 'bazooka': 'white'}
    game_guns.append(guns)

for game_gun in game_guns[0:4]:
    if game_gun['bazooka'] == 'white':
        game_gun['AK-47'] = 'brown'
        game_gun['rocket launcher'] = 'orange'
    elif game_gun['bazooka'] == 'black':
        game_gun['AK-47'] = 'golden'
```

```
        game_gun['rocket launcher'] = 'blue'
   for game_gun in game_guns[:6]:
        print(game_gun)
```

Up till now you have seen how you can insert a dictionary into a list. Now you can see why it is useful to insert a list into a dictionary. It is easier.

```
   game_guns = {'rifle': 'blue', 'arsenals': ['shotgun', 'submachine gun', 'assault rifle', 'revolver', 'bazooka'],}


   print("You have loaded up a " + game_guns['rifle'] + " color rifle. Here is the list of the items of the arsenal: ")


   for arsenal in game_guns['arsenals']:
        print("This is the weapon that you can use: " + arsenal)
```
= RESTART: C:/Users/saifia computers/Desktop/strike game.py

You have loaded up a blue color rifle. Here is the list of the items of the arsenal:

This is the weapon that you can use: shotgun

This is the weapon that you can use: submachine gun

This is the weapon that you can use: assault rifle

This is the weapon that you can use: revolver

This is the weapon that you can use: bazooka

>>>

You can create a list and nest it inside a dictionary if you want to link more than one values to a single key.

game_guns = {'rifle': ['blue', 'yellow'], 'shotgun': ['blue', 'purple'], 'submachine gun': ['white', 'green'], 'assault rifle': ['golden', 'red'], 'revolver': ['sea green', 'grey'],}

for guns, colors in game_guns.items():
    print("You have loaded up the " + guns.title() + " of the following color:")
    for color in colors:
        print("\t" + color.title())

= RESTART: C:/Users/saifia computers/Desktop/strike game.py
You have loaded up the Rifle of the following color:
    Blue
    Yellow
You have loaded up the Shotgun of the following color:
    Blue
    Purple
You have loaded up the Submachine Gun of the following color:
    White
    Green

You have loaded up the Assault Rifle of the following color:

Golden

Red

You have loaded up the Revolver of the following color:

Sea Green

Grey

>>>

You can see that Python has linked different colors to each key in the dictionary. Now the player has more than one option in terms of colors. I have used the variables of guns and colors to store the name of guns and types of colors they had. If you want to refine this program further, you can add an if statement to the start of the for loop in the dictionary to see if each gun is available in more than one color.

You also can nest a dictionary inside another dictionary.

```
game_guns = {'arsenal' : {'rifle': 'blue', 'shotgun': 'blue'},
'arsenal2': {'submachine gun': 'white', 'assault rifle': 'golden',
'revolver': 'sea green'}, }
```

This is how you write the code and develop a program.

Chapter Five

Python Loops

Python loops play a key role in user-oriented programs. Most programs in Python are written in a way to solve the problem of an end-user. To effectively do that, you have to get useful information from the user. If someone wants to know whether he is eligible for playing a game, he will see a message that will ask him to fill in the program with their age. A simple input() function can help you write a program that demands a user to enter their age. I will also explain how you can keep the program running with the help of loops.

The input() function stops the program and then waits for the next user to enter his or her age. Python will receive the input and store it the same as a variable. See the following example.

```
p_message = input("This program will repeat what you enter: ")
print(p_message)
>>>= RESTART: C:/Users/saifia computers/Desktop/strike game.py
This program will repeat what you enter: I am a Python student.
I am a Python student.
>>>
```

The input takes one argument at the prompt. When the users see the prompt, they can fill in the program with the input. The program will wait until the user enters their response. Then it goes on to the next user. You can write clear prompt. Each time you use an input() function, the program will end.

```
p_message = input("Welcome to the game! I want you to enter
your name: ")
print("Hi " + p_message + ", I wish you a brilliant gaming
session.")
= RESTART: C:/Users/saifia computers/Desktop/strike
game.py
Welcome to the game! I want you to enter your name: John
Hi John, I wish you a brilliant gaming session.
>>>
= RESTART: C:/Users/saifia computers/Desktop/strike
game.py
Welcome to the game! I want you to enter your name: Jasmine
Hi Jasmine, I wish you a brilliant gaming session.
>>>
```

A prompt can be longer than one line. You can add as many lines to the program. You will be able to store the prompt inside a variable and then go on to pass the variable to input() function. In the next example, I will attempt to write a clean input() statement.

```
p_message = input("Welcome to the game! I hope you Wil
excel in the battle ground. ")
p_message += "\nI want you to enter your name? "

username = input(p_message)
print("Hi " + p_message + ", I wish you a brilliant gaming
session.")
= RESTART: C:/Users/saifia computers/Desktop/strike
game.py
Welcome to the game! I hope you Wil excel in the battle
ground.

I want you to enter your name? John
Hi
I want you to enter your name? , I wish you a brilliant gaming
session.
>>>
```

The While Loops

The for loop accepts a list of items and then executes a certain code block once for each item in the collection. On the other hand, the while loop will keep running as long as a certain condition stands true.

A while does amazing things. You can use it for mathematical functions. You can count numbers by setting up the range. The loop will run until the last number.

```
the_present_number = 10
while the_present_number <= 25:
    print(the_present_number)
    the_present_number +=1
= RESTART: C:/Users/saifia computers/Desktop/strike
game.py
10
11
12
13
14
15
16
17
18
19
20
21
22
23
```

24

25

>>>

See another example in which I have set the difference at 3.

```
the_present_number = 10
while the_present_number <= 60:
    print(the_present_number)
    the_present_number +=3
```

= RESTART: C:/Users/saifia computers/Desktop/strike game.py

10

13

16

19

22

25

28

31

34

37

40

43

46

49

52

55

58

>>>

Python kept the loops running until the conditions I had set up stood true. Once the conditions became false, the loop stopped right away. A game needs while loop to keep running. When the user presses the exit button, this tells Python while loop that the condition has become false. The game stops running, and the user exits it. This can help explain the importance of the while loops.

If I add a while loop to the input() function, it will tell Python when to quit. I will define a specific quit value that will run the program as long as the user does not enter the quit value.

```
p_message = input("Welcome to the game! I hope you will
excel in the battle ground. I want you to enter your name. ")
p_message += "\nIf you want to quit the game, you can enter
'quit' "

p_message1 = ""
while p_message1 != 'quit':
    p_message1 = input(p_message)
    print(p_message)
```

= RESTART: C:/Users/saifia computers/Desktop/strike game.py

Welcome to the game! I hope you will excel in the battle ground. I want you to enter your name. John

John

If you want to quit the game, you can enter 'quit' quit

John

If you want to quit the game, you can enter 'quit'

>>>

The following does not print the word 'quit.' I will add an if statement to the code to make it cleaner and effective.

```
p_message = input("Welcome to the game! I hope you will
excel in the battle ground. I want you to enter your name. ")
p_message += "\nIf you want to quit the game, you can enter
'quit' "

p_message1 = ""
while p_message1 != 'quit':
    p_message1 = input(p_message)

    if p_message1 != 'quit':
        print(p_message)
```

= RESTART: C:/Users/saifia computers/Desktop/strike game.py

Welcome to the game! I hope you will excel in the battle ground. I want you to enter your name. John

John

If you want to quit the game, you can enter 'quit' quit

>>>

The program that we have developed stops running after a time. It is frustrating to restart it every time you want to use it. A short amendment in the program will fix it. I will now add an else statement to the program to make it cleaner.

```
p_message = input("Welcome to the game! I hope you will
excel in the battle ground. I want you to enter your name. ")
p_message += "\nIf you want to quit the game, you can enter 'q'
"


active = True
while active:
    p_message1 = input(p_message)

    if p_message1 == 'q':
        active = False
    else:
        print(p_message)
>>> = RESTART: C:/Users/saifia computers/Desktop/strike
game.py
```

Welcome to the game! I hope you will excel in the battle ground. I want you to enter your name. John

John

If you want to quit the game, you can enter 'q' e

John

If you want to quit the game, you can enter 'q'

John

If you want to quit the game, you can enter 'q' w

John

If you want to quit the game, you can enter 'q'

John

If you want to quit the game, you can enter 'q' t

John

If you want to quit the game, you can enter 'q'

John

If you want to quit the game, you can enter 'q' y

John

If you want to quit the game, you can enter 'q'

John

If you want to quit the game, you can enter 'q' q

>>>

You can see that the while loop keeps running until the condition stands true. I entered different words and Python while the loop kept ongoing. It stopped only when I entered 'q.'

Using Break to Exit the Loop

If you want to exit the while loop without running the rest of the code inside of the loop, you can use the *break* statement. The break statement channelizes the flow of a program and uses it to control which lines of the code must be executed and which must not. The program only executes the code when you want that. Take the example of the program that asks different users about certain places they have been visiting.

```
p_message = input("Welcome to the game! I hope you will
excel in the battle ground. I want you to enter your name. ")
p_message += "\nIf you want to quit the game, you can enter 'q'
"


while True:
    p_message1 = input(p_message)

    if p_message1 == 'q':
        break
    else:
        print(p_message)
```

= RESTART: C:/Users/saifia computers/Desktop/strike game.py

Welcome to the game! I hope you will excel in the battle ground. I want you to enter your name. John

John

If you want to quit the game, you can enter 'q' q

>>>

The next example will show how the while loop keeps running until you enter the q keyword to exit the loop.

p_message = "\nWelcome to the game! I hope you will excel in the battle ground. I want you to enter your name: "

p_message += "\n(If you want to quit the game, you can enter 'q') "


```
while True:
    p_message1 = input(p_message)

    if p_message1 == 'q':
        break
    else:
        print("Welcome to the game, " + p_message1.title() + ". I hope you will win the game.")
```

= RESTART: C:/Users/saifia computers/Desktop/strike game.py

Welcome to the game! I hope you will excel in the battle ground. I want you to enter your name:

(If you want to quit the game, you can enter 'q') John
Welcome to the game, John. I hope you will win the game.

Welcome to the game! I hope you will excel in the battle ground. I want you to enter your name:
(If you want to quit the game, you can enter 'q') Jasmine
Welcome to the game, Jasmine. I hope you will win the game.

Welcome to the game! I hope you will excel in the battle ground. I want you to enter your name:
(If you want to quit the game, you can enter 'q') Jack
Welcome to the game, Jack. I hope you will win the game.

Welcome to the game! I hope you will excel in the battle ground. I want you to enter your name:
(If you want to quit the game, you can enter 'q') Mark
Welcome to the game, Mark. I hope you will win the game.

Welcome to the game! I hope you will excel in the battle ground. I want you to enter your name:
(If you want to quit the game, you can enter 'q') Joseph
Welcome to the game, Joseph. I hope you will win the game.

Welcome to the game! I hope you will excel in the battle ground. I want you to enter your name:

(If you want to quit the game, you can enter 'q') q

>>>

The loop starts with the keywords white True. It will keep running even of you load it up with a million items. It will continue demanding the name of the player and displaying the message. When the user will enter 'q' the loop will reach its end.

The Continue Statement

Instead of breaking out of the loop without the execution of the rest of the code, you can deploy the continue statement to get back to the beginning of loop after doing the conditional test. See the following example.

```
c_number = 50

while c_number < 200:
    c_number += 3
    if c_number % 2 == 0:
        continue

    print(c_number)
= RESTART: C:/Users/saifia computers/Desktop/strike game.py
53
```

While Loops and Lists

You have seen earlier on in the book the use of for loops inside of Python lists, but you need not modify a list inside the for loop because Python will find it troubling to keep track of different items in the list. While you continue working through the list, you can use a while loop. The use of while loops in dictionaries and lists allow you to organize the input. You can use the while loop to move the items of one list to another list. Python while loop will pick items from one list and fill the other list.

```
game_guns = ['rifle', 'shotgun', 'submachine gun', 'assault rifle',
'revolver', 'bazooka']
empty_guns = []

while game_guns:
    c_guns = game_guns.pop()

    print("The gun you are using right now: " + c_guns.title())
    empty_guns.append(c_guns)
    print("\nThe following guns have been used:")
    for empty_gun in empty_guns:
        print(empty_gun.title())


= RESTART: C:/Users/saifia computers/Desktop/strike
game.py
```

The gun you are using right now: Bazooka

The following guns have been used:

Bazooka

The gun you are using right now: Revolver

The following guns have been used:

Bazooka

Revolver

The gun you are using right now: Assault Rifle

The following guns have been used:

Bazooka

Revolver

Assault Rifle

The gun you are using right now: Submachine Gun

The following guns have been used:

Bazooka

Revolver

Assault Rifle

Submachine Gun

The gun you are using right now: Shotgun

The following guns have been used:

Bazooka

Revolver

Assault Rifle

Submachine Gun

Shotgun

The gun you are using right now: Rifle

The following guns have been used:

Bazooka

Revolver

Assault Rifle

Submachine Gun

Shotgun

Rifle

>>>

Removing Instances

If you have a list that have multiple instances of the same value, you can use the remove() function to eliminate the instances.

```
game_guns = ['rifle', 'shotgun', 'rifle', 'submachine gun', 'assault rifle', 'rifle', 'revolver', 'rifle', 'bazooka']
print(game_guns)
```

```python
while 'rifle' in game_guns:
    game_guns.remove('rifle')


print(game_guns)
```

= RESTART: C:/Users/saifia computers/Desktop/strike game.py

['rifle', 'shotgun', 'rifle', 'submachine gun', 'assault rifle', 'rifle', 'revolver', 'rifle', 'bazooka']

['shotgun', 'submachine gun', 'assault rifle', 'revolver', 'bazooka']

>>>

You can take an empty dictionary and fill it up with user input with the help of a while loop. I will store the name of the gun in the empty dictionary and the color of the gun in the following example.

```python
gaming_guns = {}


gaming_active = True


while gaming_active:
    gun = input("\nWhat is the name of your gun? ")
    gaming_gun = input("Which color do you want to choose for the gun?")


    gaming_guns[gun] = gaming_gun
```

```
    repeat = input("Would you let the player choose another gun?
(yes/ no)" )
    if repeat == 'no':
        gaming_active = False


print("\n----Gun Details----")
for gun, gaming_gun in gaming_guns.items():
    print("I would like to use " + gun + " in the color " +
gaming_gun + ".")


= RESTART: C:/Users/saifia computers/Desktop/strike
game.py


What is the name of your gun? shot gun
Which color do you want to choose for the gun?green
Would you let the player choose another gun? (yes/ no)yes


What is the name of your gun? rifle
Which color do you want to choose for the gun?yellow
Would you let the player choose another gun? (yes/ no)yes


What is the name of your gun? bazooka
Which color do you want to choose for the gun?black
Would you let the player choose another gun? (yes/ no)yes
```

What is the name of your gun? rocket launcher

Which color do you want to choose for the gun?grey

Would you let the player choose another gun? (yes/ no)yes

What is the name of your gun? revolver

Which color do you want to choose for the gun?silver

Would you let the player choose another gun? (yes/ no)yes

What is the name of your gun? Ak-47

Which color do you want to choose for the gun?brown

Would you let the player choose another gun? (yes/ no)yes

What is the name of your gun? machine gun

Which color do you want to choose for the gun?red

Would you let the player choose another gun? (yes/ no)no

----Gun Details----

I would like to use shot gun in the color green.

I would like to use rifle in the color yellow.

I would like to use bazooka in the color black.

I would like to use rocket launcher in the color grey.

I would like to use revolver in the color silver.

I would like to use Ak-47 in the color brown.

I would like to use machine gun in the color red.

>>>

Chapter Six

Functions

This chapter will walk you through the techniques of writing functions. Functions are certain blocks of code that are specifically designed to do a specific job. When you look forward to performing a job in repetition, you can call the function's name and the job will be done. If you want to perform the job multiple times, you also can do that. You just have to call the function and the program will be easier to read, write, and fix.

This chapter will explain how you can pass information to different functions and use them in your programs. I will also explain how you can store different types of information in Python modules to organize your program's main files.

Definition

The following is an example of how to define a function.

```python
def gaming_guns():
    print("Hello, you can use the following gun:")


gaming_guns()
```

= RESTART: C:/Users/saifia computers/Desktop/strike game.py

Hello, you can use the following gun:

>>>

This is the simplest form of a Python function. I have defined the function name. then I added a print statement to display a message. The function in the above example is empty as you can see that the parenthesis are empty. In the next example, I will pass a piece of information to a function. In the following example, I will modify the function by passing information. Adding functions to your game can make it interactive and fun to play. Users can have the flexibility to navigate the game as per their choice.

```python
def gaming_guns(guns):
    print("Hello, you can use the following gun: " + guns + ".")


gaming_guns('rifle')
gaming_guns('machine gun')
gaming_guns('revolver')
```

= RESTART: C:/Users/saifia computers/Desktop/strike game.py

Hello, you can use the following gun: rifle.

Hello, you can use the following gun: machine gun.

Hello, you can use the following gun: revolver.

>>>

A function has certain arguments and parameters. Once we have called the function and filled it in with the requisite information, we will see the information printed in the interpreter. In the game, the user will see the same on the screen. The parenthesis in the definition of a function carry the parameters. In this code, guns is the parameter. The information that I entered in the last lines of code when I called the function's name is called arguments. You can fill in the function with as many arguments as you like.

Arguments

You have to pass the arguments to a function. If the function has multiple parameter, it will likewise have multiple arguments. You can pass certain arguments to functions in multiple ways. You also can use positional arguments that need to be in the same order as that of the parameters or the results can be funny and frustrating. When you make a function call, Python must matches each argument with the parameter. The values that are matched up like this are known as positional arguments.

```
def gaming_guns(guns, colors):
    print("\nHello, you can use the follwing gun: " + guns + ".")
    print("It is available in " + colors + " color.")


gaming_guns('rifle', 'blue')
gaming_guns('machine gun', 'yellow')
gaming_guns('revolver', 'silver')
```

```
gaming_guns('AK-47', 'brown')
gaming_guns('bazooka', 'black')
= RESTART: C:/Users/saifia computers/Desktop/strike
game.py
```

Hello, you can use the following gun: rifle.

It is available in blue color.

Hello, you can use the following gun: machine gun.

It is available in yellow color.

Hello, you can use the following gun: revolver.

It is available in silver color.

Hello, you can use the following gun: AK-47.

It is available in brown color.

Hello, you can use the following gun: bazooka.

It is available in black color.

```
>>>
```

The gun's name is stored in the variable guns while the color of the gun is stored in the variable colors. Calling the function multiple times is the most efficient style to work. Whenever you want to describe a gun, you can make the call and fill it in with the right arguments. You can pack up the function with as many arguments as you can. Positional arguments are special in the sense that you have to maintain the order of the arguments. If you change the order of the arguments, you will have funny results.

```
def gaming_guns(guns, colors):
    print("\nHello, you can use the following gun: " + guns + ".")
    print("It is available in " + colors + " color.")


gaming_guns('rifle', 'blue')
gaming_guns('machine gun', 'yellow')
gaming_guns('silver', 'revolver')
gaming_guns( 'brown', 'AK-47')
gaming_guns( 'black', 'bazooka')
```

= RESTART: C:/Users/saifia computers/Desktop/strike game.py

Hello, you can use the following gun: rifle.
It is available in blue color.

Hello, you can use the following gun: machine gun.
It is available in yellow color.

Hello, you can use the following gun: silver.

It is available in revolver color.

Hello, you can use the following gun: brown.

It is available in AK-47 color.

Hello, you can use the following gun: black.

It is available in bazooka color.

>>>

Another type of arguments is known as keyword arguments. The keyword argument is in the form of name-value pairs. You can associate the name with the value of the pair. When you pass on keyword arguments to a function, there will be no confusion. Keyword arguments will extricate you from the worry of ordering the arguments while making the function call. There will be no funny results.

```
def gaming_guns(guns, colors):
    print("\nHello, you can use the following gun: " + guns + ".")
    print("It is available in " + colors + " color.")


gaming_guns(guns = 'rifle', colors = 'blue')
gaming_guns('machine gun', colors = 'yellow')
gaming_guns(colors = 'silver', guns = 'revolver')
gaming_guns( colors = 'brown', guns = 'AK-47')
```

```
gaming_guns(colors = 'black', guns = 'bazooka')
= RESTART: C:/Users/saifia computers/Desktop/strike
game.py
```

Hello, you can use the following gun: rifle.

It is available in blue color.

Hello, you can use the following gun: machine gun.

It is available in yellow color.

Hello, you can use the following gun: revolver.

It is available in silver color.

Hello, you can use the following gun: AK-47.

It is available in brown color.

Hello, you can use the following gun: bazooka.

It is available in black color.

```
>>>
```

You can see that the same code has displayed different results when we added keyword arguments to the same. Now the order of the arguments matters the least as Python knows where to send each argument.

Error Message

You may see an error message on your screen if you do not fill in the function with the right names. A simple spelling error can trigger an error.

```
def gaming_guns(guns, colors):
    print("\nHello, you can use the following gun: " + guns + ".")
    print("It is available in " + colors + " color.")


gaming_guns(guns = 'rifle', colors = 'blue')
gaming_guns('machine gun', colors = 'yellow')
gaming_guns(colors = 'silver', guns = 'revolver')
gaming_guns( colors = 'brown', guns = 'AK-47')
gaming_guns(color = 'black', gun = 'bazooka')
```

= RESTART: C:/Users/saifia computers/Desktop/strike game.py

Hello, you can use the following gun: rifle.
It is available in blue color.

Hello, you can use the following gun: machine gun.
It is available in yellow color.

Hello, you can use the following gun: revolver.

It is available in silver color.

Hello, you can use the following gun: AK-47.

It is available in brown color.

Traceback (most recent call last):

  File "C:/Users/saifia computers/Desktop/strike game.py", line 9, in <module>

    gaming_guns(color = 'black', gun = 'bazooka')

TypeError: gaming_guns() got an unexpected keyword argument 'color'

>>>

Default Values

When you are writing a function, you have to define the default value for parameters. If a particular argument is filled in the function call, Python uses its value. If you leave a function call, Python will pick up the default value and use it to display the result. The following code snippet will help you understand the concept of default values.

```
def gaming_guns(guns, colors = 'red & black'):
    print("\nHello, you can use the following gun: " + guns + ".")
    print("It is available in " + colors + " color.")

gaming_guns(guns = 'rifle', colors = 'blue')
gaming_guns('machine gun', colors = 'yellow')
```

```
gaming_guns(guns = 'revolver')
gaming_guns( colors = 'brown', guns = 'AK-47')
gaming_guns( guns = 'bazooka')
```

= RESTART: C:/Users/saifia computers/Desktop/strike game.py

Hello, you can use the following gun: rifle.
It is available in blue color.

Hello, you can use the following gun: machine gun.
It is available in yellow color.

Hello, you can use the following gun: revolver.
It is available in red & black color.

Hello, you can use the following gun: AK-47.
It is available in brown color.

Hello, you can use the following gun: bazooka.
It is available in red & black color.
>>>

Making Equivalent Function Calls

The most interesting thing about Python is that you can use keyword arguments, default values, and positional arguments together. More often you will need different ways to make a function call. This adds diversification to your code and makes it efficient.

```
def gaming_guns(guns, colors = 'red & black'):
    print("\nHello, you can use the following gun: " + guns + ".")
    print("It is available in " + colors + " color.")


gaming_guns('rifle', 'blue')
gaming_guns('machine gun', colors = 'yellow')
gaming_guns(guns = 'revolver')
gaming_guns( colors = 'brown', guns = 'AK-47')
gaming_guns( guns = 'bazooka')
= RESTART: C:/Users/saifia computers/Desktop/strike game.py


Hello, you can use the following gun: rifle.
It is available in blue color.


Hello, you can use the following gun: machine gun.
It is available in yellow color.
```

343

Hello, you can use the following gun: revolver.

It is available in red & black color.

Hello, you can use the following gun: AK-47.

It is available in brown color.

Hello, you can use the following gun: bazooka.

It is available in red & black color.

>>>

When you have filled in the function with parameters, you must pass on arguments to the same. If you miss out on filling in the function with the right arguments, you will see an error.

```
def gaming_guns(guns, colors = 'red & black'):
    print("\nHello, you can use the following gun: " + guns + ".")
    print("It is available in " + colors + " color.")


gaming_guns('rifle', 'blue')
gaming_guns('machine gun', colors = 'yellow')
gaming_guns(guns = 'revolver')
gaming_guns()
gaming_guns( guns = 'bazooka')
```

= RESTART: C:/Users/saifia computers/Desktop/strike game.py

Hello, you can use the following gun: rifle.

It is available in blue color.

Hello, you can use the following gun: machine gun.

It is available in yellow color.

Hello, you can use the following gun: revolver.

It is available in red & black color.

Traceback (most recent call last):

  File "C:/Users/saifia computers/Desktop/strike game.py", line 8, in <module>

    gaming_guns()

TypeError: gaming_guns() missing 1 required positional argument: 'guns'

>>>

When you have set the parameters, you must fill in the code with proper arguments.

Returning Function Values

A function can return the values that you fill it up with. There is no specific need to display the output directly. Instead, you can process data and return the values. The values that the function return are known as the return value. The return statement receives the value from inside the function and forwards it to the line calling the function. I will use the same code to display the result of returned values.

```
def gaming_guns(guns, colors = 'red & black'):
    gaming_zone = "Hello, you can use the following gun: " + guns + "." + "It is available in " + colors + " color."
    return gaming_zone.title()


Player = gaming_guns('rifle', 'blue')
print(Player)


Player1 = gaming_guns('machine gun', colors = 'yellow')
print(Player1)


Player2 = gaming_guns(guns = 'revolver')
print(Player2)


Player3 = gaming_guns(guns = 'AK-47')
print(Player3)


Player4 = gaming_guns( guns = 'bazooka')
print(Player4)
```

= RESTART: C:/Users/saifia computers/Desktop/strike game.py

Hello, You Can Use The Following Gun: Rifle.It Is Available In Blue Color.

Hello, You Can Use The Following Gun: Machine Gun.It Is Available In Yellow Color.

Hello, You Can Use The Following Gun: Revolver.It Is Available In Red & Black Color.

Hello, You Can Use The Following Gun: Ak-47.It Is Available In Red & Black Color.

Hello, You Can Use The Following Gun: Bazooka.It Is Available In Red & Black Color.

>>>

You can control the output by changing the return statement.

```
def gaming_guns(guns, colors = 'red & black'):
    gaming_zone = "Hello, you can use the following gun: " + guns + "." + "It is available in " + colors + " color."
    return gaming_zone.upper()


Player = gaming_guns('rifle', 'blue')
print(Player)


Player1 = gaming_guns('machine gun', colors = 'yellow')
print(Player1)
```

347

```
Player2 = gaming_guns(guns = 'revolver')
print(Player2)


Player3 = gaming_guns(guns = 'AK-47')
print(Player3)


Player4 = gaming_guns( guns = 'bazooka')
print(Player4)
```

= RESTART: C:/Users/saifia computers/Desktop/strike game.py

HELLO, YOU CAN USE THE FOLLOWING GUN: RIFLE.IT IS AVAILABLE IN BLUE COLOR.

HELLO, YOU CAN USE THE FOLLOWING GUN: MACHINE GUN.IT IS AVAILABLE IN YELLOW COLOR.

HELLO, YOU CAN USE THE FOLLOWING GUN: REVOLVER.IT IS AVAILABLE IN RED & BLACK COLOR.

HELLO, YOU CAN USE THE FOLLOWING GUN: AK-47.IT IS AVAILABLE IN RED & BLACK COLOR.

HELLO, YOU CAN USE THE FOLLOWING GUN: BAZOOKA.IT IS AVAILABLE IN RED & BLACK COLOR.

>>>

You also can make different arguments optional. In certain situations, it makes sense to render an argument optional so the people can fill in the program with additional information if they want to. I will be changing the default values to make it happen.

```
def gaming_guns( guns, colors, bullets):
    gaming_zone = "Hello, you can use the following gun: " +
guns + "." + "It is available in " + colors + " color." + " It has "
+ str(bullets) + " bullets."
    return gaming_zone.title()


Player = gaming_guns('rifle', 'blue', 44)
print(Player)


Player1 = gaming_guns('machine gun', 'yellow', 6)
print(Player1)


Player2 = gaming_guns('revolver', 'blue', 9)
print(Player2)


Player3 = gaming_guns('AK-47', 'black')
print(Player3)


Player4 = gaming_guns( 'bazooka', 'grey', 67)
print(Player4)
= RESTART: C:/Users/saifia computers/Desktop/strike
game.py
```

Hello, You Can Use The Following Gun: Rifle.It Is Available In Blue Color. It Has 44 Bullets.

Hello, You Can Use The Following Gun: Machine Gun.It Is Available In Yellow Color. It Has 6 Bullets.

Hello, You Can Use The Following Gun: Revolver.It Is Available In Blue Color. It Has 9 Bullets.

Traceback (most recent call last):

  File "C:/Users/saifia computers/Desktop/strike game.py", line 14, in <module>

    Player3 = gaming_guns('AK-47', 'black')

TypeError: gaming_guns() missing 1 required positional argument: 'bullets'

>>>

This did not go as planned because when I missed the bullets in the arguments sections, I received an error but the color is not always needed. So, we have to fill in the code with a conditional statement so that we can make the color argument optional and we will be able to skip it at will.

```
def gaming_guns( guns, bullets, colors="):


    if colors:
        gaming_zone = "Hello, you can use the following gun: " + guns + "." + "It is available in " + colors + " color." + " It has " + str(bullets) + " bullets."
    else:
```

350

```python
    gaming_zone = "Hello, you can use the following gun: " +
guns + "." + " It has " + str(bullets) + " bullets."
    return gaming_zone.title()


Player = gaming_guns('rifle', 44, 'blue')
print(Player)


Player1 = gaming_guns('machine gun', 6, 'yellow')
print(Player1)


Player2 = gaming_guns('revolver', 10)
print(Player2)


Player3 = gaming_guns('AK-47', 40, 'black')
print(Player3)


Player4 = gaming_guns( 'bazooka', 50)
print(Player4)
```

= RESTART: C:/Users/saifia computers/Desktop/strike
game.py

Hello, You Can Use The Following Gun: Rifle.It Is Available
In Blue Color. It Has 44 Bullets.

Hello, You Can Use The Following Gun: Machine Gun.It Is
Available In Yellow Color. It Has 6 Bullets.

Hello, You Can Use The Following Gun: Revolver. It Has 10 Bullets.

Hello, You Can Use The Following Gun: Ak-47.It Is Available In Black Color. It Has 40 Bullets.

Hello, You Can Use The Following Gun: Bazooka. It Has 50 Bullets.

>>>

The conditional test has made one argument optional.

Returning Dictionary

A function returns any value that it needs to. This includes complicated data structures such as dictionaries and lists. The following function will build a dictionary of weapons in a game.

```
def gaming_guns( guns, bullets, colors):


    game_player = {'I have the following gun': guns, 'I have the following number of bullets': bullets, 'The color of my gun is': colors}
    return game_player


Player = gaming_guns('rifle', 44, 'blue')
print(Player)


Player1 = gaming_guns('machine gun', 6, 'yellow')
```

```
print(Player1)

Player2 = gaming_guns('revolver', 10, 'grey')
print(Player2)

Player3 = gaming_guns('AK-47', 40, 'black')
print(Player3)

Player4 = gaming_guns( 'bazooka', 50, 'navy blue')
print(Player4)
```

= RESTART: C:/Users/saifia computers/Desktop/strike game.py

{'I have the following gun': 'rifle', 'I have the following number of bullets': 44, 'The color of my gun is': 'blue'}

{'I have the following gun': 'machine gun', 'I have the following number of bullets': 6, 'The color of my gun is': 'yellow'}

{'I have the following gun': 'revolver', 'I have the following number of bullets': 10, 'The color of my gun is': 'grey'}

{'I have the following gun': 'AK-47', 'I have the following number of bullets': 40, 'The color of my gun is': 'black'}

{'I have the following gun': 'bazooka', 'I have the following number of bullets': 50, 'The color of my gun is': 'navy blue'}

>>>

Functions and Loops

You can pair up function with a loop to achieve complex goals. I have added an infinite while loop to the following function. See the code snippet below.

```
def gaming_guns( guns, bullets, colors):

    game_player = {'I have the following gun': guns, 'I have the following number of bullets': bullets, 'The color of my gun is': colors}
    return game_player

while True:
    print("\nPlease choose your gun.")
    g_guns = input("Gun name: ")
    g_bullets = input("Bullets: ")
    g_colors = input("Color of the gun: ")

    Player = gaming_guns(g_guns, g_bullets, g_colors)
    print(Player)

= RESTART: C:/Users/saifia computers/Desktop/strike game.py

Please choose your gun.
```

Gun name: shot gun

Bullets: 45

Color of the gun: blue

{'I have the following gun': 'shot gun', 'I have the following number of bullets': '45', 'The color of my gun is': 'blue'}

Please choose your gun.

Gun name: ak-47

Bullets: 10

Color of the gun: green

{'I have the following gun': 'ak-47', 'I have the following number of bullets': '10', 'The color of my gun is': 'green'}

Please choose your gun.

Gun name: machine gun

Bullets: 55

Color of the gun: yellow

{'I have the following gun': 'machine gun', 'I have the following number of bullets': '55', 'The color of my gun is': 'yellow'}

Please choose your gun.

Gun name: bazooka

Bullets: 10

Color of the gun: green

{'I have the following gun': 'bazooka', 'I have the following number of bullets': '10', 'The color of my gun is': 'green'}

Please choose your gun.

Gun name: revolver

Bullets: 6

Color of the gun: silver

{'I have the following gun': 'revolver', 'I have the following number of bullets': '6', 'The color of my gun is': 'silver'}

Please choose your gun.

Gun name:

Now I will add the quit statement so that users can break out of the loop whenever they want to.

```
def gaming_guns( guns, bullets, colors):

    game_player = {'I have the following gun': guns, 'I have the
following number of bullets': bullets, 'The color of my gun is':
colors}
    return game_player

while True:
    print("\nPlease choose your gun.")
    print("(Please enter 'q' to exit the game.)")
```

```python
g_guns = input("Gun name: ")
if g_guns == 'q':
    break

g_bullets = input("Bullets: ")
if g_bullets == 'q':
    break

g_colors = input("Color of the gun: ")
if g_colors == 'q':
    break

Player = gaming_guns(g_guns, g_bullets, g_colors)
print(Player)
```

= RESTART: C:/Users/saifia computers/Desktop/strike game.py

Please choose your gun.

(Please enter 'q' to exit the game.)

Gun name: shot gun

Bullets: 45

Color of the gun: green

{'I have the following gun': 'shot gun', 'I have the following number of bullets': '45', 'The color of my gun is': 'green'}

Please choose your gun.

(Please enter 'q' to exit the game.)

Gun name: ak-47

Bullets: 10

Color of the gun: brown

{'I have the following gun': 'ak-47', 'I have the following number of bullets': '10', 'The color of my gun is': 'brown'}

Please choose your gun.

(Please enter 'q' to exit the game.)

Gun name: revolver

Bullets: 6

Color of the gun: silver grey

{'I have the following gun': 'revolver', 'I have the following number of bullets': '6', 'The color of my gun is': 'silver grey'}

Please choose your gun.

(Please enter 'q' to exit the game.)

Gun name: machine gun

Bullets: q

>>>

Functions and Lists

You can pass a list to a specific function. The list can be anything like the list of numbers, objects, names, and dictionaries.

```
def gaming_guns(guns):

    for gun in guns:
        game_zone = "I have the following gun: " + gun.title()
        print(game_zone)

gun_list = ['ak-47', 'shot gun', 'machine gun', 'revolver',
'bazooka']
gaming_guns(gun_list)
= RESTART: C:/Users/saifia computers/Desktop/strike
game.py
I have the following gun: Ak-47
I have the following gun: Shot Gun
I have the following gun: Machine Gun
I have the following gun: Revolver
I have the following gun: Bazooka
>>>
```

You can modify a list while it is packed up inside a function. The changes made in the list are permanent. This allows you to work in an efficient way when you have to handle big amounts of data.

```
def gaming_guns(guns, empty_guns):

    while guns:
        c_guns = guns.pop()
        print("You have the following guns: " + c_guns)
        empty_guns.append(c_guns)

def the_empty_guns(empty_guns):
    print("\nHere is the list of the empty guns:")
    for empty_gun in empty_guns:
        print(empty_gun)

guns = ['ak-47', 'shot gun', 'machine gun', 'revolver', 'bazooka']
empty_guns = []

gaming_guns(guns, empty_guns)
the_empty_guns(empty_guns)
```

>>>= RESTART: C:/Users/saifia computers/Desktop/strike game.py

You have the following guns: bazooka

You have the following guns: revolver

You have the following guns: machine gun

You have the following guns: shot gun

You have the following guns: ak-47

Here is the list of the empty guns:

bazooka

revolver

machine gun

shot gun

ak-47

>>>

Chapter Seven

Object-Oriented Programming

Object-oriented programming is one of the most effective approaches for writing software. In the world of object-oriented programming, you have to write classes that would represent a bunch of real-world objects and situations. Classes help you create objects by allowing you to create models of real-world objects. When you create objects from classes, each object has to carry certain behavioral traits of the object. When you make an object from a class, the process is known as instantiation. This chapter will walk you through the process of creating classes and instances from the classes. Once you have created a class, you can create as many instances as you like. A proper understanding of object-oriented programming will help you see the world from the eye of a programmer. You will get to know your code from a bigger point of view.

Classes will make your life easier as you will be able to address different problems creatively. You can create a model of anything by using a class. I will start writing the class of a horse that runs fast. The horse will have a name, color, and age. H will run and leap over an obstacle on a racecourse. When I will finish writing the class, I will turn toward creating instances. Each instance will represent a separate horse. See the following code example.

```python
class Horse():
    # this is a simple Python class
    def __init__(self, hname, hage):
        # i am initializing the name & age attributes.
        self.hname = hname
        self.hage = hage

    def run(self):
        # This function will make the horse run when given a
        command.
        print(self.hname.title() + " is now running on the race
        course.")

    def leap_over(self):
        # This will make the horse leap over the obstacle.
        print(self.hname.title() + " has successfully leaped over the
        first obstacle.")
```

The __init__() method is an integral part of the class. It automatically runs when you create a brand new instance from the horse class. There are four parameters for the function, to which you will have to pass arguments when you will create an instance. I have added two methods for making the horse run and leap over the obstacle on the racecourse. The methods will create simple statements and display them on the screen. If you develop a real game, the methods will cause the horse to animate on the screen. It will quite interesting if you are looking forward to creating your own game. You can build a robot and create classes and methods to make it do things you envisioned. I will not create an instance from the same class.

```python
class Horse():
    # this is a simple Python class
    def __init__(self, hname, hage, hcolor):
        # i am initializing the name & age attributes.
        self.hname = hname
        self.hage = hage
        self.hcolor = hcolor

    def run(self):
        # This function will make the horse run when given a command.
        print(self.hname.title() + " is now running on the race course.")

    def leap_over(self):
        # This will make the horse leap over the obstacle.
        print(self.hname.title() + " has successfully leaped over the first obstacle.")

horse1 = Horse('Bond', 9, 'blue')
```

```
print("The pet name of my horse is " + horse1.hname.title() +
".")
print("My horse is " + str(horse1.hage) + " years old.")
print("My horse is of " + horse1.hcolor.title() + " color.")
= RESTART: C:/Users/saifia computers/Desktop/strike
game.py
The pet name of my horse is Bond.
My horse is 9 years old.
My horse is of Blue color.
>>>
```

Now I will call the methods that will animate the horse to make it run and leap over the obstacle to win the race. I will call the methods in the following code to make the object animate. The two lines that are required to call the methods will come at the end of the code.

```
class Horse():
    # this is a simple Python class
    def __init__(self, hname, hage, hcolor):
        # i am initializing the name & age attributes.
        self.hname = hname
        self.hage = hage
        self.hcolor = hcolor

    def run(self):
```

```python
        # This function will make the horse run when given a command.
        print(self.hname.title() + " is now running on the race course.")

    def leap_over(self):
        # This will make the horse leap over the obstacle.
        print(self.hname.title() + " has successfully leaped over the first obstacle.")

horse1 = Horse('Bond', 9, 'blue')
print("The pet name of my horse is " + horse1.hname.title() + ".")
print("My horse is " + str(horse1.hage) + " years old.")
print("My horse is of " + horse1.hcolor.title() + " color.")
horse1.run()
horse1.leap_over()
```
= RESTART: C:/Users/saifia computers/Desktop/strike game.py

The pet name of my horse is Bond.

My horse is 9 years old.

My horse is of Blue color.

Bond is now running on the race course.

Bond has successfully leaped over the first obstacle.

>>>

Multiple Instances

You can create as many instances for the same class as you want to. I will create more horses that would run on the race course in the game. See the following example.

```python
class Horse():
    # this is a simple Python class
    def __init__(self, hname, hage, hcolor):
        # i am initializing the name & age attriutes.
        self.hname = hname
        self.hage = hage
        self.hcolor = hcolor

    def run(self):
        # This function will make the horse run when given a command.
        print(self.hname.title() + " is now running on the race course.")

    def leap_over(self):
        # This will make the horse leap over the obstacle.
        print(self.hname.title() + " has successfully leaped over the first obstacle.")

horse1 = Horse('Bond', 9, 'blue')
```

```python
print("The pet name of my horse is " + horse1.hname.title() +
".")
print("My horse is " + str(horse1.hage) + " years old.")
print("My horse is of " + horse1.hcolor.title() + " color.")
horse1.run()
horse1.leap_over()


horse2 = Horse('Dragon', 12, 'Black')
print("The pet name of my horse is " + horse2.hname.title() +
".")
print("My horse is " + str(horse2.hage) + " years old.")
print("My horse is of " + horse2.hcolor.title() + " color.")
horse2.run()
horse2.leap_over()


horse3 = Horse('Saber', 8, 'White')
print("The pet name of my horse is " + horse3.hname.title() +
".")
print("My horse is " + str(horse3.hage) + " years old.")
print("My horse is of " + horse3.hcolor.title() + " color.")
horse3.run()
horse3.leap_over()


horse4 = Horse('Lilly', 13, 'Red')
```

```python
print("The pet name of my horse is " + horse4.hname.title() +
".")
print("My horse is " + str(horse4.hage) + " years old.")
print("My horse is of " + horse4.hcolor.title() + " color.")
horse4.run()
horse4.leap_over()
```

= RESTART: C:/Users/saifia computers/Desktop/strike
game.py

The pet name of my horse is Bond.

My horse is 9 years old.

My horse is of Blue color.

Bond is now running on the race course.

Bond has successfully leaped over the first obstacle.

The pet name of my horse is Dragon.

My horse is 12 years old.

My horse is of Black color.

Dragon is now running on the race course.

Dragon has successfully leaped over the first obstacle.

The pet name of my horse is Saber.

My horse is 8 years old.

My horse is of White color.

Saber is now running on the race course.

Saber has successfully leaped over the first obstacle.

The pet name of my horse is Lilly.

My horse is 13 years old.

My horse is of Red color.

Lilly is now running on the race course.

Lilly has successfully leaped over the first obstacle.

>>>

You also can add more method to animate the horses further. I will make the horse graze the grass at the river bank after it has run on the race horse. All it will take is a simple method to make it happen.

```python
class Horse():
    # this is a simple Python class
    def __init__(self, hname, hage, hcolor):
        # i am initializing the name & age attriutes.
        self.hname = hname
        self.hage = hage
        self.hcolor = hcolor


    def run(self):
        # This function will make the horse run when given a command.
        print(self.hname.title() + " is now running on the race course.")


    def leap_over(self):
        # This will make the horse leap over the obstacle.
```

```python
        print(self.hname.title() + " has successfully leaped over the
first obstacle.")

    def grass_grazing(self):
        print(self.hname.title() + " is grazing grass at the bank of
the river.")


horse1 = Horse('Bond', 9, 'blue')
print("The pet name of my horse is " + horse1.hname.title() +
".")
print("My horse is " + str(horse1.hage) + " years old.")
print("My horse is of " + horse1.hcolor.title() + " color.")
horse1.run()
horse1.leap_over()
horse1.grass_grazing()


horse2 = Horse('Dragon', 12, 'Black')
print("The pet name of my horse is " + horse2.hname.title() +
".")
print("My horse is " + str(horse2.hage) + " years old.")
print("My horse is of " + horse2.hcolor.title() + " color.")
horse2.run()
horse2.leap_over()
horse2.grass_grazing()
```

```python
horse3 = Horse('Saber', 8, 'White')
print("The pet name of my horse is " + horse3.hname.title() +
".")
print("My horse is " + str(horse3.hage) + " years old.")
print("My horse is of " + horse3.hcolor.title() + " color.")
horse3.run()
horse3.leap_over()
horse3.grass_grazing()

horse4 = Horse('Lilly', 13, 'Red')
print("The pet name of my horse is " + horse4.hname.title() +
".")
print("My horse is " + str(horse4.hage) + " years old.")
print("My horse is of " + horse4.hcolor.title() + " color.")
horse4.run()
horse4.leap_over()
horse4.grass_grazing()
```

= RESTART: C:/Users/saifia computers/Desktop/strike game.py

The pet name of my horse is Bond.

My horse is 9 years old.

My horse is of Blue color.

Bond is now running on the race course.

Bond has successfully leaped over the first obstacle.

Bond is grazing grass at the bank of the river.

The pet name of my horse is Dragon.

My horse is 12 years old.

My horse is of Black color.

Dragon is now running on the race course.

Dragon has successfully leaped over the first obstacle.

Dragon is grazing grass at the bank of the river.

The pet name of my horse is Saber.

My horse is 8 years old.

My horse is of White color.

Saber is now running on the race course.

Saber has successfully leaped over the first obstacle.

Saber is grazing grass at the bank of the river.

The pet name of my horse is Lilly.

My horse is 13 years old.

My horse is of Red color.

Lilly is now running on the race course.

Lilly has successfully leaped over the first obstacle.

Lilly is grazing grass at the bank of the river.

>>>

The Cycle Class

I will now create a cycle class. This class will store the information about cycles. I will add different methods that will help us add more information about cycles. If you are planning to launch a cycle showroom, the cycle class will help you operate the showroom efficiently. The method to creating the cycle class will be similar to that of creating the horse class. I will change the parameters, methods and arguments in the instances.

```
class Cycle():

    def __init__(self, cname, cmake, cyear, ccolor):
        self.cname = cname
        self.cmake = cmake
        self.cyear = cyear
        self.ccolor = ccolor

    def full_name(self):
        fname = self.cname + ' ' + self.cmake + ' ' + str(self.cyear) + ' ' + self.ccolor
        return fname.title()

mycycle1 = Cycle('hybrid', 'hiland', 2015, 'blue')
print(mycycle1.full_name())
```

= RESTART: C:/Users/saifia computers/Desktop/strike game.py

Hybrid Hiland 2015 Blue

>>>

I will now add more instances to the cycle class.

```
class Cycle():

    def __init__(self, cname, cmake, cyear, ccolor):
        self.cname = cname
        self.cmake = cmake
        self.cyear = cyear
        self.ccolor = ccolor

    def full_name(self):
        fname = self.cname + ' ' + self.cmake + ' ' + str(self.cyear)
+ ' ' + self.ccolor
        return fname.title()


mycycle1 = Cycle('hybrid', 'hiland', 2015, 'blue')
print(mycycle1.full_name())


mycycle2 = Cycle('hybrid retro urban', 'Eurobike', 2012, 'grey')
print(mycycle2.full_name())
```

```
mycycle3 = Cycle('hybrid', 'vilano', 2018, 'black')
print(mycycle1.full_name())
```

============ RESTART: C:\Users\saifia

computers\Desktop\strike game.py ==========

Hybrid Hiland 2015 Blue

Hybrid Retro Urban Eurobike 2012 Grey

Hybrid Hiland 2015 Blue

>>>

Default Attributes

Each attribute inside a class demands an initial value even if its value is zero. I will add to the class another attribute for reading the odometer. The attribute will start from zero. It will show that the cycle has run zero kilometers on the road. I will also add a method that will aid in reading the odometer.

```
class Cycle():

    def __init__(self, cname, cmake, cyear, ccolor):
        self.cname = cname
        self.cmake = cmake
        self.cyear = cyear
        self.ccolor = ccolor
        self.odometer_reading = 0
```

```python
    def full_name(self):
        fname = self.cname + ' ' + self.cmake + ' ' + str(self.cyear)
+ ' ' + self.ccolor
        return fname.title()
    def reading_my_odometer(self):
        print("The cycle has " + str(self.odometer_reading) + "
miles on record.")


mycycle1 = Cycle('the cycle is hybrid', 'the cycle is made by
hiland', 2015, 'its color is crazy blue')
print(mycycle1.full_name())
mycycle1.reading_my_odometer()


mycycle2 = Cycle('the cycle is hybrid retro urban', 'it is made
by Eurobike', 2012, 'it color is grey')
print(mycycle2.full_name())
mycycle2.reading_my_odometer()


mycycle3 = Cycle('the cycle is hybrid', 'it is made by vilano',
2018, 'its color is dark black')
print(mycycle1.full_name())
mycycle3.reading_my_odometer()
```

mycycle4 = Cycle('the cycle is endurance bike', 'it is made by tommaso', 2018, 'its color is brown')

print(mycycle1.full_name())

mycycle4.reading_my_odometer()

=========== RESTART: C:\Users\saifia computers\Desktop\strike game.py ==========

The Cycle Is Hybrid The Cycle Is Made By Hiland 2015 Its Color Is Crazy Blue

The cycle has 0 miles on record.

The Cycle Is Hybrid Retro Urban It Is Made By Eurobike 2012 It Color Is Grey

The cycle has 0 miles on record.

The Cycle Is Hybrid The Cycle Is Made By Hiland 2015 Its Color Is Crazy Blue

The cycle has 0 miles on record.

The Cycle Is Hybrid The Cycle Is Made By Hiland 2015 Its Color Is Crazy Blue

The cycle has 0 miles on record.

>>>

We can make the above-mentioned code cleaner by adding the statements in the method section.

class Cycle():

```python
    def __init__(self, cname, cmake, cyear, ccolor):
        self.cname = cname
        self.cmake = cmake
        self.cyear = cyear
        self.ccolor = ccolor
        self.odometer_reading = 0


    def full_name(self):
        fname = "The cycle is " + self.cname + "." + "the cycle is
made by " + self.cmake + "." + "It is made in " + str(self.cyear)
+ "." + "its color is " + self.ccolor + "."
        return fname.title()
    def reading_my_odometer(self):
        print("The cycle has " + str(self.odometer_reading) + "
miles on record.")


mycycle1 = Cycle('hybrid', 'hiland', 2015, 'crazy blue')
print(mycycle1.full_name())
mycycle1.reading_my_odometer()


mycycle2 = Cycle('retro urban', 'Eurobike', 2012, 'it color is
grey')
print(mycycle2.full_name())
mycycle2.reading_my_odometer()
```

```
mycycle3 = Cycle('the cycle is hybrid', 'it is made by vilano',
2018, 'dark black')
print(mycycle1.full_name())
mycycle3.reading_my_odometer()


mycycle4 = Cycle('endurance bike', 'tommaso', 2018, 'brown')
print(mycycle1.full_name())
mycycle4.reading_my_odometer()
```

============ RESTART: C:\Users\saifia
computers\Desktop\strike game.py ==========

The Cycle Is Hybrid.The Cycle Is Made By Hiland.It Is Made
In 2015.Its Color Is Crazy Blue.

The cycle has 0 miles on record.

The Cycle Is Retro Urban.The Cycle Is Made By Eurobike.It Is
Made In 2012.Its Color Is It Color Is Grey.

The cycle has 0 miles on record.

The Cycle Is Hybrid.The Cycle Is Made By Hiland.It Is Made
In 2015.Its Color Is Crazy Blue.

The cycle has 0 miles on record.

The Cycle Is Hybrid.The Cycle Is Made By Hiland.It Is Made
In 2015.Its Color Is Crazy Blue.

The cycle has 0 miles on record.

>>>

In the next example, I will modify the value of attributes through the instance. See the following example.

```python
class Cycle():

    def __init__(self, cname, cmake, cyear, ccolor):
        self.cname = cname
        self.cmake = cmake
        self.cyear = cyear
        self.ccolor = ccolor
        self.odometer_reading = 0

    def full_name(self):
        fname = "The cycle is " + self.cname + "." + "the cycle is made by " + self.cmake + "." + "It is made in " + str(self.cyear) + "." + "its color is " + self.ccolor + "."
        return fname.title()
    def reading_my_odometer(self):
        print("The cycle has " + str(self.odometer_reading) + " miles on record.")

mycycle1 = Cycle('hybrid', 'hiland', 2015, 'crazy blue')
print(mycycle1.full_name())
mycycle1.odometer_reading = 55
mycycle1.reading_my_odometer()
```

```python
mycycle2 = Cycle('retro urban', 'Eurobike', 2012, 'it color is
grey')
print(mycycle2.full_name())
mycycle1.odometer_reading = 20
mycycle2.reading_my_odometer()


mycycle3 = Cycle('the cycle is hybrid', 'it is made by vilano',
2018, 'dark black')
print(mycycle1.full_name())
mycycle3.reading_my_odometer()


mycycle4 = Cycle('endurance bike', 'tommaso', 2018, 'brown')
print(mycycle1.full_name())
mycycle4.reading_my_odometer()
```

============ RESTART: C:\Users\saifia
computers\Desktop\strike game.py ==========

The Cycle Is Hybrid.The Cycle Is Made By Hiland.It Is Made
In 2015.Its Color Is Crazy Blue.

The cycle has 55 miles on record.

The Cycle Is Retro Urban.The Cycle Is Made By Eurobike.It Is
Made In 2012.Its Color Is It Color Is Grey.

The cycle has 0 miles on record.

The Cycle Is Hybrid.The Cycle Is Made By Hiland.It Is Made In 2015.Its Color Is Crazy Blue.

The cycle has 0 miles on record.

The Cycle Is Hybrid.The Cycle Is Made By Hiland.It Is Made In 2015.Its Color Is Crazy Blue.

The cycle has 0 miles on record.

>>>

This is old school and worn out way to modify the value of the attributes. There is an easy and more systematic way to do that. Certain methods can update different types of attributes in the code. Instead of altering the instances, you can pass on the new value to the method that will handle the updating effectively. The new method that I will add here is named as my_update_odometer().

```
class Cycle():

    def __init__(self, cname, cmake, cyear, ccolor):
        self.cname = cname
        self.cmake = cmake
        self.cyear = cyear
        self.ccolor = ccolor
        self.odometer_reading = 0


    def full_name(self):
```

```python
        fname = "The cycle is " + self.cname + "." + "the cycle is
made by " + self.cmake + "." + "It is made in " + str(self.cyear)
+ "." + "its color is " + self.ccolor + "."
        return fname.title()
    def reading_my_odometer(self):
        print("The cycle has " + str(self.odometer_reading) + "
miles on record.")
    def my_update_odometer(self,cmileage):
        self.odometer_reading = cmileage


mycycle1 = Cycle('hybrid', 'hiland', 2015, 'crazy blue')
print(mycycle1.full_name())
mycycle1.odometer_reading = 20
mycycle1.my_update_odometer(55)
mycycle1.reading_my_odometer()


mycycle2 = Cycle('retro urban', 'Eurobike', 2012, 'it color is
grey')
print(mycycle2.full_name())
mycycle2.my_update_odometer(45)
mycycle2.reading_my_odometer()


mycycle3 = Cycle('the cycle is hybrid', 'it is made by vilano',
2018, 'dark black')
```

```
print(mycycle1.full_name())
mycycle3.reading_my_odometer()


mycycle4 = Cycle('endurance bike', 'tommaso', 2018, 'brown')
print(mycycle1.full_name())
mycycle4.reading_my_odometer()
```

============ RESTART: C:\Users\saifia
computers\Desktop\strike game.py ==========

The Cycle Is Hybrid.The Cycle Is Made By Hiland.It Is Made
In 2015.Its Color Is Crazy Blue.

The cycle has 55 miles on record.

The Cycle Is Retro Urban.The Cycle Is Made By Eurobike.It Is
Made In 2012.Its Color Is It Color Is Grey.

The cycle has 45 miles on record.

The Cycle Is Hybrid.The Cycle Is Made By Hiland.It Is Made
In 2015.Its Color Is Crazy Blue.

The cycle has 0 miles on record.

The Cycle Is Hybrid.The Cycle Is Made By Hiland.It Is Made
In 2015.Its Color Is Crazy Blue.

The cycle has 0 miles on record.

>>>

I will now add something interesting to the same code. I will add a
method that keeps the employees of the showroom from rolling back
the odometer. I will add logic to the code to ensure that no one can
roll back the odometer's reading.

```python
class Cycle():

    def __init__(self, cname, cmake, cyear, ccolor):
        self.cname = cname
        self.cmake = cmake
        self.cyear = cyear
        self.ccolor = ccolor
        self.odometer_reading = 50

    def full_name(self):
        fname = "The cycle is " + self.cname + "." + "the cycle is
        made by " + self.cmake + "." + "It is made in " + str(self.cyear)
        + "." + "its color is " + self.ccolor + "."
        return fname.title()
    def reading_my_odometer(self):
        print("The cycle has " + str(self.odometer_reading) + "
        miles on record.")
    def my_update_odometer(self, cmileage):
        self.odometer_reading = cmileage

        if cmileage >= self.odometer_reading:
            self.odometer_reading = cmileage
        else:
```

```python
        print("Dear employee! You cannot roll back the reading
of the odometer.")

mycycle1 = Cycle('hybrid', 'hiland', 2015, 'crazy blue')
print(mycycle1.full_name())
mycycle1.my_update_odometer(15)
mycycle1.reading_my_odometer()


mycycle2 = Cycle('retro urban', 'Eurobike', 2012, 'it color is
grey')
print(mycycle2.full_name())
mycycle2.my_update_odometer(10)
mycycle2.reading_my_odometer()


mycycle3 = Cycle('the cycle is hybrid', 'it is made by vilano',
2018, 'dark black')
print(mycycle1.full_name())
mycycle3.reading_my_odometer()


mycycle4 = Cycle('endurance bike', 'tommaso', 2018, 'brown')
print(mycycle1.full_name())
mycycle4.reading_my_odometer()
```

Incrementing

There is a method to increment the value of an attribute. You can add up the incremental value to the mileage of the cycle by a simple method. This makes it easier for you to maintain the record of how many miles the cycle has run during transportation. The customers need to know this.

```python
class Cycle():

    def __init__(self, cname, cmake, cyear, ccolor):
        self.cname = cname
        self.cmake = cmake
        self.cyear = cyear
        self.ccolor = ccolor
        self.odometer_reading = 50

    def full_name(self):
        fname = "The cycle is " + self.cname + "." + "the cycle is made by " + self.cmake + "." + "It is made in " + str(self.cyear) + "." + "its color is " + self.ccolor + "."
        return fname.title()
    def reading_my_odometer(self):
        print("The cycle has " + str(self.odometer_reading) + " miles on record.")
    def my_update_odometer(self, cmileage):
```

```python
        self.odometer_reading = cmileage

    if cmileage >= self.odometer_reading:
        self.odometer_reading = cmileage
    else:
        print("Dear employee! You cannot roll back the reading
of the odometer.")
    def incrementing_the_odometer(self, kilometers):
        self.odometer_reading += kilometers


mycycle1 = Cycle('hybrid', 'hiland', 2015, 'crazy blue')
print(mycycle1.full_name())
mycycle1.my_update_odometer(15)
mycycle1.reading_my_odometer()
mycycle1.incrementing_the_odometer(100)
mycycle1.reading_my_odometer()


mycycle2 = Cycle('retro urban', 'Eurobike', 2012, 'it color is
grey')
print(mycycle2.full_name())
mycycle2.my_update_odometer(10)
mycycle2.reading_my_odometer()
mycycle2.incrementing_the_odometer(5000)
mycycle2.reading_my_odometer()
```

```
mycycle3 = Cycle('the cycle is hybrid', 'it is made by vilano',
2018, 'dark black')
print(mycycle1.full_name())
mycycle3.reading_my_odometer()
mycycle3.incrementing_the_odometer(1000)
mycycle3.reading_my_odometer()


mycycle4 = Cycle('endurance bike', 'tommaso', 2018, 'brown')
print(mycycle1.full_name())
mycycle4.reading_my_odometer()
mycycle4.incrementing_the_odometer(2000)
mycycle4.reading_my_odometer()
```

=========== RESTART: C:\Users\saifia computers\Desktop\strike game.py ==========

The Cycle Is Hybrid.The Cycle Is Made By Hiland.It Is Made In 2015.Its Color Is Crazy Blue.

The cycle has 15 miles on record.

The cycle has 115 miles on record.

The Cycle Is Retro Urban.The Cycle Is Made By Eurobike.It Is Made In 2012.Its Color Is It Color Is Grey.

The cycle has 10 miles on record.

The cycle has 5010 miles on record.

The Cycle Is Hybrid.The Cycle Is Made By Hiland.It Is Made In 2015.Its Color Is Crazy Blue.

The cycle has 50 miles on record.

The cycle has 1050 miles on record.

The Cycle Is Hybrid.The Cycle Is Made By Hiland.It Is Made In 2015.Its Color Is Crazy Blue.

The cycle has 50 miles on record.

The cycle has 2050 miles on record.

>>>

The Inheritance Class

When you are righting a class, you don't always have to start from scratch. If you are writing a specialized class that is a part of the class you have already written, you can use the inheritance class feature. If a class inherits from another class, it consumes all methods and attributes of the parent class. The inherited class is labeled as the child class. You can use the _init_ () method for the class to ensure that the child class inherits all parent class values. I will create an electric bike in the next code snippet. I will now start creating a simple electric bike version that will do everything the Cycle class does.

```
class Cycle():

    def __init__(self, cname, cmake, cyear, ccolor):
        self.cname = cname
```

```python
        self.cmake = cmake
        self.cyear = cyear
        self.ccolor = ccolor
        self.odometer_reading = 50


    def full_name(self):
        fname = "The cycle is " + self.cname + "." + "the cycle is
made by " + self.cmake + "." + "It is made in " + str(self.cyear)
+ "." + "its color is " + self.ccolor + "."
        return fname.title()
    def reading_my_odometer(self):
        print("The cycle has " + str(self.odometer_reading) + "
miles on record.")
    def my_update_odometer(self, cmileage):
        self.odometer_reading = cmileage


        if cmileage >= self.odometer_reading:
            self.odometer_reading = cmileage
        else:
            print("Dear employee! You cannot roll back the reading
of the odometer.")
    def incrementing_the_odometer(self, kilometers):
        self.odometer_reading += kilometers
```

```python
class ECycle(Cycle):
    def __init__(self, cname, cmake, cyear, ccolor):
        super().__init__(cname, cmake, cyear, ccolor)
mynova = ECycle('Electric bike', 'Nova', 2020, 'silver')
print(mynova.full_name())


mycycle1 = Cycle('hybrid', 'hiland', 2015, 'crazy blue')
print(mycycle1.full_name())
mycycle1.my_update_odometer(15)
mycycle1.reading_my_odometer()
mycycle1.incrementing_the_odometer(100)
mycycle1.reading_my_odometer()


mycycle2 = Cycle('retro urban', 'Eurobike', 2012, 'it color is grey')
print(mycycle2.full_name())
mycycle2.my_update_odometer(10)
mycycle2.reading_my_odometer()
mycycle2.incrementing_the_odometer(5000)
mycycle2.reading_my_odometer()


mycycle3 = Cycle('the cycle is hybrid', 'it is made by vilano', 2018, 'dark black')
print(mycycle1.full_name())
```

mycycle3.reading_my_odometer()

mycycle3.incrementing_the_odometer(1000)

mycycle3.reading_my_odometer()

mycycle4 = Cycle('endurance bike', 'tommaso', 2018, 'brown')

print(mycycle1.full_name())

mycycle4.reading_my_odometer()

mycycle4.incrementing_the_odometer(2000)

mycycle4.reading_my_odometer()

=========== RESTART: C:\Users\saifia
computers\Desktop\strike game.py ==========

The Cycle Is Electric Bike.The Cycle Is Made By Nova.It Is
Made In 2020.Its Color Is Silver.

The Cycle Is Hybrid.The Cycle Is Made By Hiland.It Is Made
In 2015.Its Color Is Crazy Blue.

The cycle has 15 miles on record.

The cycle has 115 miles on record.

The Cycle Is Retro Urban.The Cycle Is Made By Eurobike.It Is
Made In 2012.Its Color Is It Color Is Grey.

The cycle has 10 miles on record.

The cycle has 5010 miles on record.

The Cycle Is Hybrid.The Cycle Is Made By Hiland.It Is Made
In 2015.Its Color Is Crazy Blue.

The cycle has 50 miles on record.

The cycle has 1050 miles on record.

The Cycle Is Hybrid.The Cycle Is Made By Hiland.It Is Made In 2015.Its Color Is Crazy Blue.

The cycle has 50 miles on record.

The cycle has 2050 miles on record.

>>>

You must keep in mind that when you are creating a child class, the parent class must be a part of the file in which you are creating it. The parent class is order sensitive so you have to write it before the child class. You must write name of the parent class in parenthesis when you define the child class. You might have noticed a new function named as the super() function in the code. The super() function is a very special function that aids Python in forming connections between the child class and the parent class. This informs Python that it should call on to the __init__() method from the parent class. This is how the child class takes the attributes of the parent class.

If you are using Python 2.7, the super() function will change like the following code sample but the result will be the same. Please note the super() function and the result.

```
class Cycle():

    def __init__(self, cname, cmake, cyear, ccolor):
        self.cname = cname
```

```python
        self.cmake = cmake
        self.cyear = cyear
        self.ccolor = ccolor
        self.odometer_reading = 50


    def full_name(self):
        fname = "The cycle is " + self.cname + "." + "the cycle is
made by " + self.cmake + "." + "It is made in " + str(self.cyear)
+ "." + "its color is " + self.ccolor + "."
        return fname.title()
    def reading_my_odometer(self):
        print("The cycle has " + str(self.odometer_reading) + "
miles on record.")
    def my_update_odometer(self, cmileage):
        self.odometer_reading = cmileage


        if cmileage >= self.odometer_reading:
            self.odometer_reading = cmileage
        else:
            print("Dear employee! You cannot roll back the reading
of the odometer.")
    def incrementing_the_odometer(self, kilometers):
        self.odometer_reading += kilometers
```

```python
class ECycle(Cycle):
    def __init__(self, cname, cmake, cyear, ccolor):
        super(ECycle, self).__init__(cname, cmake, cyear, ccolor)
mynova = ECycle('Electric bike', 'Nova', 2020, 'silver')
print(mynova.full_name())


mycycle1 = Cycle('hybrid', 'hiland', 2015, 'crazy blue')
print(mycycle1.full_name())
mycycle1.my_update_odometer(15)
mycycle1.reading_my_odometer()
mycycle1.incrementing_the_odometer(100)
mycycle1.reading_my_odometer()


mycycle2 = Cycle('retro urban', 'Eurobike', 2012, 'it color is
grey')
print(mycycle2.full_name())
mycycle2.my_update_odometer(10)
mycycle2.reading_my_odometer()
mycycle2.incrementing_the_odometer(5000)
mycycle2.reading_my_odometer()


mycycle3 = Cycle('the cycle is hybrid', 'it is made by vilano',
2018, 'dark black')
print(mycycle1.full_name())
```

mycycle3.reading_my_odometer()

mycycle3.incrementing_the_odometer(1000)

mycycle3.reading_my_odometer()

mycycle4 = Cycle('endurance bike', 'tommaso', 2018, 'brown')

print(mycycle1.full_name())

mycycle4.reading_my_odometer()

mycycle4.incrementing_the_odometer(2000)

mycycle4.reading_my_odometer()

=========== RESTART: C:\Users\saifia

computers\Desktop\strike game.py ==========

The Cycle Is Electric Bike.The Cycle Is Made By Nova.It Is Made In 2020.Its Color Is Silver.

The Cycle Is Hybrid.The Cycle Is Made By Hiland.It Is Made In 2015.Its Color Is Crazy Blue.

The cycle has 15 miles on record.

The cycle has 115 miles on record.

The Cycle Is Retro Urban.The Cycle Is Made By Eurobike.It Is Made In 2012.Its Color Is It Color Is Grey.

The cycle has 10 miles on record.

The cycle has 5010 miles on record.

The Cycle Is Hybrid.The Cycle Is Made By Hiland.It Is Made In 2015.Its Color Is Crazy Blue.

The cycle has 50 miles on record.

The cycle has 1050 miles on record.

The Cycle Is Hybrid.The Cycle Is Made By Hiland.It Is Made In 2015.Its Color Is Crazy Blue.

The cycle has 50 miles on record.

The cycle has 2050 miles on record.

>>>

I had to add two arguments to the super() function. The first was the reference to the child class and the second was the reference to the self object. The arguments are crucial to aid Python in forming connections between the child and parent classes.

Child Class Attributes

Now that we have created the child class, we can move on to adding new methods and attributes that are necessary to differentiate the parent class from the child class. I will now add an attribute to the ECycle class. I will add the size of the battery to the code.

```
class Cycle():

    def __init__(self, cname, cmake, cyear, ccolor):
        self.cname = cname
        self.cmake = cmake
        self.cyear = cyear
        self.ccolor = ccolor
        self.odometer_reading = 50
```

```python
    def full_name(self):
        fname = "The cycle is " + self.cname + "." + "the cycle is
made by " + self.cmake + "." + "It is made in " + str(self.cyear)
+ "." + "its color is " + self.ccolor + "."
        return fname.title()
    def reading_my_odometer(self):
        print("The cycle has " + str(self.odometer_reading) + "
miles on record.")
    def my_update_odometer(self, cmileage):
        self.odometer_reading = cmileage

        if cmileage >= self.odometer_reading:
            self.odometer_reading = cmileage
        else:
            print("Dear employee! You cannot roll back the reading
of the odometer.")
    def incrementing_the_odometer(self, kilometers):
        self.odometer_reading += kilometers


class ECycle(Cycle):
    def __init__(self, cname, cmake, cyear, ccolor):
        super(ECycle, self).__init__(cname, cmake, cyear, ccolor)
        self.c_battery_size = 80
```

```python
    def battery_description(self):
        print("This cycle has a " + str(self.c_battery_size) + " kwh battery.")


mycycle1 = Cycle('hybrid', 'hiland', 2015, 'crazy blue')
print(mycycle1.full_name())
mycycle1.my_update_odometer(15)
mycycle1.reading_my_odometer()
mycycle1.incrementing_the_odometer(100)
mycycle1.reading_my_odometer()


mycycle2 = Cycle('retro urban', 'Eurobike', 2012, 'it color is grey')
print(mycycle2.full_name())
mycycle2.my_update_odometer(10)
mycycle2.reading_my_odometer()
mycycle2.incrementing_the_odometer(5000)
mycycle2.reading_my_odometer()


mycycle3 = Cycle('the cycle is hybrid', 'it is made by vilano', 2018, 'dark black')
print(mycycle1.full_name())
mycycle3.reading_my_odometer()
mycycle3.incrementing_the_odometer(1000)
```

```
mycycle3.reading_my_odometer()

mycycle4 = Cycle('endurance bike', 'tommaso', 2018, 'brown')
print(mycycle1.full_name())
mycycle4.reading_my_odometer()
mycycle4.incrementing_the_odometer(2000)
mycycle4.reading_my_odometer()


mynova = ECycle('Electric bike', 'Nova', 2020, 'silver')
print(mynova.full_name())
mynova.battery_description()


mynova1 = ECycle('Electric bike', 'Super Nova', 2010, 'black')
print(mynova1.full_name())
mynova1.battery_description()
```

============ RESTART: C:\Users\saifia
computers\Desktop\strike game.py ==========

The Cycle Is Hybrid.The Cycle Is Made By Hiland.It Is Made In 2015.Its Color Is Crazy Blue.

The cycle has 15 miles on record.

The cycle has 115 miles on record.

The Cycle Is Retro Urban.The Cycle Is Made By Eurobike.It Is Made In 2012.Its Color Is It Color Is Grey.

The cycle has 10 miles on record.

The cycle has 5010 miles on record.

The Cycle Is Hybrid.The Cycle Is Made By Hiland.It Is Made In 2015.Its Color Is Crazy Blue.

The cycle has 50 miles on record.

The cycle has 1050 miles on record.

The Cycle Is Hybrid.The Cycle Is Made By Hiland.It Is Made In 2015.Its Color Is Crazy Blue.

The cycle has 50 miles on record.

The cycle has 2050 miles on record.

The Cycle Is Electric Bike.The Cycle Is Made By Nova.It Is Made In 2020.Its Color Is Silver.

This cycle has a 80 kwh battery.

The Cycle Is Electric Bike.The Cycle Is Made By Super Nova.It Is Made In 2010.Its Color Is Black.

This cycle has a 80 kwh battery.

>>>

You can specialize the child class as much as you need. You can add another function to describe the color of the battery. See how to create and add a function to do that successfully.

```
class Cycle():

    def __init__(self, cname, cmake, cyear, ccolor):
        self.cname = cname
        self.cmake = cmake
```

```python
        self.cyear = cyear
        self.ccolor = ccolor
        self.odometer_reading = 50


    def full_name(self):
        fname = "The cycle is " + self.cname + "." + "the cycle is
made by " + self.cmake + "." + "It is made in " + str(self.cyear)
+ "." + "its color is " + self.ccolor + "."
        return fname.title()
    def reading_my_odometer(self):
        print("The cycle has " + str(self.odometer_reading) + "
miles on record.")
    def my_update_odometer(self, cmileage):
        self.odometer_reading = cmileage


        if cmileage >= self.odometer_reading:
            self.odometer_reading = cmileage
        else:
            print("Dear employee! You cannot roll back the reading
of the odometer.")
    def incrementing_the_odometer(self, kilometers):
        self.odometer_reading += kilometers


class ECycle(Cycle):
```

```python
    def __init__(self, cname, cmake, cyear, ccolor):
        super(ECycle, self).__init__(cname, cmake, cyear, ccolor)
        self.c_battery_size = 80
        self.c_color = 'white'
    def battery_description(self):
        print("This cycle has a " + str(self.c_battery_size) + " kwh
battery.")
    def battery_color(self):
        print("This cycle's battery is of " + self.c_color + " color.")


mycycle1 = Cycle('hybrid', 'hiland', 2015, 'crazy blue')
print(mycycle1.full_name())
mycycle1.my_update_odometer(15)
mycycle1.reading_my_odometer()
mycycle1.incrementing_the_odometer(100)
mycycle1.reading_my_odometer()


mycycle2 = Cycle('retro urban', 'Eurobike', 2012, 'it color is
grey')
print(mycycle2.full_name())
mycycle2.my_update_odometer(10)
mycycle2.reading_my_odometer()
mycycle2.incrementing_the_odometer(5000)
mycycle2.reading_my_odometer()
```

```
mycycle3 = Cycle('the cycle is hybrid', 'it is made by vilano',
2018, 'dark black')

print(mycycle1.full_name())

mycycle3.reading_my_odometer()

mycycle3.incrementing_the_odometer(1000)

mycycle3.reading_my_odometer()


mycycle4 = Cycle('endurance bike', 'tommaso', 2018, 'brown')

print(mycycle1.full_name())

mycycle4.reading_my_odometer()

mycycle4.incrementing_the_odometer(2000)

mycycle4.reading_my_odometer()


mynova = ECycle('Electric bike', 'Nova', 2020, 'silver')

print(mynova.full_name())

mynova.battery_description()

mynova.battery_color()


mynova1 = ECycle('Electric bike', 'Super Nova', 2010, 'black')

print(mynova1.full_name())

mynova1.battery_description()

mynova1.battery_color()
```

The Cycle Is Hybrid.The Cycle Is Made By Hiland.It Is Made In 2015.Its Color Is Crazy Blue.

The cycle has 15 miles on record.

The cycle has 115 miles on record.

The Cycle Is Retro Urban.The Cycle Is Made By Eurobike.It Is Made In 2012.Its Color Is It Color Is Grey.

The cycle has 10 miles on record.

The cycle has 5010 miles on record.

The Cycle Is Hybrid.The Cycle Is Made By Hiland.It Is Made In 2015.Its Color Is Crazy Blue.

The cycle has 50 miles on record.

The cycle has 1050 miles on record.

The Cycle Is Hybrid.The Cycle Is Made By Hiland.It Is Made In 2015.Its Color Is Crazy Blue.

The cycle has 50 miles on record.

The cycle has 2050 miles on record.

The Cycle Is Electric Bike.The Cycle Is Made By Nova.It Is Made In 2020.Its Color Is Silver.

This cycle has a 80 kwh battery.

This cycle's battery is of white color.

The Cycle Is Electric Bike.The Cycle Is Made By Super Nova.It Is Made In 2010.Its Color Is Black.

This cycle has a 80 kwh battery.

This cycle's battery is of white color.

>>>

Overriding Parent Class's Methods

The child usually takes all the attributes of the parent class. I have added all the parent class attributes to the instance of the child class but we can override them without deleting the methods of the parent class. First of all, take a look at the following code that carries the parent class's attributes.

```
class Cycle():

    def __init__(self, cname, cmake, cyear, ccolor):
        self.cname = cname
        self.cmake = cmake
        self.cyear = cyear
        self.ccolor = ccolor
        self.odometer_reading = 50

    def full_name(self):
        fname = "The cycle is " + self.cname + "." + "the cycle is
made by " + self.cmake + "." + "It is made in " + str(self.cyear)
+ "." + "its color is " + self.ccolor + "."
        return fname.title()
```

```python
    def reading_my_odometer(self):
        print("The cycle has " + str(self.odometer_reading) + " miles on record.")

    def my_update_odometer(self, cmileage):
        self.odometer_reading = cmileage


        if cmileage >= self.odometer_reading:
            self.odometer_reading = cmileage
        else:
            print("Dear employee! You cannot roll back the reading of the odometer.")

    def incrementing_the_odometer(self, kilometers):
        self.odometer_reading += kilometers


class ECycle(Cycle):
    def __init__(self, cname, cmake, cyear, ccolor):
        super(ECycle, self).__init__(cname, cmake, cyear, ccolor)
        self.c_battery_size = 80
        self.c_color = 'white'

    def battery_description(self):
        print("This cycle has a " + str(self.c_battery_size) + " kwh battery.")

    def battery_color(self):
        print("This cycle's battery is of " + self.c_color + " color.")
```

```
mycycle1 = Cycle('hybrid', 'hiland', 2015, 'crazy blue')
print(mycycle1.full_name())
mycycle1.my_update_odometer(15)
mycycle1.reading_my_odometer()
mycycle1.incrementing_the_odometer(100)
mycycle1.reading_my_odometer()


mycycle2 = Cycle('retro urban', 'Eurobike', 2012, 'it color is
grey')
print(mycycle2.full_name())
mycycle2.my_update_odometer(10)
mycycle2.reading_my_odometer()
mycycle2.incrementing_the_odometer(5000)
mycycle2.reading_my_odometer()


mycycle3 = Cycle('the cycle is hybrid', 'it is made by vilano',
2018, 'dark black')
print(mycycle1.full_name())
mycycle3.reading_my_odometer()
mycycle3.incrementing_the_odometer(1000)
mycycle3.reading_my_odometer()


mycycle4 = Cycle('endurance bike', 'tommaso', 2018, 'brown')
```

```
print(mycycle1.full_name())

mycycle4.reading_my_odometer()

mycycle4.incrementing_the_odometer(2000)

mycycle4.reading_my_odometer()


mynova = ECycle('Electric bike', 'Nova', 2020, 'silver')

print(mynova.full_name())

mynova.my_update_odometer(15)

mynova.reading_my_odometer()

mynova.incrementing_the_odometer(100)

mynova.reading_my_odometer()

mynova.battery_description()

mynova.battery_color()


mynova1 = ECycle('Electric bike', 'Super Nova', 2010, 'black')

print(mynova1.full_name())

mynova1.my_update_odometer(15)

mynova1.reading_my_odometer()

mynova1.incrementing_the_odometer(100)

mynova1.reading_my_odometer()

mynova1.battery_description()

mynova1.battery_color()
=========== RESTART: C:\Users\saifia
computers\Desktop\strike game.py ==========
```

The Cycle Is Hybrid.The Cycle Is Made By Hiland.It Is Made In 2015.Its Color Is Crazy Blue.

The cycle has 15 miles on record.

The cycle has 115 miles on record.

The Cycle Is Retro Urban.The Cycle Is Made By Eurobike.It Is Made In 2012.Its Color Is It Color Is Grey.

The cycle has 10 miles on record.

The cycle has 5010 miles on record.

The Cycle Is Hybrid.The Cycle Is Made By Hiland.It Is Made In 2015.Its Color Is Crazy Blue.

The cycle has 50 miles on record.

The cycle has 1050 miles on record.

The Cycle Is Hybrid.The Cycle Is Made By Hiland.It Is Made In 2015.Its Color Is Crazy Blue.

The cycle has 50 miles on record.

The cycle has 2050 miles on record.

The Cycle Is Electric Bike.The Cycle Is Made By Nova.It Is Made In 2020.Its Color Is Silver.

The cycle has 15 miles on record.

The cycle has 115 miles on record.

This cycle has a 80 kwh battery.

This cycle's battery is of white color.

The Cycle Is Electric Bike.The Cycle Is Made By Super Nova.It Is Made In 2010.Its Color Is Black.

The cycle has 15 miles on record.

The cycle has 115 miles on record.

This cycle has a 80 kwh battery.

This cycle's battery is of white color.

>>>

Now I will override the methods of the parent class in the following code.

```
class Cycle():

    def __init__(self, cname, cmake, cyear, ccolor):
        self.cname = cname
        self.cmake = cmake
        self.cyear = cyear
        self.ccolor = ccolor
        self.odometer_reading = 50


    def full_name(self):
        fname = "The cycle is " + self.cname + "." + "the cycle is
made by " + self.cmake + "." + "It is made in " + str(self.cyear)
+ "." + "its color is " + self.ccolor + "."
        return fname.title()
    def reading_my_odometer(self):
        print("The cycle has " + str(self.odometer_reading) + "
miles on record.")
```

```python
    def my_update_odometer(self, cmileage):
        self.odometer_reading = cmileage

        if cmileage >= self.odometer_reading:
            self.odometer_reading = cmileage
        else:
            print("Dear employee! You cannot roll back the reading
of the odometer.")
    def incrementing_the_odometer(self, kilometers):
        self.odometer_reading += kilometers


class ECycle(Cycle):
    def __init__(self, cname, cmake, cyear, ccolor):
        super(ECycle, self).__init__(cname, cmake, cyear, ccolor)
        self.c_battery_size = 80
        self.c_color = 'white'
    def battery_description(self):
        print("This cycle has a " + str(self.c_battery_size) + " kwh
battery.")
    def battery_color(self):
        print("This cycle's battery is of " + self.c_color + " color.")
    def reading_my_odometer(self):
        print("This cycle lacks an odometer.")
```

```python
mycycle1 = Cycle('hybrid', 'hiland', 2015, 'crazy blue')
print(mycycle1.full_name())
mycycle1.my_update_odometer(15)
mycycle1.incrementing_the_odometer(100)
mycycle1.reading_my_odometer()


mycycle2 = Cycle('retro urban', 'Eurobike', 2012, 'it color is grey')
print(mycycle2.full_name())
mycycle2.my_update_odometer(10)
mycycle2.incrementing_the_odometer(5000)
mycycle2.reading_my_odometer()


mycycle3 = Cycle('the cycle is hybrid', 'it is made by vilano', 2018, 'dark black')
print(mycycle1.full_name())
mycycle3.incrementing_the_odometer(1000)
mycycle3.reading_my_odometer()


mycycle4 = Cycle('endurance bike', 'tommaso', 2018, 'brown')
print(mycycle1.full_name())
mycycle4.incrementing_the_odometer(2000)
mycycle4.reading_my_odometer()
```

```
mynova = ECycle('Electric bike', 'Nova', 2020, 'silver')
print(mynova.full_name())
mynova.my_update_odometer(15)
mynova.incrementing_the_odometer(100)
mynova.reading_my_odometer()
mynova.battery_description()
mynova.battery_color()


mynova1 = ECycle('Electric bike', 'Super Nova', 2010, 'black')
print(mynova1.full_name())
mynova1.my_update_odometer(15)
mynova1.incrementing_the_odometer(100)
mynova1.reading_my_odometer()
mynova1.battery_description()
mynova1.battery_color()
```

=========== RESTART: C:\Users\saifia computers\Desktop\strike game.py ==========

The Cycle Is Hybrid.The Cycle Is Made By Hiland.It Is Made In 2015.Its Color Is Crazy Blue.

The cycle has 115 miles on record.

The Cycle Is Retro Urban.The Cycle Is Made By Eurobike.It Is Made In 2012.Its Color Is It Color Is Grey.

The cycle has 5010 miles on record.

The Cycle Is Hybrid.The Cycle Is Made By Hiland.It Is Made In 2015.Its Color Is Crazy Blue.

The cycle has 1050 miles on record.

The Cycle Is Hybrid.The Cycle Is Made By Hiland.It Is Made In 2015.Its Color Is Crazy Blue.

The cycle has 2050 miles on record.

The Cycle Is Electric Bike.The Cycle Is Made By Nova.It Is Made In 2020.Its Color Is Silver.

This cycle lacks an odometer.

This cycle has a 80 kwh battery.

This cycle's battery is of white color.

The Cycle Is Electric Bike.The Cycle Is Made By Super Nova.It Is Made In 2010.Its Color Is Black.

This cycle lacks an odometer.

This cycle has a 80 kwh battery.

This cycle's battery is of white color.

>>>

The battery can be made a separate class in the code so that you can avoid writing lots of instances in the code. It will make the code clean, readable and short. More details add clutter to the bad code when you have to read the code at a later stage. I will create a separate class for the battery of the electronic cycle. This is how you don't have to create methods for batteries and add attributes.

class Cycle():

```python
    def __init__(self, cname, cmake, cyear, ccolor):
        self.cname = cname
        self.cmake = cmake
        self.cyear = cyear
        self.ccolor = ccolor
        self.odometer_reading = 50


    def full_name(self):
        fname = "The cycle is " + self.cname + "." + "the cycle is
made by " + self.cmake + "." + "It is made in " + str(self.cyear)
+ "." + "its color is " + self.ccolor + "."
        return fname.title()
    def reading_my_odometer(self):
        print("The cycle has " + str(self.odometer_reading) + "
miles on record.")
    def my_update_odometer(self, cmileage):
        self.odometer_reading = cmileage


        if cmileage >= self.odometer_reading:
            self.odometer_reading = cmileage
        else:
            print("Dear employee! You cannot roll back the reading
of the odometer.")
```

```python
    def incrementing_the_odometer(self, kilometers):
        self.odometer_reading += kilometers

class Battery():
    def __init__(self, c_battery_size=80, c_color = 'white'):
        self.c_battery_size = c_battery_size
        self.c_color = c_color
    def battery_description(self):
        print("This cycle has a " + str(self.c_battery_size) + " kwh
battery.")
    def battery_color(self):
        print("This cycle's battery is of " + self.c_color + " color.")


class ECycle(Cycle):
    def __init__(self, cname, cmake, cyear, ccolor):
        super(ECycle, self).__init__(cname, cmake, cyear, ccolor)
        self.battery = Battery()


mycycle1 = Cycle('hybrid', 'hiland', 2015, 'crazy blue')
print(mycycle1.full_name())
mycycle1.my_update_odometer(15)
mycycle1.incrementing_the_odometer(100)
mycycle1.reading_my_odometer()
```

```
mycycle2 = Cycle('retro urban', 'Eurobike', 2012, 'it color is grey')
print(mycycle2.full_name())
mycycle2.my_update_odometer(10)
mycycle2.incrementing_the_odometer(5000)
mycycle2.reading_my_odometer()


mycycle3 = Cycle('the cycle is hybrid', 'it is made by vilano', 2018, 'dark black')
print(mycycle1.full_name())
mycycle3.incrementing_the_odometer(1000)
mycycle3.reading_my_odometer()


mycycle4 = Cycle('endurance bike', 'tommaso', 2018, 'brown')
print(mycycle1.full_name())
mycycle4.incrementing_the_odometer(2000)
mycycle4.reading_my_odometer()


mynova = ECycle('Electric bike', 'Nova', 2020, 'silver')
print(mynova.full_name())
mynova.my_update_odometer(15)
mynova.incrementing_the_odometer(100)
mynova.reading_my_odometer()
mynova.battery.battery_description()
```

mynova.battery.battery_color()

mynova1 = ECycle('Electric bike', 'Super Nova', 2010, 'black')

print(mynova1.full_name())

mynova1.my_update_odometer(15)

mynova1.incrementing_the_odometer(100)

mynova1.reading_my_odometer()

mynova1.battery.battery_color()

=========== RESTART: C:\Users\saifia

computers\Desktop\strike game.py ==========

The Cycle Is Hybrid.The Cycle Is Made By Hiland.It Is Made In 2015.Its Color Is Crazy Blue.

The cycle has 115 miles on record.

The Cycle Is Retro Urban.The Cycle Is Made By Eurobike.It Is Made In 2012.Its Color Is It Color Is Grey.

The cycle has 5010 miles on record.

The Cycle Is Hybrid.The Cycle Is Made By Hiland.It Is Made In 2015.Its Color Is Crazy Blue.

The cycle has 1050 miles on record.

The Cycle Is Hybrid.The Cycle Is Made By Hiland.It Is Made In 2015.Its Color Is Crazy Blue.

The cycle has 2050 miles on record.

The Cycle Is Electric Bike.The Cycle Is Made By Nova.It Is Made In 2020.Its Color Is Silver.

The cycle has 115 miles on record.

This cycle has a 80 kwh battery.

This cycle's battery is of white color.

The Cycle Is Electric Bike.The Cycle Is Made By Super Nova.It Is Made In 2010.Its Color Is Black.

The cycle has 115 miles on record.

This cycle's battery is of white color.

>>>

Importing Python Classes

You can see that as I added more code lines to the program, the file got lengthy. It is presently lengthy to the extent that it is hard to read and understand. You have to keep the code as much decluttered as possible to make it readable. Python modules help us to fulfill this purpose. These modules let you store the classes inside of modules and then import the same to the program when you need them.

Importing Classes

I will not create a module for the Cycle class. You have to name it and store it on your operating system. I will slice off the Cycle class form the program and store it in a file named as cycle.py. The below-mentioned part of the code will be stored in a separate file.

```
class Cycle():

    def __init__(self, cname, cmake, cyear, ccolor):
```

```python
        self.cname = cname
        self.cmake = cmake
        self.cyear = cyear
        self.ccolor = ccolor
        self.odometer_reading = 50


    def full_name(self):
        fname = "The cycle is " + self.cname + "." + "the cycle is
made by " + self.cmake + "." + "It is made in " + str(self.cyear)
+ "." + "its color is " + self.ccolor + "."
        return fname.title()
    def reading_my_odometer(self):
        print("The cycle has " + str(self.odometer_reading) + "
miles on record.")
    def my_update_odometer(self, cmileage):
        self.odometer_reading = cmileage


        if cmileage >= self.odometer_reading:
            self.odometer_reading = cmileage
        else:
            print("Dear employee! You cannot roll back the reading
of the odometer.")
    def incrementing_the_odometer(self, kilometers):
        self.odometer_reading += kilometers
```

I am now creating a separate file to import the Cycle class and add instances.

from cycle import Cycle

mycycle1 = Cycle('hybrid', 'hiland', 2015, 'crazy blue')
print(mycycle1.full_name())
mycycle1.my_update_odometer(15)
mycycle1.incrementing_the_odometer(100)
mycycle1.reading_my_odometer()

mycycle2 = Cycle('retro urban', 'Eurobike', 2012, 'it color is grey')
print(mycycle2.full_name())
mycycle2.my_update_odometer(10)
mycycle2.incrementing_the_odometer(5000)
mycycle2.reading_my_odometer()

mycycle3 = Cycle('the cycle is hybrid', 'it is made by vilano', 2018, 'dark black')
print(mycycle1.full_name())
mycycle3.incrementing_the_odometer(1000)
mycycle3.reading_my_odometer()

mycycle4 = Cycle('endurance bike', 'tommaso', 2018, 'brown') print(mycycle1.full_name())

mycycle4.incrementing_the_odometer(2000)

mycycle4.reading_my_odometer()

============== RESTART: C:/Users/saifia

computers/Desktop/cycle1.py ==============

The Cycle Is Hybrid.The Cycle Is Made By Hiland.It Is Made In 2015.Its Color Is Crazy Blue.

The cycle has 115 miles on record.

The Cycle Is Retro Urban.The Cycle Is Made By Eurobike.It Is Made In 2012.Its Color Is It Color Is Grey.

The cycle has 5010 miles on record.

The Cycle Is Hybrid.The Cycle Is Made By Hiland It Is Made In 2015.Its Color Is Crazy Blue.

The cycle has 1050 miles on record.

The Cycle Is Hybrid.The Cycle Is Made By Hiland.It Is Made In 2015.Its Color Is Crazy Blue.

The cycle has 2050 miles on record.

>>>

The import statement tells Python to pick the code from the cycle module. It imports the code and applies it to the instances that I have just added to the new file. You have to make sure that the two modules are stored in the same directory. There will be no difference in the output. You can see that program has been decluttered. The code now is shorter than its earlier versions. There will be no effect on the functionality of the code when you import the classes.

You can store more than one classes inside a single module. I will now add another class to the module. See the following part that will now be added to the module.

```
class Cycle():

    def __init__(self, cname, cmake, cyear, ccolor):
        self.cname = cname
        self.cmake = cmake
        self.cyear = cyear
        self.ccolor = ccolor
        self.odometer_reading = 50

    def full_name(self):
        fname = "The cycle is " + self.cname + "." + "the cycle is
made by " + self.cmake + "." + "It is made in " + str(self.cyear)
+ "." + "its color is " + self.ccolor + "."
        return fname.title()
    def reading_my_odometer(self):
        print("The cycle has " + str(self.odometer_reading) + "
miles on record.")
    def my_update_odometer(self, cmileage):
        self.odometer_reading = cmileage

        if cmileage >= self.odometer_reading:
```

```python
            self.odometer_reading = cmileage
        else:
            print("Dear employee! You cannot roll back the reading
of the odometer.")
    def incrementing_the_odometer(self, kilometers):
        self.odometer_reading += kilometers


class Battery():
    def __init__(self, c_battery_size=80, c_color = 'white'):
        self.c_battery_size = c_battery_size
        self.c_color = c_color
    def battery_description(self):
        print("This cycle has a " + str(self.c_battery_size) + " kwh
battery.")
    def battery_color(self):
        print("This cycle's battery is of " + self.c_color + " color.")


class ECycle(Cycle):
    def __init__(self, cname, cmake, cyear, ccolor):
        super(ECycle, self).__init__(cname, cmake, cyear, ccolor)
        self.battery = Battery()
```

I will not import the stored classes and add instances in a
separate file.

```python
from cycle import ECycle
```

```python
mynova = ECycle('Electric bike', 'Nova', 2020, 'silver')
print(mynova.full_name())
mynova.my_update_odometer(15)
mynova.incrementing_the_odometer(100)
mynova.reading_my_odometer()
mynova.battery.battery_description()
mynova.battery.battery_color()


mynova1 = ECycle('Electric bike', 'Super Nova', 2010, 'black')
print(mynova1.full_name())
mynova1.my_update_odometer(15)
mynova1.incrementing_the_odometer(100)
mynova1.reading_my_odometer()
mynova1.battery.battery_color()
```

============== RESTART: C:/Users/saifia computers/Desktop/cycle1.py ==============

The Cycle Is Electric Bike.The Cycle Is Made By Nova.It Is Made In 2020.Its Color Is Silver.

The cycle has 115 miles on record.

This cycle has a 80 kwh battery.

This cycle's battery is of white color.

The Cycle Is Electric Bike.The Cycle Is Made By Super Nova.It Is Made In 2010.Its Color Is Black.

The cycle has 115 miles on record.

This cycle's battery is of white color.

>>>

Importing Two Classes

When you have stored more than one classes in a module, you can use them at the same time. I will import two classes this time and add instances to create objects.

```
from cycle import Cycle
from cycle import ECycle

mycycle1 = Cycle('hybrid', 'hiland', 2015, 'crazy blue')
print(mycycle1.full_name())
mycycle1.my_update_odometer(15)
mycycle1.incrementing_the_odometer(100)
mycycle1.reading_my_odometer()


mycycle2 = Cycle('retro urban', 'Eurobike', 2012, 'it color is grey')
print(mycycle2.full_name())
mycycle2.my_update_odometer(10)
mycycle2.incrementing_the_odometer(5000)
mycycle2.reading_my_odometer()
```

```
mycycle3 = Cycle('the cycle is hybrid', 'it is made by vilano',
2018, 'dark black')
print(mycycle1.full_name())
mycycle3.incrementing_the_odometer(1000)
mycycle3.reading_my_odometer()


mycycle4 = Cycle('endurance bike', 'tommaso', 2018, 'brown')
print(mycycle1.full_name())
mycycle4.incrementing_the_odometer(2000)
mycycle4.reading_my_odometer()


mynova = ECycle('Electric bike', 'Nova', 2020, 'silver')
print(mynova.full_name())
mynova.my_update_odometer(15)
mynova.incrementing_the_odometer(100)
mynova.reading_my_odometer()
mynova.battery.battery_description()
mynova.battery.battery_color()


mynova1 = ECycle('Electric bike', 'Super Nova', 2010, 'black')
print(mynova1.full_name())
mynova1.my_update_odometer(15)
mynova1.incrementing_the_odometer(100)
mynova1.reading_my_odometer()
```

mynova1.battery.battery_color()

The Cycle Is Hybrid.The Cycle Is Made By Hiland.It Is Made In 2015.Its Color Is Crazy Blue.

The cycle has 115 miles on record.

The Cycle Is Retro Urban.The Cycle Is Made By Eurobike.It Is Made In 2012.Its Color Is It Color Is Grey.

The cycle has 5010 miles on record.

The Cycle Is Hybrid.The Cycle Is Made By Hiland.It Is Made In 2015.Its Color Is Crazy Blue.

The cycle has 1050 miles on record.

The Cycle Is Hybrid.The Cycle Is Made By Hiland.It Is Made In 2015.Its Color Is Crazy Blue.

The cycle has 2050 miles on record.

The Cycle Is Electric Bike.The Cycle Is Made By Nova.It Is Made In 2020.Its Color Is Silver.

The cycle has 115 miles on record.

This cycle has a 80 kwh battery.

This cycle's battery is of white color.

The Cycle Is Electric Bike.The Cycle Is Made By Super Nova.It Is Made In 2010.Its Color Is Black.

The cycle has 115 miles on record.

This cycle's battery is of white color.

>>>

There is another method to import multiple classes from the module. See the following example.

```
from cycle import Cycle, Battery, ECycle

mycycle1 = Cycle('hybrid', 'hiland', 2015, 'crazy blue')
print(mycycle1.full_name())
mycycle1.my_update_odometer(15)
mycycle1.incrementing_the_odometer(100)
mycycle1.reading_my_odometer()

mycycle2 = Cycle('retro urban', 'Eurobike', 2012, 'it color is grey')
print(mycycle2.full_name())
mycycle2.my_update_odometer(10)
mycycle2.incrementing_the_odometer(5000)
mycycle2.reading_my_odometer()

mycycle3 = Cycle('the cycle is hybrid', 'it is made by vilano', 2018, 'dark black')
print(mycycle1.full_name())
mycycle3.incrementing_the_odometer(1000)
mycycle3.reading_my_odometer()
```

```
mycycle4 = Cycle('endurance bike', 'tommaso', 2018, 'brown')
print(mycycle1.full_name())
mycycle4.incrementing_the_odometer(2000)
mycycle4.reading_my_odometer()


mynova = ECycle('Electric bike', 'Nova', 2020, 'silver')
print(mynova.full_name())
mynova.my_update_odometer(15)
mynova.incrementing_the_odometer(100)
mynova.reading_my_odometer()
mynova.battery.battery_description()
mynova.battery.battery_color()


mynova1 = ECycle('Electric bike', 'Super Nova', 2010, 'black')
print(mynova1.full_name())
mynova1.my_update_odometer(15)
mynova1.incrementing_the_odometer(100)
mynova1.reading_my_odometer()
mynova1.battery.battery_color()
```

============== RESTART: C:/Users/saifia computers/Desktop/cycle1.py ==============

The Cycle Is Hybrid.The Cycle Is Made By Hiland.It Is Made In 2015.Its Color Is Crazy Blue.

The cycle has 115 miles on record.

The Cycle Is Retro Urban.The Cycle Is Made By Eurobike.It Is Made In 2012.Its Color Is It Color Is Grey.

The cycle has 5010 miles on record.

The Cycle Is Hybrid.The Cycle Is Made By Hiland.It Is Made In 2015.Its Color Is Crazy Blue.

The cycle has 1050 miles on record.

The Cycle Is Hybrid.The Cycle Is Made By Hiland.It Is Made In 2015.Its Color Is Crazy Blue.

The cycle has 2050 miles on record.

The Cycle Is Electric Bike.The Cycle Is Made By Nova.It Is Made In 2020.Its Color Is Silver.

The cycle has 115 miles on record.

This cycle has a 80 kwh battery.

This cycle's battery is of white color.

The Cycle Is Electric Bike.The Cycle Is Made By Super Nova.It Is Made In 2010.Its Color Is Black.

The cycle has 115 miles on record.

This cycle's battery is of white color.

>>>

This code now contains all the three classes that have been imported from the module namely cycle.py. As there were three classes in the module, we could just import the entire module instead of importing all the three one by one. If you have to use all the classes from a module, you can import the entire module and it will do the same job that importing individual classes did. Instead of writing the names of the classes, I will add a * in their place.

```
from cycle import *


mycycle1 = Cycle('hybrid', 'hiland', 2015, 'crazy blue')
print(mycycle1.full_name())
mycycle1.my_update_odometer(15)
mycycle1.incrementing_the_odometer(100)
mycycle1.reading_my_odometer()


mycycle2 = Cycle('retro urban', 'Eurobike', 2012, 'it color is grey')
print(mycycle2.full_name())
mycycle2.my_update_odometer(10)
mycycle2.incrementing_the_odometer(5000)
mycycle2.reading_my_odometer()


mycycle3 = Cycle('the cycle is hybrid', 'it is made by vilano', 2018, 'dark black')
print(mycycle1.full_name())
mycycle3.incrementing_the_odometer(1000)
mycycle3.reading_my_odometer()
```

```
mycycle4 = Cycle('endurance bike', 'tommaso', 2018, 'brown')
print(mycycle1.full_name())
mycycle4.incrementing_the_odometer(2000)
mycycle4.reading_my_odometer()


mynova = ECycle('Electric bike', 'Nova', 2020, 'silver')
print(mynova.full_name())
mynova.my_update_odometer(15)
mynova.incrementing_the_odometer(100)
mynova.reading_my_odometer()
mynova.battery.battery_description()
mynova.battery.battery_color()


mynova1 = ECycle('Electric bike', 'Super Nova', 2010, 'black')
print(mynova1.full_name())
mynova1.my_update_odometer(15)
mynova1.incrementing_the_odometer(100)
mynova1.reading_my_odometer()
mynova1.battery.battery_color()
```

============== RESTART: C:/Users/saifia computers/Desktop/cycle1.py ==============

The Cycle Is Hybrid.The Cycle Is Made By Hiland.It Is Made In 2015.Its Color Is Crazy Blue.

The cycle has 115 miles on record.

The Cycle Is Retro Urban.The Cycle Is Made By Eurobike.It Is Made In 2012.Its Color Is It Color Is Grey.

The cycle has 5010 miles on record.

The Cycle Is Hybrid.The Cycle Is Made By Hiland.It Is Made In 2015.Its Color Is Crazy Blue.

The cycle has 1050 miles on record.

The Cycle Is Hybrid.The Cycle Is Made By Hiland.It Is Made In 2015.Its Color Is Crazy Blue.

The cycle has 2050 miles on record.

The Cycle Is Electric Bike.The Cycle Is Made By Nova.It Is Made In 2020.Its Color Is Silver.

The cycle has 115 miles on record.

This cycle has a 80 kwh battery.

This cycle's battery is of white color.

The Cycle Is Electric Bike.The Cycle Is Made By Super Nova.It Is Made In 2010.Its Color Is Black.

The cycle has 115 miles on record.

This cycle's battery is of white color.

>>>

Chapter Eight

Python Program Samples

Sample 1: Python Calculator

```
# This Python program is built to create a simple calculator

# This is the Function for the addition of two numbers
def adding(num_1, num_2):
   return num_1 + num_2

# This is the Function for the subtraction of two numbers
def subtracting(num_1, num_2):
   return num_1 - num_2

# This is the Function for the multiplication of two numbers
def multiplying(num_1, num_2):
   return num_1 * num_2

# This is the Function for the division of two numbers
def dividing(num_1, num_2):
   return num_1 / num_2
```

```python
print("You have to select the operation of your choice.")
print("1. Addition of numbers.")
print("2. Subtraction of numbers.")
print("3. Multiplication of numbers.")
print("4. Dividision of numbers.")

# This will take the input from a user
selection = int(input("You have to select the operations from the
following numbers 1, 2, 3, 4 :"))

num1 = int(input("You have to enter the first number: "))
num2 = int(input("You have to enter the second number: "))

if selection == 1:
    print(num1, "+", num2, "=",
            adding(num1, num2))

elif selection == 2:
    print(num1, "-", num2, "=",
            subtracting(num1, num2))

elif selection == 3:
    print(num1, "*", num2, "=",
```

```
            multiplying(num1, num2))


    elif selection == 4:
        print(num1, "/", num2, "=",
                    dividing(num1, num2))
    else:
        print("Invalid input on the screen")
        = RESTART: C:/Users/saifia computers/Desktop/strike
        game.py
You have to select the operation of your choice.

1. Addition of numbers.

2. Subtraction of numbers.

3. Multiplication of numbers.

4. Dividision of numbers.

    You have to select the operations from the following numbers 1,
    2, 3, 4 :1
    You have to enter the first number: 67890
    You have to enter the second number: 67889
    67890 + 67889 = 135779
    >>>
= RESTART: C:/Users/saifia computers/Desktop/strike game.py
```

You have to select the operation of your choice.

    1. Addition of numbers.

    2. Subtraction of numbers.

    3. Multiplication of numbers.

    4. Dividision of numbers.

    You have to select the operations from the following numbers 1, 2, 3, 4 :2

    You have to enter the first number: 50000

    You have to enter the second number: 5678

    50000 - 5678 = 44322

    >>>

    = RESTART: C:/Users/saifia computers/Desktop/strike game.py

You have to select the operation of your choice.

1. Addition of numbers.

2. Subtraction of numbers.

3. Multiplication of numbers.

4. Dividision of numbers.

You have to select the operations from the following numbers 1, 2, 3, 4 :2

    You have to enter the first number: 5678

441

You have to enter the second number: 90000

5678 - 90000 = -84322

>>>

= RESTART: C:/Users/saifia computers/Desktop/strike game.py

You have to select the operation of your choice.

1. Addition of numbers.

2. Subtraction of numbers.

3. Multiplication of numbers.

4. Dividision of numbers.

You have to select the operations from the following numbers 1, 2, 3, 4 :3

You have to enter the first number: 5678

You have to enter the second number: 987

5678 * 987 = 5604186

>>>

= RESTART: C:/Users/saifia computers/Desktop/strike game.py

You have to select the operation of your choice.

1. Addition of numbers.

2. Subtraction of numbers.

3. Multiplication of numbers.

4. Dividision of numbers.

>You have to select the operations from the following numbers 1, 2, 3, 4 :7000

>You have to enter the first number: 7000

>You have to enter the second number: 6789

>Invalid input on the screen

>>>>

>= RESTART: C:/Users/saifia computers/Desktop/strike game.py

You have to select the operation of your choice.

1. Addition of numbers.

2. Subtraction of numbers.

3. Multiplication of numbers.

4. Dividision of numbers.

>You have to select the operations from the following numbers 1, 2, 3, 4 :4

>You have to enter the first number: 780098

>You have to enter the second number: 678

>780098 / 678 = 1150.5870206489676

>>>>

= RESTART: C:/Users/saifia computers/Desktop/strike game.py

You have to select the operation of your choice.

1. Addition of numbers.

2. Subtraction of numbers.

3. Multiplication of numbers.

4. Dividision of numbers.

You have to select the operations from the following numbers 1, 2, 3, 4 :5

You have to enter the first number: 34567

You have to enter the second number: 6677

Invalid input on the screen

>>>

= RESTART: C:/Users/saifia computers/Desktop/strike game.py

You have to select the operation of your choice.

1. Addition of numbers.

2. Subtraction of numbers.

3. Multiplication of numbers.

4. Dividision of numbers.

You have to select the operations from the following numbers 1, 2, 3, 4 :gh

Traceback (most recent call last):

    File "C:/Users/saifia computers/Desktop/strike game.py", line 27, in <module>

    selection = int(input("You have to select the operations from the following numbers 1, 2, 3, 4 :"))

ValueError: invalid literal for int() with base 10: 'gh'

>>>

Conclusion

Now that you have reached the end of the book, the next step is to practice all the knowledge you have gained. Python is an easy an interesting languages if you are fond of practicing what you learn. You can easily make robots play if you learn the language by heart. Similarly, you can easily learn the craft of animation.

I hope you will not stop at this ending but will keep practicing you have learned from the book. The most important are the basics such as data types. Once you know what they are and how to use them in coding, you can easily navigate complex concepts like object-oriented programming and looping.

References

Eric Matthes. 2016. Python Crash Course[PDF file]. San Francisco: William Pollock. http://bedford-computing.co.uk/learning/wp-content/uploads/2015/10/No.Starch.Python.Oct_.2015.ISBN_.1593 276036.pdf

Python Data Types. n.d.
https://www.w3schools.com/python/python_datatypes.asp

Python Tuples, n.d.
https://www.w3schools.com/python/python_tuples.asp

Python If … Else, n.d.
https://www.w3schools.com/python/python_conditions.asp

Global and Local Variables in Python. n.d.
https://www.geeksforgeeks.org/global-local-variables-python/

Python Dictionaries. n.d.
https://www.w3schools.com/python/python_dictionaries.asp

Python Program to Make a Simple Calculator. n.d.
https://www.programiz.com/python-programming/examples/calculator

Using IDLE (Python's IDE). n.d.
http://www2.cs.arizona.edu/people/mccann/usingidle

CODING
IN PYTHON

ADVANCED GUIDE TO CODING USING PYTHON PROGRAMMING PRINCIPLES TO MASTER THE ART OF CODING

ROBERT C. MATTHEWS

Introduction

The focus of this book will primarily be divided into two portions. The first portion will encompass the topics that will prepare the reader to work with Python as effectively as possible. The latter half will focus on enabling the user to implement the concepts outlined previously. We will start off by preparing all the necessary tools and set up the Python working environment on the system. This will make sure that the reader does not experience any inconvenience when it comes to practicing or testing out the examples shown in the upcoming chapters. The first chapter introduces the tools that the reader must have to be able to work on a system that has Python. In addition, each tool described in the first chapter is also accompanied with appropriate explanations and the methods on how the user can easily download and install them on the system. Each Operating System has its own requirements and to ensure every reader can use this book, the first chapter encompasses not only Windows but also Linux and macOS as well. Afterward, we will go over the syntaxes commonly used in advanced programming. These syntaxes will be explained and practically demonstrated on two levels, below the class level and above the class level. After this, we will come across a chapter dedicated to explain the art of naming in programming. Most people underestimate the naming process and do not give it due attention. In reality, naming packages, modules, custom functions, modules, and classes need to be done very carefully as these names are used in coding later on.

After the first four chapters, we will reach the practical portion of the book. The last two chapters are dedicated entirely to explaining the advanced techniques that can be used to create packages in Pythons and applications. These chapters will encompass the concepts discussed in this book and the techniques and practices that are commonly taught in the intermediate level of coding. This is especially important because everything we learn in this book will be useless if we cannot handle a project at the end of the day. In the last chapters, we will go through the process adopted to create packages and then also see how package creation is correlated to building complete applications.

Chapter One

Getting Ready to Work with Python

In today's day and age, Python is one of the most popular programming languages that has excellent usability in a wide variety of high-level niches, such as machine learning, data science, penetration testing, etc. Even for scenarios such as application development and standard programming, Python does not fall behind other languages such as C or C++. In this chapter, we will comprehensively discuss how to properly set up Python on the system along with the appropriate tools to allow for advanced programming and coding practices. The initial setup is very important as it is very counter-productive to find that we are missing a component and having to back and setting it up. In short, we will focus on making sure that we have everything ready and set up before we jump into practical applications and advanced practices (such as creating packages and applications).

Installing Python

Installing and using the Python programming language is easy as it runs on basically any operating system like Linus, Windows, and Macintosh. The core team responsible for the distribution and availability of this Python programming language runs a website "http://www.python.org/ download" to easily download it. The people from the Python community have also provided platforms for other users to download it, which may even have distributions for operating systems reminiscent of old times.

Different Implementations of the Python IDE

One of Python's interesting features is the ease with which it can be implemented in other programming languages as well. For instance, as the name suggests, the tool 'CPython' is an implementation of Python in 'C'. While for the time being, this is the most commonly used variant of a Python implementation, other Python implementations for up and coming fields such as machine learning, data science, and database manipulation are also becoming popular. It all depends on how popular a specialized programming field is for the implementation to enjoy wide-spread use.

Jython

Just as we discussed that 'CPython' is simply the implementation of the Python programming language in 'C', similarly, Java (a popular language used in web development) also has its own Python implementation form of the tool '**Jython**'. The main feature of this implementation is that classes that primarily belong to the Java language are able to be defined in Python modules. In addition, the cross-compatibility also extends to applications that are usually paired with Java (such as Apache). In other words, we can leverage the features provided by these applications limited to Java and bring them over to an application written in Python.

IronPython

Python is brought within the .NET framework with the help of IronPython. The developers of IronPython working at Microsoft have made version 1.1 which is the most stable and implements Python 2.4.3. IronPython with ASP.NET allows the use of Python code in .NET applications just like Jython in Java. This type of implementation of Python is useful for the promotion of the language. According to the TIOBE community index, the .NET language is becoming increasingly popular and has a big developer community comparable to Java.

PyPy

This implementation is a bit difficult to understand because it is an implementation of Python itself. To elaborate, the interpreter being used in this tool is basically responsible for translating Python code. While one might wonder what's the purpose of a Python implementation for a Python project as it doesn't make sense. But experienced programmers stack implementations over one another to bring out the true potential of tools like this one. For example, if we are working on a project, we can use the **CPython** tool and have it work on the simpler instructions, and later on, we can use the **PyPy** tool to translate the code from the **CPython** into the Python language. Many other examples such as this demonstrate the usefulness of PyPy. In the beginning, the main concern for this tool was its lackluster speed, which was even more evident when it was compared to **CPython**. But with the introduction of techniques like 'JIT', the speed of the PyPy tool's compiler has increased by an impressive margin. That said, it's not recommended to use PyPy as your main implementation as programmers are still experimenting with it.

Other implementations

Apart from the commonly used implementations, other interesting implementations and ports of Python are also available. Examples include the Python 2.2.2 available for access in the Nokia S60 phone series, and a port on ARM Linux which provides its availability in devices like Sharp Zaurus.

Linux Installation

If the operating system in question is Linux, then the Python language may already be installed. To access it, just try to call it from the shell as:

```
tarek@dabox:~$ python
Python 2.3.5 (#1, Jul 4 2007, 17:28:59)
[GCC 4.1.2 20061115 (prerelease) (Debian 4.1.1-21)] on linux2
Type "help", "copyright", "credits" or "license" for more
information.
>>>
```

Once the shell is finished executing the command from the user, it will either display an error detailing that there is no valid installation of Python on the system, or it will simply return the version of the Python installation and execute the IDE. At the end of the shell, you will notice three 'greater than' symbols (>>>). These symbols tell the user that Python will execute any valid command written in this space. The shell also tells us the compiler that is available for the Python and it depends on OS to OS. For instance, the compiler on a system running Linux will be '**GCC**' while on the other hand, the compiler for a system running Windows will be the visual studio.

If you are indeed running a Linux-based system, you can install other Python versions as well. With more than one Python installation, all you have to do is execute the command while passing the specific version you want the shell to run. In this way, the shell will not execute an entirely different version of Python or all Python versions at the same time. Here's a demonstration that explains this;

```
tarek@dabox:~$ which python
/usr/bln/python
tarek@dabox:~$ python<tab>
python python2.3 python2.5
python2.4
```

There is a chance that the system does not recognize the Python command you have executed. This can be either because you have made a typo when writing the command or the system cannot access the Python installation. In such cases, the problem can be, most of the time, fixed by simply doing a fresh installation through the package manager of the Linux distribution you are running.

The preferred way of installing Python for the Linux system is to use the package installation method, but the package-management tools may not always have the latest Python version.

Installing the Python as a Package

Python is commonly installed in Linux by using the package-management tools provided by the Linux system. In this way, it is easy to keep it upgraded as well. Based on the type of Linux system being used, there are several ways to install Python by using the following command lines:

- "apt-get install python" is the command line used for a system based on Debian such as Ubuntu.

- "urpmi python" is used for an rpm-based system namely Fedora or Red Hat series.

- "emerge python" is specified for the Gentoo system.

If the Python installation version is not specified, you need to install the latest version on the system by yourself.

For the full installation of Python, extra packages will need to be installed, but they are optional. A user can work perfectly fine without these packages, but if C extensions need to be coded or the programs need to be profiled, then they will be useful. The extra packages required for a full installation are:

- **Python-dev:** If C modules are to be compiled in Python, then the python-dev package has the Python headers needed for this task.

- **python-profiler:** This package provides non-GPL modules required for full distributions of GPL (Debian or Ubuntu)

- **gcc:** C code extensions are compiled with the help of gcc.

Source Compilation

The manual installation proceeds by the 'CMMI' process which stands for the sequence of "configure, make, make install". It is used to compile and deploy Python on the system. The latest version of the Python archive can be accessed on the website "http://python.org/download."

The programs "make" and "gcc" is used to build Python so the user should install them on the system.

- The 'make' sequence is basically responsible for double-checking that everything is according to the requirements for the program's compilation. The 'list' which the sequence tally's and double-checks is located in a config file by the name of **'makefile'**. The compilation procedure does not proceed until the sequence gives the green light.

- 'ggc' is simply the compiler responsible for creating the applications from the code.

The package "build-essentials" is available in several versions of Linux such as Ubuntu and provides the necessary build tools that can easily be installed.

The following sequence can be used to build and install Python on the system.

```
cd /tmp

wget http://python.org/ftp/python/2.5.1/Python-2.5.1.tgz

tar -xzvf tar -xzvf Python-2.5.1.tgz

cd Python-2.5.1

./configure

make

sudo make install
```

Among the things installed in the process, headers for binary installation are also included which are usually found in the package "python-dev". The source releases of the installations also contain the Hotshot profiler. After the installation process is finished, Python is enabled so it can be reached from the shell.

Windows Installation

The basic process to install and compile Python on the Windows operating system is similar to Linux, but Windows also requires a complication compilation environment to be set up which can be quite troublesome. The download section on the website "python.org" has standard Python installers for Windows and the installation wizards are easy to go through.

Installing Python on the System

The default options in Python's installation wizard choose the file path as "c:\Python25" instead of the usual " C:\Program

Files\Python25". This is done to prevent any space in the path and shortens it.

Lastly, to call Python from the DOS shell, the user has to alter the "path" environment variable. To do this during the installation of Python on Windows, follow the given steps:

- Trace the icon of **My Computer** from either the Start Menu or the desktop and activate the dialog box "System Properties" by right-clicking it.

- Click on the **Advanced** tab present in the dialog box.

- Look for the button named **Environmental Variables** and click on it.

- Change the "path" system variable by adding two new paths in it which are separated by a semicolon " ; ".

The paths which are edited into the system variable are:

- File path "c:\Python25" which is used to call "Python.exe"

- File path "c:\Python25\Scripts". This calls the third-party scripts installed in Python via extensions.

Python can be called and run in the Command Prompt. To do this, simply open **Run** from the Start menu and type in cmd. Press enter and the command prompt will be displayed from where Python is called.

C:\> python

Python 2.5.2 (#71, Oct 18 2006, 08:34:43) [MSC v.1310 32 bit (Intel)] on

win32

Type "help", "copyright", "credits" or "license" for more information.

>>>

Although Python can function in this specific environment theoretically, it will seem as if it is performing with a broken leg as compared to Linux. It is recommended always to make sure that a compatible version of **MinGW** compiler is installed on the system in addition to the set up environment.

Installing MinGW

As we have already mentioned in the previous section, '**MinGW**' is a compiler that is recommended when we are using Python on a Windows-based system. This compiler has all those features and functions that are on par and even better in terms of compatibility than the standard visual studio compiler on Windows. To get the best results on a Windows-based system, one should just use both compilers and switch between them depending on the task.

The link to access the distribution of MinGW is:

http://sourceforge.net/project/
showfiles.php?group_id=2435&package_id=240780

When we are done installing the **MinGW** compiler on the system, we cannot use the commands that come along with right out the box. Since the default compiler is still visual studio, we need to link the environment we are using to this compiler. To do this, we need to make changes to our environment's path variable, such that it specifies the system path to the **MinGW** compiler. In this case, we would need to specify the following path;

c:\MinGW\bin

The following block shows the demonstrations of the **MinGW** commands being executed in a shell.

C:\>gcc -v

Reading specs from c:/MinGW/bin/../lib/gcc-lib/mingw32/3.2.3/specs

Configured with: ../gcc/configure --with-gcc --with-gnu-ld --with-gnu-as

--host=

mingw32 --target=mingw32 --prefix=/mingw --enable-threads --disable-nls

--enable

-languages=c++,f77,objc --disable-win32-registry --disable-shared --

enable-sjljexceptions

Thread model: win32

gcc version 3.2.3 (mingw special 20030504-1)

When Python needs to run the compiler, it uses the commands only automatically. So it means these commands can't be run manually.

Installing MSYS

We will now discuss another tool that drastically increases the working results in Python coding on Windows. This is the **'MSYS'** tool. This tool offers the user all of those commands that are available in Linux and macOS Operating Systems. It is recommended to use this tool on a Windows System because it does not have access to the commands available in the '**Bourne Shell**' (specific to only Linux and macOS).

MSYS can be installed on Windows by the following download link:

http://sourceforge.net/project/
showfiles.php?group_id=2435&package_id=240780

By default, MSYS will be installed in the file path "c:\msys", so the user must edit the path to "c:\msys\1.0\bin" in the "path" variable just as done with MinGW.

Mac OS X Installation

Apple's Mac Operating System is quite similar to Linux but we will not go into that detail. Due to a certain extent of compatibility between the two operating systems, the usage process, installations, compilers, and techniques can be employed by users on either OS. But not everything is the same. For instance, the organization of the system tree is different for both Linux and Mac Operating Systems.

Following the trend from Linux and Windows, Python is installed in Mac OS X in the two ways as well,

- One is through the package installation, a simple and easy way to install Python.

- The other way is to compile it from the sources if the user wants to build it by themselves.

Installing Python as a Package

If the user has the latest version of Mac OS X, then Python may be already installed on it. An extra Python can still be installed by getting the universal binary of Python 2.5.x from:

http://www.pythonmac.org/ packages

The ".dmg" file obtained is mounted after which a ".pkg" file can be launched.

Python is installed in the "/Library" folder which creates links in the Mac OS X system. Python can then be called from the shell and run.

Source Compilation

If you choose to build Python on your own, then you will need the following tools to compile Python from the sources:

- A "gcc" compiler which can be obtained from Xcode Tools, install disk or online at the website: "http://developer.apple.com/tools/xcode."

465

- MacPorts is a package system similar to Debian's package-management system called **apt**. Just as apt installs dependencies in the Linux system, MacPorts will do the same for Mac OS X.

The rest of the process for compiling Python is the same as for Linux.

The Python Prompt

Python prompt is usually used as a small calculator and lets the user interact with the interpreter. It appears when the "python" command is called.

```
macziade:/home/tziade tziade$ python
Python 2.5 (r25:51918, Sep 19 2006, 08:49:13)
[GCC 4.0.1 (Apple Computer, Inc. build 5341)] on darwin
Type "help", "copyright", "credits" or "license" for more information.
>>>1 + 3
4
>>>5 * 8
40
```

Once we start up the Python shell and instruct Python to perform many arithmetic calculations, the interpreter translates these lines and returns a corresponding response.

Configuring the Interactive Prompt

Programmers usually customize the prompt or shell that they would interact with during the coding session. One of the easiest ways to do this is by using a '**startup**' script to perform a series of actions configured by users themselves. For example, if we create a custom startup file, then as soon as the prompt boots up, it will look for the variable '**PYTHONSTARTUP**' of the environment being used. This variable will guide the prompt to a specific file and ultimately, the prompt will access the code lines in this file and execute them. The developer distributing a package or an application usually includes a startup script as well. If you want to access these files, then you can do so by checking the system's home directory and looking for the folder '**.pythonstartup**'.

One of the simplest startup files is given below where it adds completion by using the <Tab> key, and history:

```
# python startup file
import readline
import rlcompleter
import atexit
import os
# tab completion
readline.parse_and_bind('tab: complete')
# history file
histfile = os.path.join(os.environ['HOME'], '.pythonhistory')
```

```
try:
 readline.read_history_file(histfile)
except IOError:
 pass
atexit.register(readline.write_history_file, histfile)
del os, histfile, readline, rlcompleter
```

Make a file in the home directory with the name of ".pythonstartup" and add the environment variable "PYTHONSTARTUP" by using the given file path.

Now when the interactive prompt is called and run, the script of ".pythonstartup" executes and adds new functionalities to Python. An example of such a functionality is the "Tab completion" which recalls the contents of module and makes the coding process easier:

```
>>> import md5
>>> md5.<tab>
md5.__class__ md5.__file__ md5.__name__
md5.__repr__ md5.digest_size
md5.__delattr__ md5.__getattribute__ md5.__new__
md5.__setattr__ md5.md5
md5.__dict__ md5.__hash__ md5.__reduce__
md5.__str__ md5.new
md5.__doc__ md5.__init__ md5.__reduce_ex__ md5.
blocksize
```

The automatic execution of tasks handled by the startup script shown above can be improved even further by taking advantage of the entry point that Python provides with each of its modules.

The Advanced Python Prompt 'iPython'

iPython is a tool that was designed to give a more advanced and extended prompt with interesting features such as:

- Dynamic object introspection

- Accessing the system shell from the prompt

- Profiling direct support

- Facilities for debugging

The full list of features is given at the website "http://ipython.scipy.org/doc/manual/index.html."

To install this tool, follow the website link "http://ipython.scipy.org/moin/ Download", then download and install it according to the instructions given for each platform.

An example of a working shell of iPython is given below:

```
tarek@luvdit:~$ ipython
Python 2.4.4 (#2, Apr 5 2007, 20:11:18)
Type "copyright", "credits" or "license" for more information.
IPython 0.7.2 -- An enhanced Interactive Python.
? -> Introduction to IPython's features.
```

%magic -> Information about IPython's 'magic' % functions.

help -> Python's own help system.

object? -> Details about 'object'. ?object also works, ?? prints more.

In [1]:

Installing Setuptools

In Python, some tools and modules allow programmers to build their own libraries. This is really useful when it comes to working on complex programming projects. Custom libraries can be built by using commands available in '**Perl CPAN**' but using such tools and methods have a few dependencies that need to be addressed as well;

- On Python's official site, a concentrated depository called the **Python Package Index (PyPI)**, which was previously the **Cheeseshop**.

- To send the code in archives and cooperate with PyPI, a packaging system known as setuptools that depends on distutils is required.

Prior to introducing these extensions, a couple of clarifications are important to get an entire picture.

Understanding The Working of the Tool

In Python, **distutils** is a tool that is commonly used to split the application into different packages. We will discuss this in more detail in the upcoming chapters where we will be learning how to create packages and applications. Using the **distutils** module essentially provides the following capabilities in programming projects;

- A structural definition of a package or application's metadata (you will learn more about metadata in chapters 5 and 6). This tool also allows the programmer to define custom dependencies for the packages as well

- When a package or an application has been built, the tool provides necessary commands and functions to help the programmer distribute their product to the community.

One important thing to consider is that we cannot completely depend on the **distutils** module itself. For instance, if we are simply working with a single package, then we can handle the creation of dependencies and distribution of the package by using **distutils** alone but if we are working with an application, then you will most likely split the application into several different packages and these packages will surely have overlapping dependencies. If we use the **distutils** tool alone, we cannot handle the packages' breaking because of their dependencies. This is why we use another important module in python in unison with **distutils** and this module is **'setuptools'**. The upcoming chapters will have detailed sections explaining how to use this module with **distutils**.

Installing the 'setuptools' module:

Before we can install the 'setuptools' module on the system, we first need a package that is important for this process. This package is '**EasyInstall**'. Just as the name suggests, this package handles installations of packages as well as modules. If we are installing a package from a repository or a server, EasyInstall will handle the downloading process. It's just like a third-party download and install manager that you would use on a system instead of the default one. Once we have installed **EasyInstall**, the **setuptools** module can be easily installed by executing a simple command on the system's terminal shell. The following URL is the official website for this package.

http://peak.telecommunity.com/DevCenter/EasyInstall

and the destination of this toolkit is generally found on

http://peak.telecommunity.com/dist/ez_setup.py: macziade:~ tziade$ wget

Here's the command line execution to install the **setuptools** module;

macziade:~ tziade$ wget

http://peak.telecommunity.com/dist/ez_setup.py

08:31:40 (29.26 KB/s) - « ez_setup.py » saved [8960/8960]

macziade:~ tziade$ python ez_setup.py setuptools

Searching for setuptools

Reading http://pypi.python.org/simple/setuptools/

Best match: setuptools 0.6c7

...

Processing dependencies for setuptools

Finished processing dependencies for setuptools

If you already have an older version installed, an error will pop up, and then you will have to upgrade the existing version.

macziade:~ tziade$ python ez_setup.py

Setuptools version 0.6c7 or greater has been installed.

(Run "ez_setup.py -U setuptools" to reinstall or upgrade.)

macziade:~ tziade$ python ez_setup.py -U setuptools

Searching for setuptools

Reading http://pypi.python.org/simple/setuptools/

Best match: setuptools 0.6c7

...

Processing dependencies for setuptools

Finished processing dependencies for setuptools

Since we now have **EasyInstall** on the system, it would be a waste to not use it to install other packages and extensions for the system. To instruct this software tool to initiate an installation procedure for a package, we simply need to execute the **'easy_install'** command in the system's shell. The same command can also be used to update already installed extensions as well. Here's a demonstration showing how we can use the **easy_install** command to install an extension.

tarek@luvdit:/tmp$ sudo easy_install py

Searching for py

Reading http://cheeseshop.python.org/pypi/py/

Reading http://codespeak.net/py

Reading http://cheeseshop.python.org/pypi/py/0.9.0

Best match: py 0.9.0

Downloading http://codespeak.net/download/py/py-0.9.0.tar.gz

...

Installing pytest.cmd script to /usr/local/bin

Installed /usr/local/lib/python2.3/site-packages/py-0.9.0-py2.3.egg

Processing dependencies for py

Finished processing dependencies for py

Attaching MinGW into the 'distutils' Tool

When the compiler is stimulated to build an application written in the C programming language, a communication pathway is established between the compiler MinGW and the distutils tool through a config file. This file needs to be present otherwise the compilation process will fail and return an error. To put it simply, copy the following lines shown in the block below and paste it into a cfg file named '**distutils.cfg**' and place it in the following directory

'python-installation-path\lib\distutils'

[build]

compiler = mingw32

By doing this, Python will link with MinGW so that Python will use MinGW whenever a package containing C code has to be built.

Working Environment

A proper environment is absolutely necessary for any programming project, be it creating a simple package, or an entire application. The environment is basically a space where the programmer performs most of the coding and testing and prepares the packages that will execute the code in an orderly fashion. An environment can be considered as a sort of 'work desk'. On your work desk, you make sure that you have all the tools you'll need for the project, all the components as well as the necessary materials. If your work desk is missing something, then you will most likely have to drop the entire project and fetch what you're missing, and sometimes, you don't even have the resources to prepare any substitute. The same is the case for the working environment in programming, but in here, if the environment is not set up properly, then you will have to drop most of the progress you have made and cannot continue any further until you prepare another suitable environment.

The environment needed to be set can be done in the following two ways:

- It can be built up by composing it with many small tools. This way of setting up the environment has now become old.

- A new way is to use an all-in-one tool.

These are the main methods of building the environment while many other ways in between are also available. The developer should be given the right to choose any way they would like to set up their environment.

Editor Tools and Other Components

Many programmers prefer creating the environment for their project using a suitable 'Editor tool' along with other components. Creating an environment from scratch using an editor is quite taxing on the resource of time, meaning that it takes a lot of time to do so. That said, the time one invests to create an environment in this method is paid-off pretty well as the resulting product is worth it. Environments built in this way are easily customizable after creation, which has a huge impact on the project results as well (you can tweak the environment to match the needs of your project later on in the development stage as well). If you know that the environment you have built will come in handy in the future, then you can simply make a portable version of it and store it in a removable drive, preferably a USB. In this way, you can plug it into any system you want and have it ready for the project on the fly. In the upcoming chapters, we will learn how to create a template for creating an environment as well. This dramatically decreases the time it takes to create an environment from scratch for an entirely new project.

Hence, the working environment should have the following:

- An open-source and free **code editor** that is available for use on any Operating System

- **Additional binaries** for features that can help avoid having to rewrite them in Python

A popular code editor used by many programmers is '**Vim**' but a few prefer the **'Emacs'** code editor; we will only focus on the Vim editor in this chapter.

Installing and Configuring the Vim Code Editor

The Vim code editor tool can be downloaded from their official website.

http://www.vim.org/download.php

Systems running on Linux OS usually have a version of Vim installed by default. But there are chances that the version is an older release so you should check the Vim installation version by executing the following command in the terminal.

Vim -- version

If the version is not the latest release, then it is recommended you update it.

On other systems such as Windows and macOS, Vim is not included by default and needs to be manually downloaded and installed. On Windows, users will have the option to download a Vim version that features a graphical user interface along with the standard console version. This version of Vim is commonly referred to as '**gvim**'. The official download link for the Vim tool has already been linked at the start.

If you are using a Linux or a macOS system, you will need to place a '.vimrc' file on its home directory. If your system is running Windows, then you will need to place a '**_vimrc**' file in the installation folder of the tool and simply link an environmental variable to this file, in this way, the Vim tool will be able to find this file easily.

Here's what the **vimrc** file should have;

set encoding=utf8

set paste

set expandtab

set textwidth=0

set tabstop=4

set softtabstop=4

set shiftwidth=4

set autoindent

set backspace=indent,eol,start

set incsearch

set ignorecase

set ruler

set wildmenu

set commentstring=\ #\ %s

set foldlevel=0

set clipboard+=unnamed

syntax on

Chapter Two

Syntaxes Below the Class Level

Writing a good, efficient bit of code is something of an art, and most often art is a skill that can be nurtured and learned. The syntax is important in not only pleasing the observer's eye but allowing adjustments and reducing obfuscations. A fair few projects and prototypes go under because their syntax was too dense, or incomprehensible at a glance, requiring guidance on how to look into the code and interact with it.

A lot of work has been done on the back end of Python to allow for simpler, cleaner syntax. It is an old language, its inception has been in 1991, and it has been kept updated ever since. The fundamentals have remained the same, but the instruments we have to work with have been polished and upgraded.

We will tackle five of the more integral topics in writing good Python syntax, and offer advice on how to proceed with them. They are, in our order:

- List comprehensions:

- Iterators and Generators:

- Descriptors and their properties:

- Decorators:

- *with* and *contextlib*

As you follow along, it might be helpful for you to be able to access various tips and documentation on examples of how things are done. These can be found in your compiler console's own help function, and Python's own official tutorials and guides.

List Comprehensions

Python isn't exactly C. There are inherent differences in design and interpreter that allow C to have more expansive code than Python which would be more resource intensive. An example:

```
>>> numbers = range(10)
>>> size = len(numbers)
>>> evens = []
>>> i = 0
>>> while i < size:
... if i % 2 == 0:
... evens.append(i)
... i += 1
...
>>> evens
[0, 2, 4, 6, 8]
```

This form presents Python problems, namely that one, the compiler interpreter has to recalculate what needs to be changed in the sequence per loop iteration and two, there has to be a counter to keep an eye on what element needs interaction.

We can use Python's *list comprehension* functionalities that automate the above code's processes using wired features, which ends up tidying it up and reducing our work to a singular line of code. In addition, the ease and simplicity of this allow it to be comprehended and troubleshot faster, making bugs less likely and subsequent bug fixing easier.

```
>>> [i for i in range(10) if i % 2 == 0]

[0, 2, 4, 6, 8]
```

enumerate is another example of Python's elegant simplicity. This function indexes a sequence conveniently when the sequence is used in a loop.

For instance, this:

```
>>> i = 0
>>> seq = ["one", "two", "three"]
>>> for element in seq:
... seq[i] = '%d: %s' % (i, seq[i])
```

```
... i += 1

...

>>> seq

['0: one', '1: two', '2: three']
```

reduces to this:

```
>>> seq = ["one", "two", "three"]

>>> for i, element in enumerate(seq):

... seq[i] = '%d: %s' % (i, seq[i])

...

>>> seq

['0: one', '1: two', '2: three']
```

and has a neat bow tied on it, using list comprehension, as shown below. As an aside, converting the loop into a small function vectorizes for the code, making later attempts at understanding and using it much more successful:

```
>>> def _treatment(pos, element):

... return '%d: %s' % (pos, element)

...

>>> seq = ["one", "two", "three"]

>>> [_treatment(i, el) for i, el in enumerate(seq)]
```

['0: one', '1: two', '2: three']

Iterators and Generators

An iterator is a container object that simply causes iteration inside it. It comprises of two parts, *next* which produces the next item in containment and *_iter_*, which returns the iterator object. Let's use a sequence to help in understanding iterators.

```
>>> i = iter('abc')
>>> i.next()
'a'
>>> i.next()
'b'
>>> i.next()
'c'
>>> i.next()
Traceback (most recent call last):
File "<stdin>", line 1, in <module>
StopIteration
```

At the end of the sequence, we use *StopIteration*, which handily allows iterator use in loops due to the condition allowing it to break out and stop.

We can also create an iterator in a class as follows, which uses the *next* method and uses _*iter*_ to return an iterator instance:

```
>>> class MyIterator(object):
... def __init__(self, step):
... self.step = step
... def next(self):
... """Returns the next element."""
... if self.step == 0:
... raise StopIteration
... self.step -= 1
... return self.step
... def __iter__(self):
... """Returns the iterator itself."""
... return self
...
>>> for el in MyIterator(4):
... print el
...
3
2
```

```
1

0
```

Iterators are a basic and low-level construction, and their use is fairly unnecessary, but they do form the bedrock for the concept of generators. Introduced in Python version 2.2, it serves to create functions that return a list of elements. We can use *yield* to pause said function and get an intermediate value. The following example describes how we might create a generator to produce the Fibonacci sequence.

```
>>> def fibonacci():
... a, b = 0, 1
... while True:
... yield b
... a, b = b, a + b
...
>>> fib = fibonacci()
>>> fib.next()
1
>>> fib.next()
1
```

```
>>> fib.next()

2

>>> [fib.next() for i in range(10)]

[3, 5, 8, 13, 21, 34, 55, 89, 144, 233]
```

The function defined returns a *generator* object, a special kind of iterator, which can save the execution context. We can call it as many times as we might please, and it would produce the element that comes after the one we left it on. Consider the syntax in which it is written: it is clean, simple, and concise, and even though the series is infinite we do not need to worry about it anymore.

Most Python programmers do not use generators due to the more accessible ideas of using simpler functions and have never been comfortable using them. It is ideal that one considers a generator whenever there's a function that is used in a loop or produces a sequence of items uniquely, which improves the code's overall performance.

To expand on the former, let's consider a generator that returns sequential values. The values of that sequence don't need loading immediately because the generator produces each in its turn, and since every generator loop should use less processing time than the system would take loading a possibly infinite sequence (such as the Fibonacci sequence) beforehand, it would be a much faster solution. An example of this in practice is in its use in stream buffers, where we can have complete control over how much data we need to stream in, and whether we might need to pause it or completely shut it down temporarily.

Let's now have a look at the *tokenize* module. A pre-defined member of Python's standard library, it is a generator reads a stream of text, produces tokens (i.e. a subdivision of the given body of text) for it, and returns an iterator, which can be used to process the data further via applying it into external functions. We use *Open* to load up and read the text stream to be able to pass it into *tokenize,* and *generate_tokens* to work on this data stream.

```
>>> import tokenize
>>> reader = open('amina.py').next
>>> tokens = tokenize.generate_tokens(reader)
>>> tokens.next()
(1, 'from', (1, 0), (1, 4), 'from amina.quality import
similarities\n')
>>> tokens.next()
(1, 'amina', (1, 5), (1, 10), 'from amina.quality import
similarities\n')
>>> tokens.next()
```

generator also assists in simplifying code; for instance, we can combine several modules of, say, data transformation algorithms into one higher function, by considering each module as an *iterator* object. This also has the benefit of producing live feedback on the process. An example is given below, wherein each function transforms a sequence, and each of them is connected; one function after the other. All of them manipulate the value and return an output:

```
>>> def power(values):
... for value in values:
... print 'powering %s' % value
... yield value
...
>>> def adder(values):
... for value in values:
... print 'adding to %s' % value
... if value % 2 == 0:
... yield value + 3
... else:
... yield value + 2
...
>>> elements = [1, 4, 7, 9, 12, 19]
>>> res = adder(power(elements))
>>> res.next()
```

```
powering 1

adding to 1

3

>>> res.next()

powering 4

adding to 4

7

>>> res.next()

powering 7

adding to 7

9
```

We'll end our section about iterators and generators by mentioning how generators can use code that was called using *next,* wherein *yield* becomes an expression, and we can move the resulting output to somewhere else using a new tool; *send*

The Send Tool

```
>>> def psychologist():

... print 'Please tell me your problems'

... while True:

... answer = (yield)
```

```
... if answer is not None:

... if answer.endswith('?'):

... print ("Don't ask yourself

... "too much questions")

... elif 'good' in answer:

... print "A that's good, go on"

... elif 'bad' in answer:

... print "Don't be so negative"

...

>>> free = psychologist()

>>> free.next()

Please tell me your problems

>>> free.send('I feel bad')

Don't be so negative

>>> free.send("Why I shouldn't ?")

Don't ask yourself too much questions

>>> free.send("ok then i should find what is good for me")

A that's good, go on
```

Send is similar to *next*, but changes the functionality of *yield* to return the generator's output. Two functions exist to assist *send*; *throw* and *close*. These are error flags for the generator, and they work as follows:

- *throw* is a catch-all to allow client code to send any kind of exception flag.

- *close* only allows a specific flag to be raised, *GeneratorExit*. This can only be cleared by using *GeneratorExit* again or using *StopIteration*.

An example is given below:

```
>>> def my_generator():
... try:
... yield 'something'
... except ValueError:
... yield 'dealing with the exception'
... finally:
... print "ok let's clean"
...
>>> gen = my_generator()
>>> gen.next()
'something'
```

```
>>> gen.throw(ValueError('mean mean mean'))

'dealing with the exception'

>>> gen.close()

ok let's clean

>>> gen.next()

Traceback (most recent call last):

File "<stdin>", line 1, in <module>

StopIteration
```

Finally, a method called *'finally'*, clears any *close* or *throw* that wasn't caught, and is a simple way of tying up loose ends. Care must be given to distancing *GeneratorExit* from the generator, to ensure its clean exit on calling *close*, otherwise, a system error will be called for the interpreter.

Now, we can move on to using generators to form coroutines, which utilizes the last three methods we've discussed just prior

Coroutines

Coroutines are a type of function whose purpose is to allow multiple processes to work together by permitting them to stop and resume execution when necessary. These are handy in a variety of situations where something may occur randomly, such as event loops and handling exceptions (such as error statements).

Coroutines assist in setting up multitasking within a body of code, and in cleaning up process pipelines. Generators are similar to Io and Lua's version of coroutines, but not quite; it requires *send*, *throw*, and *close*. Another technique similar to this would be threading, which allows blocks of code to interact, though the resources it requires, the necessity of pre-definition of its manner of execution, and the complexity of the code make it troublesome for simpler projects.

An example of using the above mentioned to make a coroutine is given in Python's official documentation, and the particular method is referred to as Trampoline. It can be accessed by using the following weblink: http://www.python.org/dev/peps/pep-0342 (PEP 342).

Trampoline is described by a bit of example code from PyPI (a Python interpreter):

```
>>> import multitask
>>> import time
>>> def coroutine_1():
... for i in range(3):
... print 'c1'
... yield i

...
```

```
>>> def coroutine_2():

... for i in range(3):

... print 'c2'

... yield i

...

>>> multitask.add(coroutine_1())

>>> multitask.add(coroutine_2())
```

A perfect example for coroutines is server management, where multiple threads of processing occur in tandem. Clients trying to access and use the server send a request to do so, which is processed by the server via two coroutines, a server coroutine to read through these requests and allow or deny them, and a handler coroutine to work through these requests. A call to the handler is placed by the server coroutine everytime a new input is received from the client.

The multitask package adds a few cool API's to allow us to work with sockets. Let's try and use this to make an echo server:

```
from __future__ import with_statement

from contextlib import closing

import socket

import multitask

def client_handler(sock):
```

```python
with closing(sock):
    while True:
        data = (yield multitask.recv(sock, 1024))
        if not data:
            break
        yield multitask.send(sock, data)

def echo_server(hostname, port):
    addrinfo = socket.getaddrinfo(hostname, port,
        socket.AF_UNSPEC,
        socket.SOCK_STREAM)
    (family, socktype, proto,
     canonname, sockaddr) = addrinfo[0]
    with closing(socket.socket(family,
        socktype,
        proto)) as sock:
        sock.setsockopt(socket.SOL_SOCKET,
            socket.SO_REUSEADDR, 1)
        sock.bind(sockaddr)
        sock.listen(5)
        while True:
```

```
multitask.add(client_handler((

yield multitask.accept(sock))[0]))f __name__ ==
'__main__':

import sys

hostname = None

port = 1111

if len(sys.argv) > 1:

hostname = sys.argv[1]

if len(sys.argv) > 2:

port = int(sys.argv[2])

multitask.add(echo_server(hostname, port))

try:

multitask.run()

except KeyboardInterrupt:

pass
```

Generator Expressions

There's a simple shortcut to writing generators for a sequence, included in Python's libraries. The syntax used for it is similar to list comprehensions, but we can use it in place of yield. And instead of parentheses, we use brackets.

```
>>> iter = (x**2 for x in range(10) if x % 2 == 0)

>>> for el in iter:

... print el

...

0

4

16

36

64
```

These expressions are referred to as generator expressions, or genexp to abbreviate it. As we have mentioned, they can be used to replace *yield* loops, or replace a list comprehensions that act as iterators. Also similar to the latter, they help in trimming down code blocks to make it look nice and clean, and like generators themselves, only one element at a time is produced as an output.

The 'itertools' Module

Python introduced a toolkit module to introduce and implement iterators, written in C, which makes them fairly efficient iterators. The more eye-catching tools in the module include *islice, groupby,* and *tee.*

The 'islice Window Iterator

This *itertools* method produces an iterator that works over a sequence subgroup. Let's use an example to explain that.

The following reads lines from an input and, as long as the line has greater than four elements, yields the element of each line, beginning from the fifth in the order:

```
>>> import itertools
>>> def starting_at_five():
... value = raw_input().strip()
... while value != '':
... for el in itertools.islice(value.split(),
... 4, None):
... yield el
... value = raw_input().strip()
...
>>> iter = starting_at_five()
>>> iter.next()
one two three four five six
'five'
>>> iter.next()
'six'
```

```
>>> iter.next()

one two

one two three four five six

'five'

>>> iter.next()

'six'

>>> iter.next()

one

one two three four five six seven eight

'five'

>>> iter.next()

'six'

>>> iter.next()

'seven'

>>> iter.next()

'eight'
```

islice returns data from a stream in an increment (via inputting a step argument) or all of it in sequence, starting and stopping where we tell it to be. Arguments for the iterable stream include things like wrapped data (e.g. a SOAP envelope). This start and stop of data stream can be visualized as a sheet or window that we place over the data, which is received via *islice* and sent forth to other functions.

The Back and Forth 'tee' Iterator

Only one iterator can run a sequence at a time, after which the sequence is "consumed" but we can use *tee* to run multiple iterators on sequences, which can prove helpful in recomputing data in a loop. An example of a case where this would be useful is in reading the header of a file to determine its function, before running the code.

Consider the following example:

```
>>> import itertools
>>> def with_head(iterable, headsize=1):
... a, b = itertools.tee(iterable)
... return list(itertools.islice(a, headsize)), b
...
>>> with_head(seq)
([1], <itertools.tee object at 0x100c698>)
>>> with_head(seq, 4)
([1, 2, 3, 4], <itertools.tee object at 0x100c670>)
```

By the use of tee, two iterators are generated in this code, out of which the list is produced on the usage of *islice* to have headsize elements for the iterations. The other element or the secondary element works over the entire process that is returned as a new iterator.

The Unix's Uniq Iterator 'Groupby'

Groupby reduces and reorders iterables based on various parameters and its method of execution. These generally work by taking the object apart, processing the split elements in a function, and fusing the (generally smaller) results to be worked on a function.

Let's try and use *groupby* to make a function that uses run-length encoding (RLE). As a reminder, run-length encoding replaces repeated characters in a string by representing that repetition, which contains the number of duplicates and the character present in that space. In the case of no repetition, the number of duplicates will be one.

SPARTAAAAAAAAA

will be replaced by

1S1P1A1R1T9A.

The code for this would be simple. Let's use the example string 'get uuuuuuuuuuuuuuuuup' to demonstrate:

```
>>> from itertools import groupby
>>> def compress(data):
... return ((len(list(group)), name)
```

```
... for name, group in groupby(data))

...

>>> def decompress(data):

... return (car * size for size, car in data)

...

>>> list(compress('get uuuuuuuuuuuuuuuuuuup'))

[(1, 'g'), (1, 'e'), (1, 't'), (1, ' '),

(18, 'u'), (1, 'p')]

>>> compressed = compress('get uuuuuuuuuuuuuuuuuuup')

>>> ''.join(decompress(compressed))

'get uuuuuuuuuuuuuuuuuuup'
```

groupby is a useful tool to summarize data. To do this, we use the function *sorted* to line up similar elements and the data passed to it.

A few other useful functions are described as follows.

- *chain(*iterables)* receives multiple iterables, and works on them in order.

- *Count([n])* produces a periodic sequence in a given range and with a given step size.

- *cycle(iterable)* returns a list of members of an iterable and saves the same list, which it iterates over when the original list is exhausted, causing this loop to occur infinitely

- *dropwhile(predicate, iterable)* removes elements from an iterable while the predicate is true, and then returns the rest of the elements.

- *ifilter(predicate, iterable)* is similar to *filter* in Python's default library.

- *ifilterfalse(predicate, iterable)* is akin to the above, but functions on the iterable when the predicate is false. For example, for a range of ten and a predicate that asks for when values are divisible by two (via $x\%2$), this function returns even numbers (whose remainder is zero).

- *imap(function, *iterables)* shares similarities to *map* but works over multiple iterables, discontinuing its function when the shortest iterable is completely functioned on.

- *izip(*iterables)* combines iterator elements. Functions like *zip* but returns an iterator.

- *repeat(object[, times])* returns the object *times* many times, or infinitely if no *times* argument exists for it.

- *starmap(function, iterable)* passes the iterable values onto the function. A useful in place of *imap* for when the elements are tuples.

- *takewhile(predicate, iterable)* produces elements from the iterable while the predicate is true, and stops when it becomes false.*chain(*iterables)* receives multiple iterables, and works on them in order.

Fuller, more exhaustive documentation for all the functions in *itertools* is available at http://docs.python.org/lib/itertools-functions.html.

Decorators

To help in making objects in Python easier to modify on the fly, decorators were introduced into the language in update 2.4. Decorators are constructions in Python that changes how a class or a function behaves. In the past, static or class methods were used for this purpose, as follows:

```
>>> class WhatFor(object):

... def it(cls):

... print 'work with %s' % cls

... it = classmethod(it)

... def uncommon():

... print 'I could be a global function'
```

```
... uncommon = staticmethod(uncommon)
...
```

This would become cumbersome to go through, and thus decorators were introduced. The syntax for them is as follows:

```
>>> class WhatFor(object):
... @classmethod
... def it(cls):
... print 'work with %s' % cls
... @staticmethod
... def uncommon():
... print 'I could be a global function'
...
>>> this_is = WhatFor()
>>> this_is.it()
work with <class '__main__.WhatFor'>
>>> this_is.uncommon()
I could be a global function
```

The ease and simplicity it offered attracted many followers, and it was adopted fairly quickly.

Now, we shall examine how to implement decorators, via a few examples.

Writing a Decorator

An easy way to make a decorator is to create a function nested into another function, as follows:

```
>>> def mydecorator(function):
... def _mydecorator(*args, **kw):
... # do some stuff before the real
... # function gets called
... res = function(*args, **kw)
... # do some stuff after
... return res
... # returns the sub-function
... return _mydecorator
...
```

A good habit to follow while creating a sub-function like so is to give it a unique, explicit name, such as _mydecorator, for debugging purposes. Now, if the decorator requires arguments, we make a second wrapper layer:

```
def mydecorator(arg1, arg2):

def _mydecorator(function):

def __mydecorator(*args, **kw):

# do some stuff before the real

# function gets called

res = function(*args, **kw)

# do some stuff after

return res

# returns the sub-function

return __mydecorator

return _mydecorator
```

Be careful to use decorators only with wrappers whose application is generic and does not have complex interactions with the rest of the class, since the decorator is loaded first. If this isn't possible, it would be a good idea to redo it into a regular callable; this method reduces the function's complexity. Either way, the best practice, in this case, is to group them in a module.

Decorators come in a variety of shapes and serve a variety of functions. A few common patterns include:

- Argument checking

- Caching

- Proxy

- Context provision

Argument checking

One might want to keep check of what kind of arguments a function receives. For example, consider if an XML-RPC (a lightweight Remote Procedure Call protocol that uses XML to encode its calls) call is received by a function. Python cannot provide a full signature using the statically-typed languages; it needs something more. We can use decorators for such cases.

```
>>> from itertools import izip
>>> rpc_info = {}
>>> def xmlrpc(in_=(), out=(type(None),)):
... def _xmlrpc(function):
... # registering the signature
... func_name = function.func_name
... rpc_info[func_name] = (in_, out)
...
... def _check_types(elements, types):
... """Subfunction that checks the types."""
... if len(elements) != len(types):
... raise TypeError('argument count is wrong')
```

```
... typed = enumerate(izip(elements, types))

... for index, couple in typed:

... arg, of_the_right_type = couple

... if isinstance(arg, of_the_right_type):

... continue

... raise TypeError('arg #%d should be %s' % \

... (index, of_the_right_type)

...

... # wrapped function

... def __xmlrpc(*args): # no keywords allowed

... # checking what goes in

... checkable_args = args[1:] # removing self

... _check_types(checkable_args, in_)

... # running the function

... res = function(*args)

...

... # checking what goes out

... if not type(res) in (tuple, list):

... checkable_res = (res,)

... else:
```

```
... checkable_res = res

... _check_types(checkable_res, out)

...

... # the function and the type

... # checking succeeded

... return res

... return __xmlrpc

... return _xmlrpc

...
```

A list is kept by the argument checker that keeps stock of the types of arguments received and values returned by the function. A globally-defined dictionary is used for this purpose.

We must note that this is an ideal case of a decorator use, and it wouldn't hold up in practical use. A more realistic example is given below, where a dictionary is populated by a class definition which is then used for argument checking.

```
>>> class RPCView(object):

...

... @xmlrpc((int, int)) # two int -> None

... def meth1(self, int1, int2):

... print 'received %d and %d' % (int1, int2)
```

```
...

... @xmlrpc((str,), (int,)) # string -> int

... def meth2(self, phrase):

... print 'received %s' % phrase

... return 12

>>> rpc_infos

{'meth2': ((<type 'str'>,), (<type 'int'>,)),

'meth1': ((<type 'int'>, <type 'int'>),

(<type 'NoneType'>,))}

>>> my = RPCView()

>>> my.meth1(1, 2)

received 1 and 2

>>> my.meth2(2)

Traceback (most recent call last):

File "<stdin>", line 1, in <module>

File "<stdin>", line 16, in _wrapper

File "<stdin>", line 11, in _check_types

TypeError: arg #0 should be <type 'str'>
```

Other uses for argument-checker decorators exist, such as type enforcers that define what type can be used and predicated on a global configuration value. More information about type enforcers can be found here:

http://wiki.python.org/moin/PythonDecoratorLibrary#head-308f2b3507ca91800def19d813348f78db34303e

Caching

Similar to argument checking, this kind of decorator instead focuses on functions whose internal state has no bearing on the output, i.e. each unique input argument produces a unique output. We can use this when the set of inputs is finite. We can use caching decorator to track the relationship between output and input, and return it on call. This is called memoizing, and decorators make it easy to implement.

```
>>> import time
>>> import hashlib
>>> import pickle
>>> from itertools import chain
>>> cache = {}
>>> def is_obsolete(entry, duration):
... return time.time() - entry['time']> duration
...
>>> def compute_key(function, args, kw):
... key = pickle.dumps((function.func_name, args, kw))
```

```
... return hashlib.sha1(key).hexdigest()

...

>>> def memoize(duration=10):

... def _memoize(function):

... def __memoize(*args, **kw):

... key = compute_key(function, args, kw)

...

... # do we have it already ?

... if (key in cache and

... not is_obsolete(cache[key], duration)):

... print 'we got a winner'

... return cache[key]['value']

...

... # computing

... result = function(*args, **kw)...

... # storing the result

... cache[key] = {'value': result,

... 'time': time.time()}

... return result

... return __memoize

... return _memoize
```

The *SHA* hash key is a construction of argument values placed in order, and this result is stored in a global dictionary. We use a pickle to create this hash, which is something of a shortcut that "freezes" the states of objects that are presented as input arguments. This allows us to make sure that every argument is valid.

In case of too long a period of time passing between function calls, *duration* clears the cached value.

Let's continue with describing its use:

```
>>> @memoize()
... def very_very_very_complex_stuff(a, b):
... # if your computer gets too hot on this calculation
... # consider stopping it
... return a + b
...
>>> very_very_very_complex_stuff(2, 2)
4
>>> very_very_very_complex_stuff(2, 2)
we got a winner
4
>>> @memoize(1) # invalidates the cache after 1 second
... def very_very_very_complex_stuff(a, b):
```

```
... return a + b

...

>>> very_very_very_complex_stuff(2, 2)

4

>>> very_very_very_complex_stuff(2, 2)

we got a winner

4

>>> cache

{'c2727f43c6e39b3694649ee0883234cf': {'value': 4,
'time':

1199734132.7102251)}

>>> time.sleep(2)

>>> very_very_very_complex_stuff(2, 2)

4
```

Two-level wrapping or you can refer to as dual-level wrapping uses an empty parenthesis as you might have observed in the first call to function.

Caching is a useful tool; it can massively reduce the resources required for complex and expensive functions to work. But as always, care must be taken that it isn't used in such a way that it causes detriment. Either way, more efficient decorators (such as

Memcached) use a specialized cache library, which is developed using advanced caching methods and algorithms.

Proxy

Consider a security layer that protects access to internal, more important code. This can be implemented using decorators, which are called proxies; these serve to register and identify functions using a global mechanism. We can create the above using a centralized checker, and associated permission that the callable would require.

```
>>> class User(object):
... def __init__(self, roles):
... self.roles = roles
...
>>> class Unauthorized(Exception):
... pass
...
>>> def protect(role):
... def _protect(function):
... def __protect(*args, **kw):
... user = globals().get('user')
... if user is None or role not in user.roles:
... raise Unauthorized("I won't tell you")
```

```
... return function(*args, **kw)

... return __protect

... return _protect

...
```

Python-based web frameworks often use this syntax to create a security layer for publishable classes. Another example demonstrates a variation where a value denoting the current user is kept in a global value, which is checked when there's an access call:

```
>>> tarek = User(('admin', 'user'))

>>> bill = User(('user',))

>>> class MySecrets(object):

... @protect('admin')

... def waffle_recipe(self):

... print 'use tons of butter!'

...

>>> these_are = MySecrets()

>>> user = tarek

>>> these_are.waffle_recipe()

use tons of butter!

>>> user = bill
```

```
>>> these_are.waffle_recipe()

Traceback (most recent call last):

File "<stdin>", line 1, in <module>

File "<stdin>", line 7, in wrap

__main__.Unauthorized: I won't tell you
```

Context Provider

To make sure that a function works in the correct context, or run code after or before a function, we use a context decorator. This allows us to edit the context that we require the function to operate in.

Consider a situation where we might need to share data among several threads working simultaneously. We would need to create a lock so that it isn't accessible via multiple access. We can create such a lock using decorators, as follows:

```
>>> from threading import RLock

>>> lock = RLock()

>>> def synchronized(function):

... def _synchronized(*args, **kw):

... lock.acquire()

... try:

... return function(*args, **kw)
```

```
... finally:

... lock.release()

... return _synchronized

>>> @locker

... def thread_safe(): # make sure it locks the resource

... pass

...
```

Sadly, these have been phased out with the introduction of '*with*' in Python 2.5, which complements the *try...finally* pattern and even covers the niche of use of cases where we might've used context decorator instead.

'with' and 'contextlib'

We mentioned the '*try...finally*' pattern, which is applied for cases where we need to have the memory clean-up code when an error is raised, such as when closing files, making temporary code patches, and running protected code. To implement this, we use '*with*'; it factors out these blocks of code by allowing us to call another method before and after a section of other code.

An example of file access is as follows:

```
>>> hosts = file('/etc/hosts')
>>> try:
... for line in hosts:
... if line.startswith('#'):
... continue
... print line
... finally:
... hosts.close()
...
127.0.0.1 localhost
255.255.255.255 broadcasthost
::1 localhost
```

We can rewrite this block of code using *with* as follows:

```
>>> from __future__ import with_statement
>>> with file('/etc/hosts') as hosts:
... for line in hosts:
... if line.startswith('#'):
... continue
```

```
... print host

...

127.0.0.1 localhost

255.255.255.255 broadcasthost

::1 localhost
```

We can use *thread* and *threading* module classes with this statement, such as:

- thread.LockType

- threading.RLock

- threading.Lock

- threading.Semaphore

- threading.BoundedSemaphore

- Threading.Condition

These classes share two methods: __*enter*__ and __*exit*__, which form the basic protocol for *with*. This means that any of these classes can be used to make *with*:

```
>>> class Context(object):

... def __enter__(self):
```

```
... print 'entering the zone'
... def __exit__(self, exception_type, exception_value,
... exception_traceback):
... print 'leaving the zone'
... if exception_type is None:
... print 'with no error'
... else:
... print 'with an error (%s)' % exception_value
...
>>> with Context():
... print 'i am the zone'
...
entering the zone
i am the zone
leaving the zone
with no error
>>> with Context():
... print 'i am the buggy zone'
... raise TypeError('i am the bug')
...
```

```
entering the zone

i am the buggy zone

leaving the zone

with an error (i am the bug)

Traceback (most recent call last):

File "<stdin>", line 3, in <module>

TypeError: i am the bug
```

__exit__ receives four arguments; one for itself and three from the code block. These are generated in the case of an error; in its absence, the arguments are set to None but if an error is raised, exit__ shouldn't reraise it, as that is the callers duty. Nonetheless, __exit__ can suppress an error flag exception by returning *True*, though this tool is useful for only a select few cases such as for a decorator called *contextmanager*, and in most cases cleaning up the code is usually the better option.

00000000000000000000

We can use *with* to log the code decorated when the context is entered, and resetting it as it was after. This can be useful in various cases, such as allowing a unit test to test the code and get feedback. We create a context for equipping the public APIs of a custom class in the following example:

```
>>> import logging
```

```python
>>> from __future__ import with_statement
>>> from contextlib import contextmanager
>>> @contextmanager
... def logged(klass, logger):
... # logger
... def _log(f):
... def __log(*args, **kw):
... logger(f, args, kw)
... return f(*args, **kw)
... return __log
...
... # let's equip the class
... for attribute in dir(klass):
... if attribute.startswith('_'):
... continue
... element = getattr(klass, attribute)
... setattr(klass, '__logged_%s' % attribute, element)
... setattr(klass, attribute, _log(element))
...
... # let's work
```

```
... yield klass

...

... # let's remove the logging

... for attribute in dir(klass):

... if not attribute.startswith('__logged_'):

... continue

... element = getattr(klass, attribute)

... setattr(klass, attribute[len('__logged_'):],

... element)

... delattr(klass, attribute)

...
```

We can then use *logger* to record what APIs are being used in our particular context.

In our next example, these calls are compiled into a list, used to track APIs and perform assertions, such as reprogramming the public signature of a class to have it avoid duplicate calls if it is noticed that an API is called more than once:

```
>>> class One(object):

... def _private(self):

... pass
```

```
... def one(self, other):

... self.two()

... other.thing(self)

... self._private()

... def two(self):

... pass

...

>>> class Two(object):

... def thing(self, other):

... other.two()

...

>>> calls = []

>>> def called(meth, args, kw):

... calls.append(meth.im_func.func_name)

...

>>> with logged(One, called):

... one = One()

... two = Two()

... one.one(two)

...
```

```
>>> calls

['one', 'two', 'two']
```

Chapter Three

Syntaxes Above the Class Level

This chapter focuses on developing an understanding the more nuanced and advanced parts of Python's syntax, particularly focused on tinkering with and enhancing code for class structures. Python's object model presents unique language internals intended to work with classes, which should be kept an eye on to avoid odd mistakes. We'll focus on the following:

- Subclassing built-in types

- Accessing methods from superclasses

- Slots

- Meta-level programming

Subclassing Built-in Types

Classes and types were unified in Python's 2.2 update. and a common form for the types was created, *object*, which serves as a hierarchical ancestor for all later types. This allows programmers to subclass built-in types such as *list*, *tuple*, and *dict*. It's a good habit to subtype one of the library's own types when a new class with similar functionality is added.

Let's look at an example: *distinctdist*. A subclass of *dict*, it differs in the fact that it raises a *ValueError* (alongside a help message) when a new entry with an identical value to previous entries is submitted:

```
>>> class DistinctError(Exception):
... pass
>>> class distinctdict(dict):
... def __setitem__(self, key, value):
... try:
... value_index = self.values().index(value)
... # keys() and values() will return
... # corresponding lists
... # as long as the dict is not changed
... # between the two calls
... # otherwise the dict type does not guarantee
... # the ordering.
... existing_key = self.keys()[value_index]
... if existing_key != key:
... raise DistinctError(("This value already
... "exists for '%s'") % \
... str(self[existing_key]))
```

```
... except ValueError:

... pass

...

... super(distinctdict, self).__setitem__(key, value)

...

>>> my = distinctdict()

>>> my['key'] = 'value'

>>> my['other_key'] = 'value'

Traceback (most recent call last):

File "<stdin>", line 1, in <module>

File "<stdin>", line 14, in __setitem__

ValueError: This value already exists for 'value'

>>> my['other_key'] = 'value2'

>>> my

{'other_key': 'value2', 'key': 'value'}
```

Go through your code now and then, and you may find that many of the class structures you create are similar to Python's own types. Using them will clean up your code and improve performance.

```
>>> class folder(list):

... def __init__(self, name):
```

```
... self.name = name

... def dir(self):

... print 'I am the %s folder.' % self.name

... for element in self:

... print element

...

>>> the = folder('secret')

>>> the

[]

>>> the.append('pics')

>>> the.append('videos')

>>> the.dir()

I am the secret folder:

pics

videos
```

Python 2.4 introduced *collections*, a module that can be used to create more resource-efficient container classes. It consists of the following types:

- *deque,* used to create a double-ended memory queue.

- *defaultdict,* used to provide default values for a dictionary-esque object.

Methods Belonging to Superclasses that Allow Access

Python's library includes a built-in type called *super* that allows an object to access its superclass attributes. Keep in mind that the documentation mentions it as a function and it is applied similarly, instead of a type. This might prove somewhat misleading, so let's look at an example:

```
>>> class Mama(object): # this is the old way
... def says(self):
... print 'do your homework'
...
>>> class Sister(Mama):
... def says(self):
... Mama.says(self)
... print 'and clean your bedroom'
...
>>> anita = Sister()
>>> anita.says()
do your homework
and clean your bedroom
```

Here, we use the *says()* method by calling the parent class *Mama* with *self* as the argument (in *Mama.says(self)*). The instance on which it is called will return *self*, which here is an instance of *Sister*.

Using *super,* this simplifies to:

```
>>> class Sister(Mama): # this is the new way

... def says(self):

... super(Sister, self).says()

... print 'and clean your bedroom'

...
```

This is a basic case, and unfortunately not everything can be as simple. Multiple inheritances can start to become clustered and confusing, and *super* usage starts to become unintuitive. To comprehend these problems further (which also includes cases where super use is not optimal), we must understand Python's Method Resolution Order (MRO).

Python's Method Resolution Order

A new MRO, based on a language called Dylan's MRO named C3, was added in version 2.3. A description of its function is linked here:

http://www.python.org/download/releases/2.3/mro.

Basically, C3 linearizes a class, also mentioned as precedence, by creating an ordered list of ancestor classes, and this list is used by *super* to look for attributes in parent classes. This served to clear up a problem that Python's older MRO method had, which resulted from combining types and classes into objects. For example, suppose a class has two ancestors:

```
>>> class Base1:
... pass
...
>>> class Base2:
... def method(self):
... print 'Base2'
...
>>> class MyClass(Base1, Base2):
... pass
...
>>> here = MyClass()
>>> here.method()
Base2
```

In this older MRO implementation process, *here.method* is called, and then the interpreter looks for it in *MyClass*, *Base1* and *Base2,* in that order. But adding a *BaseBase* class above *Base1* and *Base2* would make the search move from *MyClass* to *Base1* to *BaseBase* as a result of its "left to right, depth first" search algorithm, before moving to *Base2* as follows:

```
>>> class BaseBase:
... def method(self):
... print 'BaseBase'
...
>>> class Base1(BaseBase):
... pass
...
>>> class Base2(BaseBase):
... def method(self):
... print 'Base2'
...
>>> class MyClass(Base1, Base2):
... pass
...
>>> here = MyClass()
>>> here.method()
BaseBase
```

Prior to the introduction of objects, this was merely a theoretical problem; it would have rare to have encountered such a hierarchy of classes in practice. The introduction of *object* at the top of every hierarchy made this problem was making this issue appear throughout the entire system, thus introducing issues in subtyping. This made the previous MRO simply unfeasible, and a new MRO was introduced. Let's use a similar example to see how it works:

```
>>> class BaseBase(object):
... def method(self):
... print 'BaseBase'
...
>>> class Base1(BaseBase):
... pass
...
>>> class Base2(BaseBase):
... def method(self):
... print 'Base2'
...
>>> class MyClass(Base1, Base2):
... pass
...
```

```
>>> here = MyClass()

>>> here.method()

Base2
```

This new MRO uses a recursive call over all the base classes.

According to the documentation we mentioned, the symbolic notation of our example would be:

```
L[MyClass(Base1, Base2)] =

MyClass + merge(L[Base1], L[Base2], Base1, Base2)
```

wherein *L[MyClass]* refers to the *MyClass* linearization and *merge* is an algorithm that merges these linearized results. This algorithm is what keeps the ordering correct and removes duplications. It is described in further detail in the documentation as follows, (and we will substitute our example as necessary to help this description):

> Take the head of the first list, i.e L[Base1][0]; if this head is not in the tail of any of the other lists, then add it to the linearization of MyClass and remove it from the lists in the merge,

> otherwise, look at the head of the next list and take it, if it is a
>
> good head.
>
> Then repeat the operation until all the class is removed or it is
>
> impossible to find good heads. In this case, it is impossible to
>
> construct the merge, Python 2.3 will refuse to create the class
>
> MyClass and will raise an exception.

In this description *tail* is the first element and *head* refers to the remaining elements of a list. For instance, *Base1* would be the head of (*Base1, ... ,BaseN*), and the tail for (*Base2, ... ,BaseN*).

C3, thus, does a recursive loop, checking each parent. This produces a list that is then combined via a left-to-right rule into a hierarchy to allow a class to exist in multiple lists. This is the result:

```
>>> def L(klass):
... return [k.__name__ for k in klass.__mro__]
...
```

```
>>> L(MyClass)

['MyClass', 'Base1', 'Base2', 'BaseBase', 'object']
```

Things to Look out for When Using 'Super'

Super can prove quite treacherous to use, considering Python's method of initialization of classes. *__init__* does not call the base class implicitly, and the programmer themselves have to call it. What follow are examples of a few ways of how this can become a problem:

1. Mixing Super and Classic Calls

The following example depicts a C class using *__init__ to call base classes, which results in class B in the exampl*e called twice.

```
>>> class A(object):

... def ___init___(self):

... print "A"

... super(A, self).___init___()

...

>>> class B(object):

... def ___init___(self):

... print "B"

... super(B, self).___init___()
```

```
...
>>> class C(A,B):
... def ___init___(self):
... print "C"
... A.___init___(self)
... B.___init___(self)
...
>>> print "MRO:", [x.__name__ for x in C.__mro__]
MRO: ['C', 'A', 'B', 'object']
>>> C()
C A B B
<__main__.C object at 0xc4910>
```

Here, *A.__init__(self)* calls makes *super(A, self).__init__()* call *B*'s constructor. To clarify, *super* should be used in the whole class hierarchy, but a common issue is that a bit of this hierarchy would exist third-party code. Keep an eye out for whether there's a __mro__ attribute for the class before subclassing to minimize this issue. If there isn't, we can understand that this is an old-style class, and we should keep our use of *super* well away.

```
>>> from SimpleHTTPServer import
SimpleHTTPRequestHandler
```

```
>>> SimpleHTTPRequestHandler.__mro__

Traceback (most recent call last):

File "<stdin>", line 1, in <module>

AttributeError: class
SimpleHTTPRequestHandler has no attribute '__

mro__'
```

But if __mro__ is present, look at the constructors for the classes in the lists. If super is already there, it's safe to use them inside the subclasses. Again, if it isn't there, try not to deviate from the existing syntax.

A second example shows that we can use *collections.deque* safely because it is an immediate subclass of *object*, and thus we can use *super* safely.

```
>>> from collections import deque

>>> deque.__mro__

(<type 'collections.deque'>, <type 'object'>)
```

A third example demonstrates that *random.Random* is a wrapper, that lives in a *_random* module and exists around another class. Again, this should be stable due to it being a C module:

```
>>> from random import Random

>>> random.Random.__mro__

(<class 'random.Random'>, <type
'_random.Random'>, <type 'object'>)
```

Our last example is a Zope class, and it would be wise to thoroughly check the classes' constructors:

```
>>> from zope.app.container.browser.adding
import Adding

>>> Adding.__mro__

(<class
'zope.app.container.browser.adding.Adding'>,

<class 'zope.publisher.browser.BrowserView'>,

<class 'zope.location.location.Location'>,

<type 'object'>)
```

2. Heterogenous Arguments

Using *super* comes with another problem to consider: often passing an argument during initialization proves challenging. For example, a child class cannot call a parent class' __init__ code if it doesn't have the same signature. Consider the following:

```
>>> class BaseBase(object):
... def __init__(self):
... print 'basebase'
... super(BaseBase, self).__init__()
...
>>> class Base1(BaseBase):
... def __init__(self):
... print 'base1'
... super(Base1, self).__init__()
...
>>> class Base2(BaseBase):
... def __init__(self, arg):
... print 'base2'
... super(Base2, self).__init__()
...
>>> class MyClass(Base1 , Base2):
... def __init__(self, arg):
... print 'my base'
... super(MyClass, self).__init__(arg)
...
```

```
>>> m = MyClass(10)

my base

Traceback (most recent call last):

File "<stdin>", line 1, in <module>

File "<stdin>", line 4, in __init__

TypeError: __init__() takes exactly 1 argument
(2 given)
```

This might be solved using *args and **kw, making every class constructor pass along their parameters to all subclasses, even if they may prove redundant or go unused.

```
>>> class BaseBase(object):

... def __init__(self, *args, **kw):

... print 'basebase'

... super(BaseBase, self).__init__(*args, **kw)

...

>>> class Base1(BaseBase):

... def __init__(self, *args, **kw):

... print 'base1'

... super(Base1, self).__init__(*args, **kw)

...
```

```
>>> class Base2(BaseBase):

... def __init__(self, arg, *args, **kw):

... print 'base2'

... super(Base2, self).__init__(*args, **kw)

...

>>> class MyClass(Base1 , Base2):

... def __init__(self, arg):

... print 'my base'

... super(MyClass, self).__init__(arg)

...

>>> m = MyClass(10)

my base

base1

base2

basebase
```

But, due to constructors being able to accept any parameters in our fix, it's not optimal. Anything can be accepted, passed through and cause errors. One might consider using _init_ calls again in MyClass, but this would come back to the aforementioned problem.

A few tips to stay clear of these problems are as follows:

- Avoid multiple inheritance structures: Alternative syntaxes are discussed in a later section.

- Be mindful while using *super*: When using it, use it through all the structure or none of it, to remove possible confusion. Often, people shy away from *super* due to its more expansive code.

- Stay clear of mixing old style and new style classes: This interferes with Python's MRO.

- Class hierarchy needs to be looked over every time a parent class is to be called: Take a glance at the involved MRO (using __mro__) to debug any problem before they take root.

Descriptors and Properties

Python does not have a *private* keyword, which often throws programmers of other languages for a loop. The closest Python gets to it is its concept of 'name mangling': the interpreter renames any attribute prefixed by double underscores.

```
>>> class MyClass(object):
... __secret_value = 1
...
>>> instance_of = MyClass()
>>> instance_of.__secret_value
```

```
Traceback (most recent call last):
File "<stdin>", line 1, in <module>
AttributeError: 'MyClass' object has no attribute
'__secret_value'
>>> dir(MyClass)
['_MyClass__secret_value', '__class__', '__delattr__',
'__dict__',
'__doc__', '__getattribute__', '__hash__', '__init__',
'__module__',
'__new__', '__reduce__', '__reduce_ex__', '__repr__',
'__setattr__',
'__str__', '__weakref__']
>>> instance_of._MyClass__secret_value
1
```

Double underscores are used to reduce collision during inheritance, wherein the attribute is renamed to include a prefix, the class name, to identify it. It can still be accessed using this composed name, and thus it isn't a good idea to use the "__" prefix. Instead, a "_" prefix is conventional to use when an attribute is private. This doesn't mangle the name via the internal algorithms; it just provides documentation. Similar designs exist to allow public and private code parts to develop alongside, and they should be used to make a streamlined API.

Descriptor

A descriptor is, simply put, something that allows us to change what happens when an object's attribute is called.

To be more precise, they're a powerful (but technical) method of complex attribute access in Python. This makes them a fundamental puzzle piece of the language, and they're written into the libraries to define and implement things such ascvproperties, classes, static methods, and the *super* type. One can think of them as classes that define how other classes' attributes can be accessed, i.e. one class can act as a manager for other classes.

Three special methods define a descriptor class, and are what is implemented in the code to create one:

- *__set__* is called when a class attribute is set. We'll refer to this as a setter.

- *__get__* is called when a class attribute is read. We'll refer to this as a getter,

- *__delete__* is called when del is used on the attribute.

These are called before *__dict__*.

We present the following example:

```
# 1- looking for definition
if hasattr(MyClass, 'attribute'):
attribute = MyClass.attribute
AttributeClass = attribute.__class__
# 2 - does attribute definition has a setter ?
if hasattr(AttributeClass, '__set__'):
# let's use it
AttributeClass.__set__(attribute, instance,
value)
return
# 3 - regular way
instance.__dict__['attribute'] = value
# or 'attribute' is not found in __dict__
writable = (hasattr(AttributeClass, '__set__') or
'attribute' not in instance.__dict__)
if readable and writable:
# 4 – let's call the descriptor
return AttributeClass.__get__(attribute,
instance, MyClass)
```

```
# 5 - regular access with __dict__

return instance.__dict__['attribute']
```

Notice *instance*, an instance of *MyClass*, and how it's used. The getter and setter methods apply before the __dict__ mapping.

Let us create a data descriptor, and use an instance to work with it:

```
>>> class UpperString(object):
... def __init__(self):
... self._value = ''
... def __get__(self, instance, klass):
... return self._value
... def __set__(self, instance, value):
... self._value = value.upper()
...
>>> class MyClass(object):
... attribute = UpperString()
...
>>> instance_of = MyClass()
>>> instance_of.attribute
''
```

```
>>> instance_of.attribute = 'my value'

>>> instance_of.attribute

'MY VALUE'

>>> instance.__dict__ = {}
```

__dict__ will store any new attribute in the instance:

```
>>> instance_of.new_att = 1

>>> instance_of.__dict__

{'new_att': 1}
```

But the addition of a data descriptor will cause it to claim precedence over the __dict__:

```
>>> MyClass.new_att = MyDescriptor()

>>> instance_of.__dict__

{'new_att': 1}

>>> instance_of.new_att

''

>>> instance_of.new_att = 'other value'

>>> instance_of.new_att

'OTHER VALUE'
```

```
>>> instance_of.__dict__

{'new_att': 1}
```

This does not work with non-data descriptors, where the opposite precedence will occur:

```
>>> class Whatever(object):
... def __get__(self, instance, klass):
... return 'whatever'
...
>>> MyClass.whatever = Whatever()
>>> instance_of.__dict__
{'new_att': 1}
>>> instance_of.whatever
'whatever'
>>> instance_of.whatever = 1
>>> instance_of.__dict__
{'new_att': 1, 'whatever': 1}
```

The last rule avoids recursion while looking up class attributes.

The following example lays out an algorithm that sets an attribute to a value, similar to the one used to delete it as well:

```
# 1- looking for definition

if hasattr(MyClass, 'attribute'):

attribute = MyClass.attribute

AttributeClass = attribute.__class__

# 2 - does attribute definition has a setter ?

if hasattr(AttributeClass, '__set__'):

# let's use it

AttributeClass.__set__(attribute, instance,

value)

return

# 3 - regular way

instance.__dict__['attribute'] = value
```

We can use descriptor structures to create two very interesting things:

- Introspection descriptors, which uses the host class' singnature to compute something and

- Meta descriptors, which compute values using class methods.

Introspection Descriptors

Oftentimes, an inspection might be required by a class of its attributes. A method to achieve this is to create a property class that calculates and produces a documentation that can make methods to present to the code's public attributes and methods. Using the built-in function *dir,* we can build an example non-data descriptor that can work with any object of any type:

```
>>> class API(object):
... def _print_values(self, obj):
... def _print_value(key):
... if key.startswith('_'):
... return "
... value = getattr(obj, key)
... if not hasattr(value, 'im_func'):
... doc = type(value).__name__
... else:
... if value.__doc__ is None:
... doc = 'no docstring'
... else:
... doc = value.__doc__
... return ' %s : %s' % (key, doc)
... res = [_print_value(el) for el in dir(obj)]
... return '\n'.join([el for el in res
... if el != "])
```

```
... def __get__(self, instance, klass):

... if instance is not None:

... return self._print_values(instance)

... else:

... return self._print_values(klass)

...

>>> class MyClass(object):

... __doc__ = API()

... def __init__(self):

... self.a = 2

... def meth(self):

... """my method"""

... return 1

...

>>> MyClass.__doc__

' meth : my method'

>>> instance = MyClass()

>>> print instance.__doc__

a : int

meth : my method
```

The descriptor is defined so that it functions to filter away a particular kind of element; namely, those whose names begin with an underscore and use *docstrings.*

Meta-Descriptor

A meta-descriptor performs its function using the methods defined in a host class. This has a variety of uses, such as in trimming away code in writing a class that returns steps.

An example with a chaining descriptor, which calls a list of methods from a class and produces an array, is given as follows. We can also add a callback to control the code, and we can stop the process when it encounters an error.

```
>>> class Chainer(object):
... def __init__(self, methods, callback=None):
... self._methods = methods
... self._callback = callback
... def __get__(self, instance, klass):
... if instance is None:
... # only for instances
... return self
... results = []
... for method in self._methods:
```

```
... results.append(method(instance))

... if self._callback is not None:

... if not self._callback(instance,

... method,

... results):

... break

... return results
```

Following this example, we can allow for complex computation and even more complex structures by adding external methods, like a logger.

```
>>> class TextProcessor(object):

... def __init__(self, text):

... self.text = text

... def normalize(self):

... if isinstance(self.text, list):

... self.text = [t.lower()

... for t in self.text]

... else:

... self.text = self.text.lower()

... def split(self):
```

```
... if not isinstance(self.text, list):
... self.text = self.text.split()
... def threshold(self):
... if not isinstance(self.text, list):
... if len(self.text) < 2:
... self.text = ''
... self.text = [w for w in self.text
... if len(w) > 2]
...
>>> def logger(instance, method, results):
... print 'calling %s' % method.__name__
... return True
...
>>> def add_sequence(name, sequence):
... setattr(TextProcessor, name,
... Chainer([getattr(TextProcessor, n)
... for n in sequence], logger))
```

Here, *add_sequence* allows a programmer to dynamically define a new descriptor to continue the chain, which functions the same as the same and calls the same methods. We can save this new combination in the class' definition.

```
>>> add_sequence('simple_clean', ('split', 'treshold'))
>>> my = TextProcessor(' My Taylor is Rich ')
>>> my.simple_clean
calling split
calling treshold
[None, None]
>>> my.text
['Taylor', 'Rich']
>>> # let's perform another sequence
>>> add_sequence('full_work', ('normalize',
... 'split', 'treshold'))
>>> my.full_work
calling normalize
calling split
calling treshold
[None, None, None]
>>> my.text
['taylor', 'rich']
```

Remember, Python allows for a lot of flexibility in its structures, and descriptors are no exception; they can be added during program runtime to perform meta-programming.

Properties

Python has its own, pre-built descriptor in its library, called Properties. This is a generally powerful tool which can link methods to attributes.

Four arguments, *fget, fset, fdel,* and *doc*, can be passed to it, though it can do something when only the first is passed, the rest of them being optional additions. *doc*, the last argument, defines a *docstring* attached to the attribute in similar fashion as a method:

```
>>> class MyClass(object):
... def __init__(self):
... self._my_secret_thing = 1
...
... def _i_get(self):
... return self._my_secret_thing
...
... def _i_set(self, value):
... self._my_secret_thing = value
...
... def _i_delete(self):
... print 'neh!'
...
```

```
... my_thing = property(_i_get, _i_set, _i_delete,

... 'the thing')

...

>>> instance_of = MyClass()

>>> instance_of.my_thing

1

>>> instance_of.my_thing = 3

>>> instance_of.my_thing

3

>>> del instance_of.my  thing

neh !

>>> help(instance_of)

Help on MyClass in module __main__ object:

class MyClass(__built-in__.object)

| Methods defined here:

|

| __init__(self)

|

| ----------------------------------------------------

| Data descriptors defined here:
```

```
| ...
| my_thing
| the thing
```

Properties make descriptors easier to implement, though care must be taken when inheritance between classes is involved. The attribute that it creates is dynamic, using the current class, and does not mesh with derived classes' methods, against common and intuitive language implementor syntax. For example:

```
>>> class FirstClass(object):
... def _get_price(self):
... return '$500'
... price = property(_get_price)
...
>>> class SecondClass(FirstClass):
... def _get_price(self):
... return '$20'
...
...
>>> plane_ticket = SecondClass()
>>> plane_ticket.price
'$500'
```

The above code does not work as intended.

We can remedy the issue by manually redirecting the property instance towards the method that we want it to interact with, using another method:

```
>>> class FirstClass(object):
... def _get_price(self):
... return '$500'
... def _get_the_price(self):
... return self._get_price()
... price = property(_get_the_price)
...
>>> class SecondClass(FirstClass):
... def _get_price(self):
... return '$20'
...
>>> plane_ticket = SecondClass()
>>> plane_ticket.price
'$20'
```

But often, this would prove to be a bad practice, since properties mask complexity and its methods are not public. We might want to override the property instead, as follows:

```
>>> class FirstClass(object):

... def _get_price(self):

... return '$500'

... price = property(_get_price)

...

>>> class SecondClass(FirstClass):

... def _cheap_price(self):

... return '$20'

... price = property(_cheap_price)

...

>>> plane_ticket = SecondClass()

>>> plane_ticket.price

'$20'
```

Slots

Slots are a curious feature of Python that, rather unfortunately, goes underused by most programmers. This method allows users to create a list of static attributes for a given class, and permits users to ignore '__dict__' initialization. Slots can also be used to create a form of class whose signature can be frozen, which can be a useful tool for a variety of things.

```
>>> class Frozen(object):

... __slots__ = ['ice', 'cream']

...

>>> '__dict__' in dir(Frozen)

False

>>> 'ice' in dir(Frozen)

True

>>> glagla = Frozen()

>>> glagla.ice = 1

>>> glagla.cream = 1

>>> glagla.icy = 1

Traceback (most recent call last):

File "<stdin>", line 1, in <module>

AttributeError: 'Frozen' object has no attribute 'icy'
```

This won't work for derived classes, since new attributes will be added to __dict__

Meta-Programming

The newer methods of making classes in Python, referred to as *new-style,* have a few neat tricks up their sleeves. We can change the definitions of classes and objects as and when we please. To this end, _new__ and_metaclass__ were introduced; two special methods that serve to allow us to change definitions. Let's have a look at them now.

The '__new__' method

__new__ is a special, purpose-built method. It is a meta-constructor; it is called every time a new instance of an object is produced, such as by the class *factory* in the following example:

```
>>> class MyClass(object):
... def __new__(cls):
... print '__new__ called'
... return object.__new__(cls) # default factory
... def __init__(self):
... print '__init__ called'
... self.a = 1
...
>>> instance = MyClass()
__new__ called
__init__ called
```

An instance of the class is returned by this method, making it useful in determining the object constructor's state by allowing us to access the class and make changes after or before an object is created. We can monitor the constructor's state, for example, or add a forced initialization method for the constructor to obey.

Let's look at another example of how we can use __new__. __init__ calls aren't implicit in child classes, and our new method can be used to make sure that such an initialization occurs through all the hierarchy.

```
>>> class MyOtherClassWithoutAConstructor(MyClass):
... pass
>>> instance = MyOtherClassWithoutAConstructor()
__new__ called
__init__ called
>>> class MyOtherClass(MyClass):
... def __init__(self):
... print 'MyOther class __init__ called'
... super(MyOtherClass, self).__init__()
... self.b = 2
>>> instance = MyOtherClass()
__new__ called
MyOther class __init__ called
__init__ called
```

In particular, things like database initialization and network socketing are easily achieved using this method, because it tells us when the class must be initialized and when it can simply be derived from somewhere else.

Threading, using the *Thread* class and the *threading* module, uses this process to make sure all instances are initialized properly. This occurs through assertions over the methods (*assert self.__initialized*), and can be reduced to a single call in __new__, otherwise the instance will not be functional:

```
>>> from threading import Thread
>>> class MyThread(Thread):
... def __init__(self):
... pass
...
>>> MyThread()
Traceback (most recent call last):
File "<stdin>", line 1, in <module>
File "/Library/Frameworks/Python.framework/Versions/2.5/lib/python2.5/threading.py", line 416, in __repr__
```

```
assert self.__initialized, "Thread.__init__() was not
called"

AssertionError: Thread.__init__() was not called
```

The '__metaclass__' Method

Metaclasses allow a programmer to interact, via a factory, with class objects as soon as they are created. The standard factory is the built-in type '*type*', which takes in arguments such as names, base classes, and attributes, and produces a new class instance. This behavior is like how __new__ functions, but only in the domain of classes.

```
>>> def method(self):
... return 1
...
>>> klass = type('MyClass', (object,), {'method':
method})
>>> instance = klass()
>>> instance.method()
1
```

You might notice how this bears similarities to how classes are defined explicitly:

```
>>> class MyClass(object):
```

```
... def method(self):

... return 1

...

>>> instance = MyClass()

>>> instance.method()

1
```

This metaclass method often proves valuable to have in a developer's mental toolkit, allowing to interact with class creation before or after a *type* call has gone through. A specially constructed attribute links a custom factory to a class.

A class definition can accept __metaclass__, permitting it to interact with newly-initialized objects. This attribute must be set to something accept the same arguments as *type*. This something can be anything (that follows the rule) such as an unbound function. An example describes such a function, where an API descriptor is added to the class if the *docstring* is empty.

```
>>> def equip(classname, base_types, dict):

... if '__doc__' not in dict:

... dict['__doc__'] = API()

... return type(classname, base_types, dict)

...
```

```
>>> class MyClass(object):

...     __metaclass__ = equip

...     def alright(self):

...         """the ok method"""

...         return 'okay'

...

>>> ma = MyClass()
>>> ma.__class__
<class '__main__.MyClass'>
>>> ma.__class__.__dict__['__doc__'] # __doc__
is replaced !
<__main__.API object at 0x621d0>
>>> ma.y = 6
>>> print ma.__doc__
alright : the ok method
y : int
```

We need __new__ to do this since __doc__ is a read-only attribute of type, the language's built-in base metaclass.

Metaclasses do have drawbacks, but code written that includes them is often extremely dense and complicated. Their interaction with class hierarchy structures threatens the stability and security of the code. This can prove to be the case in things like implementing slots. Also, easier methods exist for situations where this complexity becomes redundant; simpler things such as changing readwrite attributes. Often, these prove easier to work with since the restriction of working in one class is removed.

We can change class attributes by creating an enhancement function, which we can use to apply two particular behaviours, as follows:

```
>>> def enhancer_1(klass):
... c = [l for l in klass.__name__ if l.isupper()]
... klass.contracted_name = ''.join(c)
...
>>> def enhancer_2(klass):
... def logger(function):
... def wrap(*args, **kw):
... print 'I log everything !'
... return function(*args, **kw)
... return wrap
... for el in dir(klass):
... if el.startswith('_'):
... continue
... value = getattr(klass, el)
```

```
... if not hasattr(value, 'im_func'):

... continue

... setattr(klass, el, logger(value))

...

>>> def enhance(klass, *enhancers):

... for enhancer in enhancers:

... enhancer(klass)

...

>>> class MySimpleClass(object):

... def ok(self):

... """I return ok"""

... return 'I lied'

...

>>> enhance(MySimpleClass, enhancer_1,
enhancer_2)

>>> thats = MySimpleClass()

>>> thats.ok()

I log everything !

'I lied'

>>> thats.score
```

```
>>> thats.contracted_name
'MSC'
```

This is a powerful tool to have, since this allows us to create multiple variations on the fly, in one pre-instantiated class.

To conclude, metaclasses and dynamic enhancers are only "addons" of sorts and, if not used carefully, can make clean code turn into a giant mess. We suggest using them at the framework level, where multiple classes need to be made to adhere to a specific behavior. Also, when sure, the behaviors that we add aren't interacting with class features; logging, for example.

Chapter Four

Selecting Appropriate Names

Today, the majority of Python's standard library is built while keeping the convenience and usability level for the programmer as a priority. To understand this better, consider built-in types for a second. They have been designed so that the process of implementing these types feels not only nature but also easy to understand and use. Similarly, if we take the usability, understandability, and ease of use of the Python programming language as a whole, we can even compare it to pseudo-codes. To elaborate, most times Python code can be easily comprehended by almost anyone due to the simplicity of the syntax. Take these two lines of Python code as an example;

```
>>> if 'd' not in my_list:
... my_list.append('d')
```

Just from reading the if statement, one can understand the purpose of the second line of code and the condition without even needing to know that the **my_list.append** argument is a function. One naturally obtains the context which makes Python more preferable over technical and old-school programming languages such as C and C++. Due to the ease and convenience of using Python, the programmer's focus isn't stressed to the maximum, instead, programmers usually find their thought flow to be transferred into lines of code swiftly.

In this chapter, we will be mainly discussing a few of the best, easy to understand, and easy to implement practices in writing codes are:

1. PEP 8 and naming best practices (naming conventions use)

Python Enhanced Proposal (PEP) 8 and Naming Best Practices

You can find basic guidance on python code writing by PEP which includes the following:

1.   Style guide

2.   Basic rules i.e. detail about the layout of the code

3.   Naming conventions which are referred for codebases

Under the current heading, a summarized view of the PEP and guidance on naming best practices for the various elements are given.

Naming Styles

There are five naming styles given below which are applied in Python:

1. **CamelCase**

2. **_leading** and **trailing_** underscores, and sometimes **__doubled__**

3. **lowercase** and **lower_case_with_underscores**

4. **mixedCase**

5. **UPPERCASE**, and
   UPPER_CASE_WITH_UNDERSCORES

The above styles in a glance show the type of style followed for writing code with the use of underscores and different case types e.g. Words are capitalized and grouped in CamelCase, this style is similar to mixedCase with the difference that the latter starts with characters of the lower case.

The elements whether uppercase or lowercase are mostly one-word or grouped words. Whereas usually abbreviated phrases are written with underscores. Still, for writing codes, single words used are a better option. In codes, special elements and privacy are marked by underscores (leading and trailing). The styles discussed above have application in the following elements:

- Classes
- Functions and methods
- Properties
- Variables

Variables: In python, these are of two types, i.e Constants, Public and Private variables

Constants: for this type of variable style used is Uppercase with an underscore. This is also referred to as constant global variables. The developer is able to identify that the variables used are of a constant value.

An example of this is the '**doctest**' module. To define the purpose for the given options, a list is available in this module stating the directives and option flags written as short sentences. (for further details http://docs.python.org/lib/doctest-options.html):

>>> from doctest import IGNORE_EXCEPTION_DETAIL

>>> from doctest import REPORT_ONLY_FIRST_FAILURE

The names of the two variables as given above might seem long initially, but the need to clearly define these is more important. These variables play their part in the initialization code and not within the code hence the length of it can be ignored.

In the same way, names of constant variables are given on the basis of their application or connection to technology. For example in the '**os**' module, the EX_XXX is a constant defined on the C side which describes exception numbers.

```
>>> import os
>>> try:
...     os._exit(0)
... except os.EX_SOFTWARE:
...     print 'internal software error'
...     raise
```

When constants are intended for the similar operations the preferred practice is collecting them at the top of the module which is using these constants and combining the same under newer variables:

```
>>> import doctest
>>> TEST_OPTIONS = (doctest.ELLIPSIS |
...             doctest.NORMALIZE_WHITESPACE |
...             doctest.REPORT_ONLY_FIRST_FAILURE)
```

Naming and Usage

A Python program is based on a list of values, which are defined using constant variables. The file name used for default configuration is an example of such a value. It would be a comfortable habit to place all such constant variables into one place, i.e. a file.

This is exactly the basis on which the Python tool '**Django**' functions. Here's a module '**config.py**' which contains all of the necessary constants.

```
# config.py SQL_USER = 'tarek'
SQL_PASSWORD = 'secret'
SQL_URI = 'postgres://%s:%s@localhost/db' % \
        (SQL_USER, SQL_PASSWORD)
MAX_THREADS = 4
```

Alternate approaches exist towards this problem, such as making a configuration file that can be read using *ConfigParser* (a Python library module) or even something like *ZConfig* (a very advanced tool that parses through the file in *Zope*). This might prove to be excessive, since Python's native file format already allows a good amount of freedom up front in editing files. A good habit is to use Boolean operations with all the options that can be used as flags, akin to the **doctest** and **re** modules.

The simplicity of the **doctest** pattern can be seen below:

```
>>> OPTIONS = {}
>>> def register_option(name):
...     return OPTIONS.setdefault(name, 1 << len(OPTIONS))
>>> def has_option(options, name):
...     return bool(options & name)
>>> # now defining options
>>> BLUE = register_option('BLUE')
>>> RED = register_option('RED')
>>> WHITE = register_option('WHITE')
>>>
>>> # let's try them
>>> SET = BLUE | RED
>>> has_option(SET, BLUE)
True
>>> has_option(SET, WHITE)
False
```

Whenever another set of constants is created, keep in mind that the module's name is a common prefix in and of itself. Thus, it would be a good idea to not use such a name, unless the module already contains multiple sets of constants.

Public and Private Variables

The lower case accompanied by an underscore is used to protect mutable and public global variables.

But for the protection of global variables, mostly the module itself provides getters and setters which work with these variables, thus making the use of the aforementioned variables obsolete.

Note here that the variable can be marked as private element of the package by addition of a leading underscore:

```
>>> _observers = []
>>> def add_observer(observer):
...     _observers.append(observer)
>>> def get_observers():
...     """Makes sure _observers cannot be modified."""
...     return tuple(_observers)
```

Variables are considered local to the context when they are stored in a function or method, which prohibits them from being flagged as private. This also means that they are bound to the same rules. The private marker is only used for instances or class variables in situations where the information received isn't significant or relevant enough to be acted upon or simply ignored, via making the variable part of the function's public signature.

Before we go any further, we must understand the use of the 'private marker' (remember that the private marker refers to the underscore symbol in the leading position). The recommended use of private markers in the case of classes or even instance variables is extremely limited due to high potentials of redundancy. The only case that makes sense to employ private markers is when the given public signature's variable is named in such a way that it does not propagate a context or if it is simply redundant.

To better understand this, consider that the variable has a specified role of providing a public feature and is being used internally in the method, then in this scenario, making the variable private is obviously the better option. An example of this is given below:

```
>>> class Citizen(object):
...    def __init__(self):
...        self._message = 'Go boys'
...    def _get_message(self):
...        return self._message
...    kane = property(_get_message)
>>> Citizen().kane
'Go boys'
```

A variable maintaining an internal state would also be a relevant example. The value takes part in the class's behavior even though the rest of the code does not get any benefit from it:

```
>>> class MeanElephant(object):
...     def __init__(self):
...         self._people_to_kill = []
...     def is_slapped_on_the_butt_by(self, name):
...         self._people_to_kill.append(name)
...         print 'Ouch!' ...     def revenge(self):
...         print '10 years later...'
...         for person in self._people_to_kill:
...             print 'Me kill %s' % person
>>> joe = MeanElephant()
>>> joe.is_slapped_on_the_butt_by('Tarek')
Ouch!
>>> joe.is_slapped_on_the_butt_by('Bill')
Ouch!
>>> joe.revenge()
10 years later...
Me kill Tarek
Me kill Bill
```

Functions and Methods

The rules of using lower cases with underscores in functions and methods are not universally true. In the standard library, the use of style *mixedCase* can be located in modules e.g. in the *threading* modules *currentThread* is evidence of the *mixedCase* style.

The *mixedCase* style of methods writing became obsolete because of lowercase use, which has become the standard. But the use of this style can be seen in frameworks like *Zope,* which has a rather large community of developers working it. The definite drive behind opting between the two i.e lowercase with underscore or mixedCase is the library being used.

Developing such an application is not an easy feat which intermixes modules importing Zope code and modules of pure Python, because doing so requires the developer's consistency.

Still, classes in Zope mix both these conventional types of modules because of the evolution of a codebase into an egg-based framework. In such frameworks, each module is comparatively closer to pure Python.

Having a library environment of the type discussed above, the acceptable standard of practice is that all the code be kept in PEP 8 style except for elements that are exposed in the framework for which mixedCase can be used.

The Private Controversy

Conventionally the addition of a leading underscore is for private functions and methods. The feature of Python mangling names made this rule very debatable.

In the instances where a method is named such that it has two underscores, the interpreter changed the name during the process to prevent any name clashes between the method and that of the subclass. Many people also prevent name classes in subclasses, by using double leading underscores in naming private attributes:

```
>>> class Base(object):
... def __secret(self):
... print "don't tell"
... def public(self):
... self.__secret()
>>> Base.__secret
Traceback (most recent call last):
File "<stdin>", line 1, in <module>
AttributeError: type object 'Base' has no attribute '__secret'
>>> dir(Base)
['_Base__secret', ..., 'public']
>>> class Derived(Base):
... def __secret(self):
... print "never ever"
>>> Derived().public()
don't tell
```

The drive behind the feature of name mangling / decoration in Python was to make sure that clashes in subclasses are subtly prevented by base classes, in particular cases of multiple inheritance contexts unlike that of a private trick in C++. It was the opinion of a few that name mangling should at all times be clear-cut because the feature makes the code in private complicated when used for every attribute, which fails the purpose of Pyhton:

> >>> class Base(object):
>
> ... def _Base_secret(self): # don't do this !!!
>
> ... print "you told it ?"

Special Methods
Double underscores are added at the start and end of a name in special methods only and it is required that the same convention not be used in normal methods the given link can be referred for this topic (http://docs.python.org/ref/specialnames.html)

Special methods have application for container definitions, operator overloading etc. Gathering these at the start of class definitions is for the ease of interpretation:

> ... def __add__(self, other):
>
> ... return int.__add__(self, other) + 1
>
> ... def __repr__(self):
>
> ... return '<weirdo %d>' % self
>
> ... #

```
... # public API
... #
... def do_this(self):
... print 'this'
... def do_that(self):
... print 'that'
```

Names of this type should not be used in any case for a normal method. The given example is for understanding that for normal methods you should not create such names:

```
>>> class BadHabits(object):
... def __my_method__(self):
... print 'ok'
```

Arguments

For expressing arguments lowercase characters are used and underscores are added where needed. Similar rules for naming are followed as those for variables.

Properties

Lowercase or lowercase with underscores are used to express the names of properties. These names usually represent the state of the object. This state is expressed in the form of an adjective, a noun or it can be a small phrase where needed:

```
>>> class Connection(object):
... _connected = []
```

```
...     def connect(self, user):
...         self._connected.append(user)
...     def _connected_people(self):
...         return '\n'.join(self._connected)
...     connected_people = property(_connected_people)
>>> my = Connection()
>>> my.connect('Tarek')
>>> my.connect('Shannon')
>>> print my.connected_people
Tarek
Shannon
```

Classes

The most common and widespread way to name classes is in CamelCase. These may have a leading underscore to denote the fact that it is privately inside a module. These variables are often nouns and noun phrases, which helps develop an intrinsic and intuitive logic in relating these names to the verb-based method names.

```
>>> class Database(object):
...     def open(self):
...         pass
>>> class User(object):
...     pass
>>> user = User()
```

```
>>> db = Database()
>>> db.open()
```

Modules and Packages

Commonly names of modules are written in lowercase without any underscores, but in special modules underscores are used e.g. __*init*__. From the standard library common module names are given here as an example:

1. *os*

2. *sys*

3. *shutil*

The addition of a leading underscore to the module name indicates that it is private to the package. Most of the assembled C / C++ modules have underscores in their names and imported into the pure Python modules. Packages follow similar rules because in the namespace they are not much different from modules.

Naming Guide

For naming functions, methods, properties, and variables a common set of rules are applied. Names given to modules and classes hold a significant place due to their impact on the construction of namespace, as a result, their impact is also reflected in the readability of the code. A comprehensive guide is given here to gain an understanding of picking names through familiar patterns and antipatterns.

Use "has" or "is" Prefix for Boolean Elements:

When the value of an element is of Boolean nature, then adding a prefix i.e is / has etc. improve readability and names are easily understood in the namespace:

```
>>> class DB(object):
...     is_connected = False
...     has_cache = False
>>> database = DB()
>>> database.has_cache
False
>>> if database.is_connected:
...     print "That's a powerful class"
... else:
...     print "No wonder..."
No wonder...
```

Use Plural for Elements That Are Sequences

Opting to use plural forms is a better choice where elements are holding a sequence. On sequence-like exposure, mappings can are also likely to gain an advantage.

```
>>> class DB(object):
... connected_users = ['Tarek']
... tables = {'Customer': ['id', 'first_name',
... 'last_name']}
```

Use Explicit Names for Dictionaries

It is required that a clear / explicit name be used in all possibilities whenever a variable holds a mapping. An example is that the name *person_contact* can be assigned to a *dict* if it has contacts of a few persons:

>>> person_address = {'Bill': '6565 Monty Road',

... 'Pamela': '45 Python street'}

>>> person_address['Pamela']

'45 Python street'

Avoiding Generic Names

Names such as dict, elements, list, and sequences are fairly commonplace and generic. As such, they stand to cause much confusion and make understanding the code harder by obfuscating what variable stands for what. But these can be used by the code in creating an abstract datatype. Another tip is to refrain from using prebuilt names, so that names in the current namespace database stay clear of shadowing. Use generic verbs only if they make sense in context, and use terms specific to your current topic instead of more generic catch-all terms (such as *displayNumber* as opposed to a generic *compute*).

>>> def compute(data): # too generic

... for element in data:

... yield element * 12

>>> def display_numbers(numbers): # better

... for number in numbers:

... yield number * 12

Avoid Redundancy from Existing Names

It becomes very confusing and is also considered an unlikable practice when such names that have been given in the context are used. Readability in general and debugging in specific becomes confusing and difficult to interpret.

```
>>> def bad_citizen():
... os = 1
... import pdb; pdb.set_trace()
... return os
>>> bad_citizen()
> <stdin>(4)bad_citizen()
(Pdb) os
1
(Pdb) import os
(Pdb) c
<module 'os' from
'/Library/Frameworks/Python.framework/Versions/2.5/
lib/python2.5/os.
pyc'>
```

It's evident in the example above that *os* is shadowed by the code. Take care to avoid using module names and built-in names that already exist and are in use by the standard library.

The creation of original names regardless of their being local to the context is a good practice. A trailing underscore is used to avoid a collision for a keyword:

```
>>> def xapian_query(terms, or_=True):
... """if or_ is true, terms are combined
... with the OR clause"""
... pass
```

It should be noted here how the term *class* is mostly substituted with *klass* or *cls*:

```
>>> def factory(klass, *args, **kw):
... return klass(*args, **kw)
```

Tips for Dealing with Arguments

Function signatures and methods are the first line of defense for code integrity. These serve to build up a code block's API and drive its usage. Special care must be taken in naming the arguments for these, in compliance with the rules for naming things that we've discussed. These guidelines should be kept in mind:

- Building arguments using Iterative Design.

- Trusting your tests and the arguments.

- Careful use of *args and **kw magic arguments.

Building Arguments by Iterative Design

A clean, well-defined list of arguments that each function should accept helps make a code stronger and more robust, but this isn't something that can be done in one go. This problem nudges us towards exploring an iterative ideology of designing arguments. These arguments should be built so that they show the exact purpose and use of their elements, and change as required by the system.

In cases where arguments are to be joined, it is required that the individual default values are maintained for prevention of any setback:

```
>>> class BD(object): # version 1
... def _query(self, query, type):
... print 'done'
... def execute(self, query):
... self._query(query, 'EXECUTE')
>>> BD().execute('my query')
done
>>> import logging
>>> class BD(object): # version 2
... def _query(self, query, type, logger):
... logger('done')
... def execute(self, query, logger=logging.info):
... self._query(query, 'EXECUTE', logger)
>>> BD().execute('my query') # old-style call
```

```
>>> BD().execute('my query', logging.warning)
WARNING:root:done
```

The change in the argument of public element is brought by deprecation process for making the previous state obsolete.

Have Confidence in the Arguments and Tests

Benefiting from Python's dynamic typing nature, assertions are employed on top of functions and methods by programmers, to ensure that the arguments being written are correct.

```
>>> def division(dividend, divisor):
... assert type(dividend) in (long, int, float)
... assert type(divisor) in (long, int, float)
... return dividend / divisor
>>> division(2, 4)
0
>>> division(2, 'okok')
Traceback (most recent call last):
File "<stdin>", line 1, in <module>
File "<stdin>", line 3, in division
AssertionError
```

The technique is mostly adopted by those developers quite familiar with static typing and feels the need to add something to Python. The Design by Contract style of programming checks argument in such a way, that before running the code, preconditions have to be verified. But this style has a few problems as well which are given below:

1. Its readability is negatively impacted because the DbC's code explains its use.

2. And it is lag-prone due to an assertion being made on every call.

Choosing a Name for the Class

Whenever you are defining a class, it is recommended to specify a corresponding name with the following features; conciseness, precision, and enough context that the user immediately has an idea of the main purpose of the class. To accommodate all of these features within the namespace for a class, experienced programmers usually choose a suitable suffix. This suffix allows the class's name to propagate its intricate features like its type or even the nature of the class. Here's a list of classes whose name follow the suggestions we have discussed so far in this section;

- SQL**Engine**

- Mime**Types**

- String**Widget**

- Test**Case**

By now, you must have gotten a pretty good idea of what we're talking about. For the purpose of naming classes that are either **base** or **abstract**, using a suffix is not sufficient anymore. For such cases, it is recommended to add a prefix instead that explicitly states the class type, i.e, whether it is a base class or an abstract class. The following examples demonstrate this.

- **Base**Cookie

- **Abstract**Formatter

Out of all these things, the most important thing to always be wary of is consistency and avoiding redundancy. This can be easily avoidable if one is conscious of his naming scheme so as to take care that no name becomes redundant. Usually, the most commonplace for redundancy is to repeat the name of the attribute in the class's name as well. For instance;

```
>>> SMTP.smtp_send()   # redundant information in the
namespace
>>> SMTP.send()              # more readable and
mnemonic
```

Names of Modules and Packages

Generally, the names of modules and packages are purposed so that the user reading them immediately has an idea of its corresponding contents and useful function, but this is done so that the names are not lengthy. Instead, the standard names of modules and packages are usually kept concise, without any uppercases (only lowercase is used as standard). Most of all, there is no preference for symbols such as underscores. Here's an example of the names of modules and packages. Notice how they are easy to comprehend, concise, lowercase, and have no special characters or symbols.

- **sqlite**

- **postgres**

- **shal**

If a module or a package is supposed to implement a protocol, then the common approach to accommodate such a feature into their names is to include the suffix of '**lib**'. Examples have been listed below;

>>> import smtplib
>>> import urllib
>>> import telnetlib

Another important thing to be wary of when naming modules and packages is that the corresponding namespaces should always be consistent. If the naming scheme of modules and packages are inconsistent, i.e, a few modules follow one pattern while others follow a different pattern, it causes inconsistency, and using the modules in code becomes a pain. The same is the case for packages as well.

>> from widgets.stringwidgets import TextWidget   # bad
>>> from widgets.strings import TextWidget   # better

Before wrapping things up for this chapter, there's one final tip when naming modules. There are times when a module is not as simple as its name makes it out to be. For instance, a module's contents can be quite diverse, i.e, featuring a plethora of classes. Since we discussed at the start that the naming scheme for a module should reflect its contents and purpose, naming such a module becomes quite tricky. The recommended way to tackle such a hurdle is to simply build a package and then divide its contents into different modules and name them accordingly. In this way, we simplify the module and simplify the naming process for the module.

Chapter Five

Creating Packages in Python

Creating software packages is one of the most common applications of the Python programming language. As such, the discussion will be focused on going through the process that will allow us to create Python packages and release them as well. In addition, the process of creating and releasing Python packages can be repeated several times in one coding session enabling the user to make several packages for different applications.

One might wonder as to what is the underlying purpose or even the advantages of learning how to create packages when coding in Python. To answer as well as explain the productivity of creating Python packages, here are a few key points that might help provide the appropriate context;

- Packages basically prime the resources that the programmer needs in later stages of app development. In simpler terms, the programmer won't need to allocate his time towards doing the initial set-ups.

- The process explained in this chapter to create Python packages does not revolve around experimental techniques or workarounds. The method that we will explore is not only preferred by many programmers due to its popularity but it is also easy to understand.

- The discussion of creating Python packages will also facilitate programmers that adopt the 'test-driven' approach towards the development of their projects making the implementation relatively easier.

- The releasing process is also made easier with the help of packages.

A Common Pattern for Every Python Package

Whenever we create an application, we will usually have to throw in many code lines. Even the most simple of applications can have anywhere from 25 to 150 lines of code. This can make the readability, maintenance, updates, patches, bug fixes, and even debugging of the application quite overwhelming for anyone. To keep things as simple as possible, we employ different techniques to organize the application's source code. One such approach towards organizing lines of code is to use 'eggs'.

An 'egg' is basically a term that is used to refer to a specific portion of the application's source code. Apart from being a simply definitive term, 'egg' is also a functional element in Python programming as well. In other words, we divide the entire code into different sections, and each section is then put into different packages by using eggs. In this way, the application's source code becomes much easier to work with and if needed, the programmer can also reuse portions for another project as well. This definitely makes the life of programmers considerably easier as they can reuse code conveniently. From this perspective, packages function as individual components that, together, build the entire application. In this way, we can simply create every Python package by incorporating an egg structure to split different code blocks for an application.

This section will mainly be using the functionality provided by the two Python modules, which are **'distutils'** and **'setuptools'** to create **'namespaced packages'**. You will learn the process of organizing, releasing, and distributing a **'namespaced package'** using these Python modules as well.

Creating eggs is pretty simple and straight-forward. Just as how an egg can be broken to reveal the yellow and white parts of the egg (yolk and albumen respectively), in programming, an egg can be created by putting different portions of code inside a nested folder. To elaborate, we create a parent folder and then put one package inside this folder, then we create a sub-folder and place another package inside it, and so on. When creating 'namespaced packages' using eggs, the important thing is for every sub-folder to have a name used by the parent folder. For instance, if we create a 'namespace package' by using eggs and the root folder's name is 'python.advanced', then the name of the subfolders should always have at least a prefix that's common with the root folder's namespace. In this case, if we were to create two sub-folders, then we could name the first one 'python' and the other 'advanced'.

A good practice when creating 'namespace packages' is to define the nature of the code in the namespace itself. For instance, if the code lines in our package are meant to deal with an SQL database, we can have something like this for the root folder's namespace; 'python.sql'. We can then have two folders with 'python' and 'sql' namespaces accordingly.

Using the 'setup.py' Script in Namespaced Packages

Since we are dealing with nested folders, it is important to have a script capable of managing the successive executions of the packages housed in different sub-folders. We can think of this script as a game's installation wizard that decompresses an entire game even though the game data is split into several individual zip files.

The 'setup.py' script is always placed within the root directory of the nested folders to ensure that this script is the first to be executed. What's the point if the main controlling mechanism is the first one? initialized later on? The anatomy of this script isn't too complex as well. It only consists of the metadata leveraged from the Python module 'distutils' bundled into arguments which ultimately set a call to a function known as 'setup()'. By using the 'setuptools' module, we can extend this function to create the necessary egg structure for our different packages.

Depending on the programmer's needs, they can easily create their own custom setup.py script file but the bare minimum to make one is to use the following two lines of code;

```
from setuptools import setup

setup(name='acme.sql')
```

Now let's briefly discuss the function being used to specify the egg's parent folder's name, i.e, **setup()**. What we see here is a slight demonstration of the arguments that can be used with the functions. In the upcoming sections, you will see that we will define many other package elements using this particular function. The setup.py file's purpose is to set the stage for us to execute more instructions (through commands) needed for creating packages. While we cannot discuss every available command right here and now, the module provides a full command list that users can review. To bring up the command list, we simply access an option known as '--help-commands'. This has been demonstrated below for the sake of convenience;

```
$ python setup.py --help-commands
Standard commands:
 build                   build everything needed to install
 ...
install install       everything from build directory
sdist                   create a source distribution
register                register the distribution
bdist                   create a built (binary) distribution
Extra commands:
develop               install package in 'development mode'
 ...
```

test	run unit tests after in-place build
alias	defines a shortcut
bdist_egg	create an "egg" distribution

The commands that are used commonly and are emphasized more than the rest belong to none other than the 'Standard Commands' family. But this doesn't mean that the extra commands are useless, on the contrary, they offer extended functionality making certain tasks possible which would otherwise require unnecessary workarounds. Before we move on to discussing a few of the most important commands, it's important to note that if we do not have any extension modules installed in our Python IDE, such as the **setuptools** module, then we won't have access to the 'Extra Commands' list. By installing the '**distutils**' module, we gain access to the 'Standard Commands' and by installing the '**setuptools**' module, we can use its corresponding commands listed under 'Extra Commands'.

The 'sdist' Command

Not only is the '**sdist**' command the most commonly used, but it is also the simplest command out of the bunch. This command is responsible for copying all the files necessary for the package to run properly in a 'release tree'. It then proceeds to archive this tree. The tree can be either archived in a single file or in several files.

This command is primarily executed when a programmer wants to distribute a particular package from a 'target system independently'.

All things said and done, this is arguably one of the most easiest approaches to performing such a task. As soon as the 'sdist' command is executed, a folder named 'dist' is generated which houses the archive files containing a copy of the package's source tree (which was initially created). In this way, when we distribute this 'dist' file, we are essentially distributing the package itself.

We can execute the 'sdist' command by passing a version= ' ' argument to the setup() function. If no value is specified to the 'version' argument, then the default value will be set to "0.0.0". The following lines of code demonstrate how to pass this argument;

```
from setuptools import setup
setup(name='acme.sql', version='0.1.1')
```

Just as the name suggests, the 'version=0.1.1' argument literally specifies the package's version being distributed using the 'sdist' command. In this way, if we make changes to the package (in other words update it), then we change the version value. This tells the target system that has changed since its original release. Similarly, each time we release a package using the 'sdist' command, we need to change the version value accordingly.

Here's a quick demonstration showing the use of the 'sdist' command accompanied by another argument.

```
$ python setup.py sdist
running sdist
...
```

```
creating dist
tar -cf dist/python.advanced-0.1.1.tar python.advanced-0.1.1
gzip -f9 dist/python.advanced-0.1.1.tar
removing 'python.advanced-0.1.1'          (and everything under
it)
$ ls dist/
python.advanced-0.1.1.tar.gz
```

Generally, the version we include when using the 'sdist' command also serves as an identifier for the archive containing the package itself. A package archived using 'sdist' can be distributed and used on any system with a Python installation. There are cases when the contents of the package contain application data that have been coded using 'C++ or C language' which are also relatively popular programming languages. If such packages are distributed using the 'sdist' command in Python, then the responsibility of compiling the lines of 'C code' lies entirely on the target system itself. One should consider that such a scenario is unlikely as Linux and macOS based systems also feature compilers to handle such distributed packages, especially when the package is meant to be distributed to different Operating Systems. This is why it is always a good idea to include a pre-built distribution with the package if you intend to distribute it to different Operating Systems.

The MANIFEST.in File

When we use the 'sdist' command to create a distributable package, the one responsible for going through the entire file directory of the package to fetch and list the appropriate files to put into the archive is none other than the '**distutils**' tool.

When the 'distutils' tool is tasked to gather the files and put them in the archive, it will generally fetch files such as;

- Every Python source file that has been specified by the following options; '**py_modules**', '**packages**', and '**scripts**'.

- If the package contains instructions written in C language, then every C language source file as specified by the '**ext_modules**' option.

- All those files that correspond to the following glob pattern; '**test/test*.py**'.

- Every informative file and controlling scripts present in the directory, such as '**README.txt**', '**setup.py**', and '**setup.cfg**'.

After the necessary files have been scouted by the 'distutils' tool, the next task is to fetch these files from their respective directory and include them in the distributable archive. This is done by the 'sdist' command. To do this, the 'sdist' command generates a file named '**MANIFEST**' and creates the list for all of the package's files, and then proceeds to add them into the archive sequentially.

When we use tools and commands that handle the responsibility of searching for the files and including them in the package archive, this process is automatic and cannot be controlled. If users want to include additional files in the archive, they will have to do it manually by creating a template file named '**MANIFEST.in**' and then place this file in the same directory where the **setup.py** script is located. We then specify the files along with their respective directories to include in the archive. The 'sdist' file then reads the instructions contained in the 'MANIFEST.in' file and proceeds to fetch and include the files that have been specified.

In this template, each line can feature one of two rules; an inclusion and an exclusion rule. For instance, here's a demonstration showing a manifest template including several files;

```
include HISTORY.txt
include README.txt
include CHANGES.txt
include CONTRIBUTORS.txt
include LICENSE
recursive-include *.txt *.py
```

'build' and 'bdist' Commands

If we have a pre-built distribution package and we want to distribute it, then we can do so by using the 'build' and 'bdist' commands available from the 'distutils' tool. These commands basically work by compiling the package. This is done in a total of four stages which have been elaborated by Tarek Ziade in his book 'Expert Python Programming';

1. **build_py**: Builds pure Python modules by byte-compiling them and copying them into the build folder.

2. **build_clib:** Builds C libraries, when the package contains any, using Python compiler and creating a static library in the build folder.

3. **build_ext:** Builds C extensions and puts the result in the build folder like build_clib.

4. **build_scripts:** Builds the modules that are marked as scripts. It also changes the interpreter path when the first line was set (!#) and fixes the file mode so that it is executable.

You might have noticed that these four stages basically include a different command on each step. Moreover, each command belongs to the 'build' family and can be executed independently as well. Once this entire process is completed successfully, the end product is a '**build folder**' that features all those elements and files necessary for the package installation procedure. But one thing to be wary of is that the 'distutils' tool does not support different compiler integration within the same 'build' compilation process. In other words, if we execute the 'build' command, the resulting folder will only be compatible with a specific system for which it was built for. But this might change in the near future as third-party patches and workarounds enable cross-compiler compatibility for the distutils tool.

When we use the build command procedure to create, let's say, a C language extension, the process will simply make use of the system's default compiler alongside a Python header file. In packaged distributions, the header file, and the system's mainly used compiler is stored within an additional package named as '**python-dev**' but we will have to install this package manually on the system before we can use it.

For Windows-based computer systems, the main system compiler used is 'C'. On the other hand, for Linux-based and macOS-based systems, the main compiler used by the system is not 'C', instead, it's '**ggc**'.

Now let's talk a bit more about the **build** and **bdist** commands. Both of these commands and the commands explained at the start of this section are dependent on each other. To elaborate, the **bdist** command is dependent on the **build** command to generate an initial binary distribution. Similarly, the **build** command uses four additional dependant commands to successfully generate an archive in the same manner the **sdist** command does.

Now let's see a demonstration of how we can generate a binary distribution using the **bdist** command. This time, we will be doing so for a macOS-based target system instead of a Windows system.

```
$ python setup.py bdist
running bdist
running bdist_dumb
```

running build

...

running install_scripts

tar -cf dist/acme.sql-0.1.1.macosx-10.3-fat.tar .

gzip -f9 acme.sql-0.1.1.macosx-10.3-fat.tar

removing 'build/bdist.macosx-10.3-fat/dumb'   (and everything under it)

$ ls dist/

acme.sql-0.1.1.macosx-10.3-fat.tar.gz acme.sql-0.1.1.tar.gz

If you look closely, you will notice that the resulting archive generated by the **bdist** command specifies the original package's name and the target system for which it was built (in this case, it would be Mac OS X).

If we want to use the same process for creating a distributable archive intended for Windows-based systems, then we can do so as shown below;

C:\acme.sql> python.exe setup.py bdist

...

C:\acme.sql> dir dist

25/02/2008 08:18 <DIR> .

25/02/2008 08:18 <DIR> ..

25/02/2008 08:24   16 055 acme.sql-0.1.win32.zip

    1 File(s) 16 055 bytes

    2 Dir(s) 22 239 752 192 bytes free

When the **bdist** command creates a binary distribution release, the main contents are a 'tree' which can be easily copied over to a Python tree. In simpler terms, the binary distribution has a folder that is simply copied to a Python directory named '**site-packages**'.

The 'bdist_egg' Command

Another mode of distribution in parallel with the **bdist** command is the **bdist_egg** command. This is basically an additional command which can be used by installing the **setuptools** module in Python. Its function is mainly similar to that of the **bdist** command. Instead of creating a simple binary distribution archive like bdist, the one generated by the bdist_egg command features a very similar tree to the tree of the source distribution. This allows users to simply download the distribution archive onto their systems, uncompress the file and then use it by putting the unzipped folder inside the Python search path which is specified by '**sys.path**'.

Generally, this mode of distribution is preferred over the one provided by the **bdist** command.

The 'install' Command

Just as the name suggests, the '**install**' command is executed when installing a Python package. If the package called with the install command does not have any prior builds, then Python will automatically attempt to create a build version of this package and then copy the contents to the Python tree. If we call the **install** command on a distribution package that has its source distribution, then the command will simply unzip the contents of the archive file in a temporary folder and then install it from there. Most of the time, a package also has dependencies, without which, it cannot function properly. For packages that have dependencies, the **install** command looks through the metadata file '**install_requires**' and installs the corresponding dependencies for the package.

To elaborate, the dependency list is created by Python through analyzing the 'PyPI', also known as 'Python Package Index'. In this way, if we want to install a distribution package and other packages as its dependencies, we can manually specify these packages in the call to the '**setup()**' function. For example, let's say that we have a package file we created by the name of '**acme.sql**' and we want to install the '**pysqlite**' and '**SQLAlchemy**' at the same time as its dependencies. To do so, we will simply call the '**setup()**' function and provide an argument named '**instal_requires**'. The packages specified within this argument will be considered as the original package's dependencies. The following demonstration explains this process;

from setuptools import setup

```
setup(name='acme.sql', version='0.1.1',
    install_requires=['pysqlite', 'SQLAlchemy'])
```

As soon as the **install** command is executed to install the '**acme.sql**' package, the **pysqlite** and **SQLAlchemy** packages will be installed alongside as well.

The 'develop' Command

This section will talk about another very productive command made available by the '**setuptools**' module in Python, which is '**develop**'. The **develop** command essentially performs three tasks;

- Building the package

- Installing the package

- Adding a link of the package to the '**site-packages**' folder of Python

In this way, the user is able to work on the code contained in the package itself, even though this code is a local copy.

When we use the **develop** command to install a package, we can uninstall it fairly easily as well. The process of uninstallation can be executed by using an option known as '**-u**'. Here's a demonstration;

```
$ sudo python setup.py develop
running develop
...
Adding iw.recipe.fss 0.1.3dev-r7606 to easy-install.pth file
Installed
/Users/repos/ingeniweb.sourceforge.net/iw.recipe.fss/trunk
Processing dependencies ...
$ sudo python setup.py develop -u
running develop
```

Removing

...

Removing iw.recipe.fss 0.1.3dev-r7606 from easy-install.pth file

Another important thing to note is that a package can be installed by using **sdist** and **bdist** as well. If we use either of these two commands to install a package, then a specific version of the package will be available on the user's system for use. If we use the **develop** command to install the same package on the system as well, then the package installed through the **develop** command will have precedence over the versions installed using **sdist** and **bdist**.

The 'test' Command

Just as how building and developing tasks are important for working with packages, testing the package we created to see if it works properly is also equally important. The 'test' command can do this. The command works by searching through the specified file directory and executing the testing procedure, afterward, it displays an aggregated result but the tests run by the command are quite limited in functionality. To counter this, it is recommended to use an external test runner (such as **zope.testing** or **Nose**) to extend the command's functionality and make up for its limitations.

Here's a quick demonstration of how we can attach the **Nose** as an extended test runner with the **test** command.

setup(

```
...

test_suite='nose.collector',

test_requires=['Nose'],

...

)
```

You will see that to hook the **Nose** test runner, we are primarily using two arguments; **test_suite** and **test_requires**. In the first argument, we include **nose.collector** in the command's metadata and then add a dependency to the command's execution, which is the **Nose** test runner itself.

The 'register' and 'upload Commands

Once you are done with creating a distributable package, the next step is to distribute it to other systems. Otherwise, there's no point in going through all these steps and creating a package. The following two commands generally perform package distribution tasks;

- **Register**: this command takes the entire metadata of a package and uploads it to a target server.

- **Upload**: this command takes all of the archive files which are present in the **dist** folder and uploads it to the target server.

The major server for Python Packages can be accessed through the following address;

http://pypi.python.org/pypi

This server is commonly used by the Python community and features a large number of packages uploaded by individual developers and teams. Moreover, the **distutils** tool uses this specific server by default for uploading the packages when a call to the **register** command is executed. Once the user executes the **register** command, the system automatically creates a '**.pypric**' file in its main home file directory.

By now, you must be aware of the fact that a package is not only created once and left afterward. Developers and programmers work to improve, add new features, and even update their existing packages by uploading a newer version of it but the default PyPI server requires users their packages to create a user account for authentication purposes. Without a user account, one cannot upload their packages on to the server or even update the existing version of the packages. A user account can be created directly through the prompt as shown below;

```
$ python setup.py register
running register
...
```

We need to know who you are, so please choose either:

1. use your existing login,

2. register as a new user,

3. have the server generate a new password for you (and email it to

you), or

 4. quit

Your selection [default 1]:

Once you are done, a '**.pypric**' file will be generated by the system and placed in its home directory. This file contains your user account's information for the PyPI server (the username and password). Whenever you execute the **register** or **upload** commands, the upload process will automatically prompt the user to enter the user account's name and password. An example of the contents of the '**.pypric**' file has been shown below;

> [server-index]
>
> username: loki
>
> password: asgard

When we upload the file using the **register** command, we need to either include the metadata for the package's download URL or specify the URL itself. If the URL is checked to be valid, the server will then register the package on the web-page for other people to access and download the package for their systems.

On the other hand, if we use the **upload** command, the archive file will be uploaded directly to the server without the user's need to specify the **download_url** metadata.

Whenever a package is uploaded to the server, it also needs to be classified. This way, the end-user can easily find the package if he's looking through a broad catalog. By default, the **distutils** tool employs a type of classification known as '**Trove Categorization**' to classify the package being uploaded. This is a static list which can be accessed by going to the following address;

http://pypi.python.org/pypi?%3Aaction=list_classifiers

New entries are added to this list periodically. Here's what a typical trove list will look like;

...

Topic :: Terminals

Topic :: Terminals :: Serial

Topic :: Terminals :: Telnet

Topic :: Terminals :: Terminal Emulators/X Terminals

Topic :: Text Editors Topic :: Text Editors :: Documentation

Topic :: Text Editors :: Emacs

...

Just as one movie cannot be classified into a single genre, several genres are associated with one movie. Similarly, there are cases where it is insufficient to classify a package into a single category. In such a scenario, we can associate several categories to a particular package by including the appropriate '**classifiers**' from the trove list into the metadata. For instance, a GPL package can be classified into more than one categories as shown below;

Programming Language :: Python

Topic :: Software Development :: Libraries :: Python Modules

License :: OSI Approved :: GNU General Public License (GPL)

The 'setup.py' Usage Summary

To summarize the entire discussion, the main tasks which are to be included in the **setup.py** script of a package are the following;

1. Build the package using the appropriate commands (sdist or even bdist).

2. Install the package in standard mode (using sdist) or in develop mode (using the **develop** command).

3. Using the **register** and **upload** commands to upload the package to the PyPI server.

All of these tasks can be incorporated within a single consistent call, here are a few general usage patterns that you can adopt;

```
# register the package with PyPI, creates a source and
# an egg distribution, then upload them
$ python setup.py register sdist bdist_egg upload
# installs it in-place, for development purpose
$ python setup.py develop
# installs it
$ python setup.py install
```

A Bunch of Significant Metadata

Until now, we have emphasized the namespace of the package we are distributing as well as its version. Although these arguments are considered important but there are other arguments that are equally important as well such as;

- **description:** this argument contains a string which is acts as a brief summary or description of the package being distributed.

- **long_description:** this argument allows the user to create a lengthy description of the package. The description made henceforth can also be in '**reStructuredText**'.

- **keywords:** this argument defines a list that specifies the keywords for the search queries of the package.

- **author:** this argument is used to specify the name of the developer of the package. The name can be an individual or an entire organization.

- **Author_email:** this argument is used to specify the developer's email address so that users of the package can reach out to the developer if they have any problems or want to report any bugs to the developer.

- **url:** this argument specifies the Uniform Resource Link of the project containing the distributed package.

- **License:** this argument specifies the package's licensing (GPL, LGPL, etc.)

- **Packages:** this argument is used to specify every name that has been defined in the package. This list can be calculated by using the function '**find_packages**' which becomes available when installing the **setuptools** module.

- **namespace_packages:** this is used to provide a list of every namespaced package.

Here's an example of what the contents of an actual **setup.py** file will look like.

```
import os
from setuptools import setup, find_packages
version = '0.1.0'
README = os.path.join(os.path.dirname(__file__),
'README.txt')
long_description = open(README).read() + '\n\n'
setup(name='acme.sql',
 version=version,
 description=("A package that deals with SQL, "
 "from ACME inc"),
 long_description=long_description,
 classifiers=[
 "Programming Language :: Python",
```

```
("Topic :: Software Development :: Libraries ::
"Python Modules"),
],
keywords='acme sql',
author='Tarek',
author_email='tarek@ziade.org',
url='http://ziade.org',
license='GPL',
packages=find_packages(),
namespace_packages=['acme'],
install_requires=['pysqlite','SQLAchemy']
)
```

The Template-Based Approach

If we look at the underlying code of the '**acme.sql**' file, we will come to know that the file itself comprises an organization of folders in the form of a 'tree' that defines the namespace for specific files in the root directory. To ensure that the organizational structure of all of the packages is identical, we can create a code template containing this structural information. This template is then extracted and provided to the tool to create further codes for packages accordingly. Formally, this approach is termed as '**Generative Programming**' and it is particularly resourceful for programmers that are working on projects at the organizational tier. Using a template not only sets a standard for the code structure, but it also increases the efficiency and productivity of the developers working on the project. This is due to the fact that since they don't have to worry about keeping the organization of the code coherent throughout the project, they can allocate their entire concentration and focus on coding.

In the Python community, many tools have surfaced which facilitate generative programming. Out of these bundle of tools, the most commonly used and preferred tool is '**Python Paste**'. The Python Paste tool can be downloaded from the following URL;

http://pythonpaste.org

Python Paste

If you have spent a considerable amount of time in Python programming, then there are chances that you must have used frameworks like '**Pylons**' or at least heard of them. The popularity of these frameworks was partly due to the project of Python Paste. Nowadays, developers have become even more efficient in programming due to the use of such tools. This allows them to generate the overall 'skeletal structure' of the application in a considerably short time. In the past, this would require hours of work, and even then, a team of developers would often have to painfully check their code's structure and make sure it aligns with the application's structure perfectly.

There are numerous detailed tutorials available that extensively explain the use of such frameworks and tools in generative programming. There is even an official tutorial for users to follow as well. Here's a demonstration that uses generative programming to create an entire web-application in just three lines;

$ paster create -t pylons helloworld

$ cd helloworld

$ paster serve --reload development.ini

There are many useful tools available in Python Paste that offer extended functionalities for the purpose of generative programming. In this section, we will primarily be using the 'PasteScript' template engine. To install the template engine, we simply need to execute the command '**easy_install**' and the template engine along with its dependencies will be installed on the system automatically. Here's a demonstration showcasing the installation process;

$ easy_install PasteScript

Searching for PasteScript

Reading http://pypi.python.org/simple/PasteScript/

Reading http://pythonpaste.org/script/

Best match: PasteScript 1.6.2

Downloading

Processing dependencies for PasteScript

Searching for PasteDeploy

...

Searching for Paste>=1.3

...

Finished processing dependencies for PasteScript

Once the template engine has been installed, we now have access to the commands made available by PasteScript. For example, PasteScript features a command '**paster**' that comes with a few templates by default. To check what templates are available for use, we just need to access the '**-list-templates**' option from the command '**create**' as demonstrated below;

$ paster create --list-templates

Available templates:

>   basic_package: A basic setuptools-enabled package
>
>   paste_deploy: A web application deployed through
>   paste.deploy

From this list, by using the **basic_package** template, we can build an entire namespaced package that includes the **setup.py** script file. When we choose a template and run it, the command line interface prompts the user to fulfill a bunch of queries. These answered queries are then used to include the necessary information within the template. Here's an example;

$ paster create -t basic_package mypackage

Selected and implied templates:

>   PasteScript#basic_package A basic setuptools-enabled package
>
>   ...

Enter version (Version (like 0.1)) ["]: 0.1

Enter description ["]: My package

Enter long_description ["]: this is the package

Enter keywords ["]: package is mine

Enter author (Author name) ["]: Tarek

Enter author_email (Author email) ["]: tarek@ziade.org

Enter url (URL of homepage) ["]: http://ziade.org

Enter license_name (License name) ["]: GPL

Enter zip_safe [False]:

Creating template basic_package

...

By doing so, we end up with a single-tiered structure that is 'setuptools-compliant'.

$ find mypackage

mypackage

mypackage/mypackage

mypackage/mypackage/__init__.py

mypackage/setup.cfg

mypackage/setup.py

Creating a Package Template

We can also use different template engines with Python Paste depending on the developmental needs of an application. For instance, we can use the '**Cheetah**' template engine as well if the application we are creating requires a lot of user input. The Cheetah template engine can be downloaded from its official website which has been linked below;

http://cheetahtemplate.org

Apart from using pre-built templates, we can also create our own custom template as well. But we need to keep in mind that a template needs to have the following elements to be valid;

1. A derivative class that has been created from 'paste.script.templates.Template'.

2. A structure that defines the organization of the files and folders (we can use Cheetah templates or even static files for this purpose).

3. An entry point that leads from **setuptools** to 'paste.paster_create_template'. This is necessary for the class to be registered.

Now let's proceed to create a proper template for the package **'acme.sql'** which we have used in the preceding sections.

First things first, we need to have a structure according to which the package's content will be organized. The following lines demonstrate how we can generate this structure;

$ mkdir -p pbp.skels/pbp/skels
$ find pbp.skels
pbp.skels

pbp.skels/pbp

pbp.skels/pbp/skels

After this, we need to create an '**__init__.py**' file and place it within the **pbp** file directory. The code within this file is responsible for detailing the package's nature to the **distutils** tool. In this case, it will declare the package as a 'namespaced package' to the distutils tool.

try:

    __import__('pkg_resources').declare_namespace(__name__)
    except ImportError:
    from pkgutil import extend_path
    __path__ = extend_path(__path__, __name__)

In the next step, we have to build the **setup.py** file and place it in the root directory

    path_to_pbp_package/pbp.skels/__init__.py

It is important that the setup.py file has the necessary metadata for the acme.sql package. The contents of the setup.py file in this case has been shown below;

    from setuptools import setup, find_packages
    version = '0.1.0'
    classifiers = [
    "Programming Language :: Python",
    ("Topic :: Software Development :: "

```
    "Libraries :: Python Modules")]
setup(name='pbp.skels',
version=version,
description=("PasteScript templates for the Expert "
"Python programming Book."),
classifiers=classifiers,
keywords='paste templates',
author='Tarek Ziade',
author_email='tarek@ziade.org',
url='http://atomisator.ziade.org',
license='GPL',
packages=find_packages(exclude=['ez_setup']),
namespace_packages=['pbp'],
include_package_data=True,
install_requires=['setuptools',
'PasteScript'],
entry_points="""
# -*- Entry points: -*-
[paste.paster_create_template]
pbp_package = pbp.skels.package:Package
""")
```

At the end, you will see a portion dedicated to entry points. These entry points are responsible for the inclusion of another template in the Pyton Paste tool.

Now, we need to define the **package** class in a module. We will name this module as 'package' and place it within the **pbp** file directory (**pbp/skels**). The following lines of code demonstrate this;

```
from paste.script.templates import var
from paste.script.templates import Template
class Package(Template):
 """Package template"""
 _template_dir = 'tmpl/package'
 summary = "A namespaced package with a test environment"
 use_cheetah = True
 vars = [
 var('namespace_package', 'Namespace package',
 default='pbp'),
 var('package', 'The package contained',
 default='example'),
 var('version', 'Version', default='0.1.0'),
 var('description',
 'One-line description of the package'),
 var('author', 'Author name'),
 var('author_email', 'Author email'),
 var('keywords', 'Space-separated keywords/tags'),
 var('url', 'URL of homepage'),
 var('license_name', 'License name', default='GPL')
```

```
]
def check_vars(self, vars, command):
    if not command.options.no_interactive and \
        not hasattr(command, '_deleted_once'):
        del vars['package']
        command._deleted_once = True
    return Template.check_vars(self, vars, command)
```

The **package** class is responsible for defining the following;

- The directory where the template we are creating is stored in.

- A template summary which will be displayed by the Python Paste tool.

- An indicator that will tell us if the Cheetah template is being used. In this case, the indicator is a flag.

- A variable list. Each of the variables within this list has the following elements; name, label, and standard value. When using this template, the Python Paste tool uses these variables to process user input. For instance, the variables initially have a default value. When using the template, users can change this value according to their needs.

- Finally, the '**check_vars**' method. This method ensures that the corresponding package variable is called up at the prompt.

Finally, all that's left is to create a new directory, specifically **'tmpl/package'**, and copy the template that has been generated for the **acme.sql** package into this directory. The important thing to remember is that every file we know has variables that will be changed in the future, need to contain the '**_tmpl**' suffix.

For example, we know that the **setup.py** file has variables that will be changed according to the user's input. So, we will add the **_tmpl** suffix to the setup.py file such that its name becomes **'setup.py_tmpl'**. The contents of this file are as follows;

```
from setuptools import setup, find_packages
import os
version = ${repr($version) or "0.0"}
long_description = open("README.txt").read()
classifiers = [
 "Programming Language :: Python",
 ("Topic :: Software Development :: "
 "Libraries :: Python Modules")]
setup(name=${repr($project)},
 version=version,
 description=${repr($description) or $empty},
 long_description=long_description,
 classifiers=classifiers,
 keywords=${repr($keywords) or $empty},
 author=${repr($author) or $empty},
```

```
author_email=${repr($author_email) or $empty},

url=${repr($url) or $empty},

license=${repr($license_name) or $empty},

packages=find_packages(exclude=['ez_setup']),

namespace_packages=[${repr($namespace_package)}],

include_package_data=True,

install_requires=[

'setuptools',

# -*- Extra requirements: -*-

],

test_suite='nose.collector',

test_requires=['Nose'],

entry_points="""

# -*- Entry points: -*-

""",

)
```

Quotation marks are automatically added to the string values because we are using the **repr** function.

In this way, we can add the '**_tmpl**' suffix to every file that is present within the **acme.sql** package, thus creating a template. For example, the 'README.txt' file in the package will be changed to 'README.txt_tmpl' and copied to the '**tmpl/package**' directory. Afterward, every reference to the **acme.sql** package is taken over by the values which have been defined according to the **package** class.

So, if we want to fetch the name of the package, we will have to refer to it in the following way;

${namespace_package}.${package}

Lastly, if we want to employ a variable to refer to a folder name, then the folder's namespace has to include the '+' sign in the start and at the end, such that a folder named '**package**' will become '**+package+**'.

Here's the concluding structure of the **pbp.skels** file once the **acme.sql** package has been generalized;

$ cd pbp.skels

$ find .

setup.py

pbp

pbp/__init__.py

pbp/skels

pbp/skels/__init__.py

pbp/skels/package.py

pbp/skels/tmpl

pbp/skels/tmpl/package

pbp/skels/tmpl/package/README.txt_tmpl

pbp/skels/tmpl/package/setup.py_tmpl

pbp/skels/tmpl/package/+namespace_package+

pbp/skels/tmpl/package/+namespace_package+/__init__.py_tm
pl

pbp/skels/tmpl/package/+namespace_package+/+package+

pbp/skels/tmpl/package/+namespace_package+/+package+/__in
it__.py

At this point, we can use the **'develop'** command to link the package to the **'site-packages'** directory. By doing this, the Python Paste tool has access to this package.

$ python setup.py develop

...

Finished processing dependencies for pbp.skels==0.1.0dev

Once we execute the **develop** command, the template will become available for use in the Python Paster tool;

$ paster create --list-templates

Available templates:

 basic_package: A basic setuptools-enabled package

 pbp_package: A namespaced package with a test environment

 paste_deploy: A web application ... paste.deploy

$ paster create -t pbp_package trying.it

Selected and implied templates:

 pbp.skels#package A namespaced package with a test environment

Variables:

egg: trying.it

 package: tryingit

 project: trying.it

Enter namespace_package (Namespace package) ['pbp']: trying

Enter package (The package contained) ['example']: it

...

Creating a template package

...

The resulting tree generated by the running the **develop** command will feature the organizational structure we have built. We can now use the custom generated template directly from the Python Paste tool and begin creating applications through generative programming.

Chapter Six

Working on an Application Project

In the previous chapter, we discussed a method to create packages and organize the code of different packages in a nested directory based on namespaces. Moreover, this method can be easily repeated making it more convenient to create several packages in one go. In this chapter, we will take this a step further and create an application from these packages. To summarize the entire process, we simply assemble all of the packages and then create another package responsible for handling the interaction between the packages that will make up the application. In other words, we take all of the components and then add in one final element which ties everything together.

The topic of creating applications from packages can lead to an extremely lengthy discussion but such a discussion will be pointless and become boring. In this chapter, we will look at a relatively brief case study to explain the process of building, releasing, and distributing an application this time instead of a package.

An Introduction to Atomisator

In simple terms, an 'Atomisator' is an application and in this section, we will learn how to implement it. When we install the Atomisator application on our system, the Python command-line interface gains a new tool available to be used by the user. This application tool is capable of creating 'RSS XML' files. These files are basically a unification of different streams of news feeds. Here's a demonstration showing the use of the atomisator tool in the command-line interface;

    $ atomisator

    Reading source http://feeds.feedburner.com/dirtsimple Phillip Eby

    10 entries read.

    Reading source http://blog.ianbicking.org/feed/ Ian Bicking

    10 entries read.

    20 total.

    Writing feed in atomisator.xml

    Feed ready.

As soon as we execute the command to call the atomisator tool, it checks the configuration file and fetches all of the sources listed within it. It then reads these sources (which are essentially web pages) and then stores the appropriate data into a database. Once the data is stored within the database, the tool then creates a file in XML format while keeping this database as the template ensuring that only the latest entries are included in the XML file. If you have worked on such a task before, then you will most likely have heard of the **Planet** tool which does the same task but in a slightly different manner, in the sense that the atomisator tool stores the data it has fetched from the sources into a database instead of unifying it at the same time, the data is being fetched.

The way Atomisator handles data from the sources lets its users apply filters on the entries being recorded into the database. Let's elaborate on this, consider for a moment that the tool is recording entries to an already existing database. During the process of reading and storing the entries into the database, we can apply a smart filter that will cross-check the new entry with the existing entries in the database. In this way, we can ensure that no duplicate entries will be recorded within the database.

The Big Picture

We know how the Atomisator tool is supposed to store entries to the database, which is by fetching the source web pages from the configuration file and reading them. We will now proceed with the main project of this chapter, which will be to create an application.

First, since the application will comprise multiple packages, we need to list all of them. Since we will be creating an Atomisator application, it is important to note that we can use a single package for this purpose but our focus is to keep the application as maintainable as possible, for this purpose, we will split the application into different packages.

If we look back to the previous chapter, we will find the four stages of building a package. For building the application in this chapter, we will follow the standard steps as well. Keeping in mind these four stages, we will split the application into four packages. The details have been listed below;

1. **atomisator.parser**: This package defines the application's feed parser. This package is responsible for imparting the functionality of reading a news feed from a source and then returning a list of entries corresponding to the feed.

2. **atomisator.db:** This package enables the application to perform read and write operations on the database. In this way, the application will be able to read the database and write new entries to the database and store them as well.

3. **atmosiator.feed**: This package has the instructions necessary for generating an RSS XML file. The XML file will consist of entries read from the database by the application.

4. **atomisator.main**: This is the application's main package. This package features two elements, a configuration file, and utilities that can be used in the command-line interface. These utilities are a total of three in number and they have been further elaborated below;

   - **load_feeds:** This utility executes the function of fetching the data from the listed sources.

   - **generate_feed:** This utility allows the user to issue a command to the application for generating the corresponding XML file.

- **atomisator:** It combines all of the preceding commands into a single unified call.

Here's a diagram that illustrates the communication and interaction of different packages of an application among themselves;

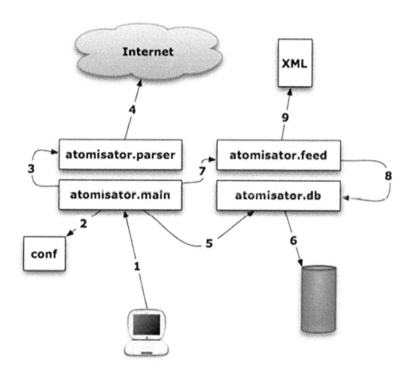

Now let's explain the process of interaction between the packages;

1. The end-user initiates a request to the command-line interface to call the **atomisator.main** package to generate a feed.

2. The **atomisator.main** package then refers to the configuration file and fetches the resources mentioned within.

3. The control is then passed on to the **atomisator.parser** which processes the read request from **atomisator.main**. As a result, **atomisator.parser** provides a list of entries collected from the different sources it has gone through.

4. The **atomisator.parser** then performs a read operation on the news feeds and then creates corresponding data structures.

5. Once the **atomisator.parser** is done with its job, the control is passed over to the **atomisator.main** package along with the entries fetched from the sources. The **atomisator.main** then passes the entries to the **atomisator.db** package which accesses the database and performs a write operation, updating the entries. Moreover, it also employs a smart filter to avoid the duplication of entries. This process covers both steps 5 and 6.

7. Once the entries have been stored, the control is then passed back to **atomisator.main** to which the **atomisator.main** sends a feed generation request to the **atomisator.feed** package. The feed is created with the newly updated database.

8. The **atomisator.feed** and **atomisator.db** packages work together in the way that the feed package accesses and reads

the database through the '.db' package and creating an RSS XML file from the data it has gathered. This entire process spans over step 8 to step 9.

The Working Environment

We know that certain packages are necessary for the system to have already installed before we can proceed with the main package's installation procedure. Once we have specified the dependencies, we execute the develop command to install the package through the setup.py script, this call will be '**python setup.py develop**'. All of the dependencies needed for the package's code to execute properly will be automatically installed, but there's a slight workaround that you might encounter. Depending on the type of package you are installing, the dependencies sometimes also have to cohere to the main package's code structure. For instance, if we have a namespaced package organized in an egg structure, then the dependencies we specify must also have an egg structure in PyPI or those dependencies need to be already installed in the Python before-hand. In this case, we are building an **Atomisator** application and the building process of its packages is parallel to each other and no package is released before the other. All of them are released at the same time.

Hence, we need to set up a proper working environment to build the application without any hiccups. At the application level, it is imperative for the working environment to have the ability to isolate the corresponding dependencies of the application.

A recommended solution is to use a project tool '**virtualenv**'. This tool basically provides the user with an 'isolated Python interpreter' stacked on top of an existing Python installation on the system. This tool can be downloaded from the official PyPI server. The URL has been linked below;

http://pypi.python.org/pypi/virtualenv

As a result, we have set up a working environment where we can install and develop whatever libraries we need and create a specialized working environment. The following block demonstrates how we are creating a working environment for the **Atomisator** application project;

```
mkdir my_env
cd my_env/
$ easy_install -U virtualenv
Searching for virtualenv
Reading http://pypi.python.org/simple/virtualenv/
Best match: virtualenv 1.0
Processing virtualenv-1.0-py2.5.egg
Adding virtualenv 1.0 to easy-install.pth file
...
Finished processing dependencies for virtualenv
$ virtualenv --no-site-packages .
New python executable in ./bin/python
```

Installing setuptools............done.

```
$ ls bin/
activate    easy_install    easy_install-2.5
python      python2.5
```

Upon executing the '**virtualenv**' command, a folder is created which is used to store the isolated interpreter for the project. Two scripts also accompany the interpreter; the '**easy_install**' script and the '**activate**' script. The function of the '**active**' script is to primarily provide more convenience to users when they wish to change the scope of the 'environment variable', i.e, from isolated to system-wide (or global). To remove the dependencies of every package being used in the main Python environment, we can simply access the '**—no-site-packages**'. This option is particularly useful when working on a clean Python environment and avoiding dependency complications on the system.

We will now proceed to generate a clean Python environment for the Atomisator application in a new directory. The process has been demonstrated below;

```
$ mkdir Atomisator
$ cd Atomisator
$ virtualenv --no-site-packages .
New python executable in ./bin/python
Installing setuptools............done.
```

Another point that makes using the **virtualenv** tool even more useful is that whenever we use the **easy_install** command or the local Python interpreter to install any package, the installation will also carry over to the local system as well.

Choosing a Test Runner

Just as we needed a test runner to ensure that a package was being built properly, we also need to choose a test runner for the building and development process of an application. If you recall the previous chapter, we used the **Nose** tool as the test runner for the package templates. Similarly, we will be using this tool for this project as well. The following command demonstrates how we can globally include the **Nose** test runner in the environment we are using;

$ bin/easy_install nose

Once the **Nose** tool package has been installed on the system, we will now have access to the commands it features, such as '**nosetests**'. The **bin** folder being used by the local Python interpreter will be the default directory where the **Nose** package will be installed. This allows the tool to be able to have access to any package that is added to the Python environment.

Choosing the Packages Structure

The **Atomisator** project has a single file directory '**bin**' and this directory contains an isolated Python interpreter and a test runner. The corresponding packages of the application need to be placed in a sub-folder. We will name this folder as '**packages**'. This will be the package structure for the application project.

Creating the Packages

When creating packages, we need to follow a strict order so that there is no conflict in dependencies. The order in which the packages will be built is;

1. **atomisator.parser**

2. **atomisator.db**

3. **atomisator.feed**

4. **atomisator.main**

The overall process of creating a package is summarized below;

- Choosing an appropriate template and building the first package with this template.

- Building '**doctest**'

- Creating the appropriate 'test environment'

- Coding for the application according to the initial **doctest**

The atomisator.parser Package

Building the First Package

We will be using the template '**pbp_package**' to create the application's first package. The template needs to be in the '**packages**' sub-folder located in the **application project's bin directory**.

```
$ cd Atomisator/packages
$ paster create -t pbp_package atomisator.parser
```

We then execute the **develop** command to link the package to the project's Python interpreter.

```
$ cd atomisator.parser
$ atomisator-python setup.py develop
running develop
...
Finished processing dependencies for atomisator.parser==0.1.0
```

Now, we need to run the tests. A default **doctest** file for the template is available so we will execute the **'nosetest'** command within this hollow package.

```
$ atomisator-nosetests --doctest-extension=.txt
----------------------------------------------------------------
Ran 1 test in 0.162s
OK
```

We will now include a dependency on the initial package (**atomisator.parser**). The dependency will be on **'feedparser'** which can be downloaded from the PyPI server. The dependency will be included as an argument in the package's setup.py file.

```
...
setup(name='atomisator.parser',
```

```python
version=version,
description=("A thin layer on the top of "
"the Universal Feed Parser"),
long_description=long_description,
classifiers=classifiers,
keywords='python best practices',
author='Tarek Ziade',
author_email='tarek@ziade.org',
url='http://atomisator.ziade.org',
license='GPL',
packages=find_packages(exclude=['ez_setup']),
namespace_packages=['atomisator'],
include_package_data=True,
zip_safe=False,
install_requires=[
'setuptools',
'feedparser'
# -*- Extra requirements: -*-
],
entry_points="""
# -*- Entry points: -*-
""",
)
```

To wrap things up, we will execute the **"atomisator-python setup.py develop"** call once more to ensure that it links to the environment in which we will build the application. Now, we are ready to put the necessary code in this package.

Building the Initial Doctest

The document that the end-user will read to understand how to use the package and its intended purposes, is the '**README.txt**' file. This file can be found in the following directory;

atomisator.parser/atomisator/parser/

We will adopt the '**Test-Driven Development**' approach with the help of the '**reStructuredText**' tool to create the code for the package. Here's an initial draft for the **doctest** file.

=================

atomisator.parser

=================

The parser knows how to return a feed content, with

the 'parse' function, available as a top-level function::

    >>> from atomisator.parser import parse

This function takes the feed url and returns an iterator

over its content. A second parameter can specify a maximum

number of entries to return. If not given, it is fixed to 10::

```
>>> res = parse('http://example.com/feed.xml')
>>> res
<generator ...>
```

Each item is a dictionary that contain the entry::

```
>>> res.next()
```

From this text file, we have enough data to begin the building stage of the package. But before we do that, we need to double-check if an error is encountered when we execute the script '**bin/test**' because the package still does not contain any code;

```
$ atomisator-nosetests --doctest-extension=.txt

...

File "atomisator.parser/atomisator/parser/docs/README.txt",
line 8, in

README.txt

Failed example:

 from atomisator.parser import parse

Exception raised:

 Traceback (most recent call last):

 ...

File "<doctest README.txt[0]>", line 1, in ?

 from atomisator.parser import parse

 ImportError: cannot import name parse

------------------------------------------------------------------

Ran 1 test in 0.170s
```

FAILED (failures=1)

From here on out, we can just keep on working in the test-driven development mode and making changes in the code we include in the package until we no longer encounter this error.

Creating the Test Environment

When creating packages, one should always try to run tests that can be executed without having to include any dependencies from other packages. In this case, the most convenient and easiest way to avoid having the '**atomisator.parser**' package to depend on a URL is to use a simple XML file. This is because the **feedparser** tool is also compatible with feeds contained within XML files. We will now create an XML file named '**sample.xml**' and save the feed we want to test. Once this is done, we will put the XML file within the '**tests**' folder.

```
cd atomisator/parser/tests

wget http://ziade.org/atomisator/sample.xml
```

The other thing we have to do make slight changes to the 'README.txt' file. These changes have been shown below;

```
...

>>> res = parse(os.path.join(test_dir, 'sample.xml'))

...
```

We can now test the package without having it to depend on a connection to the internet.

Writing the Code for the Package

We will now add a function **'parse()'** to the package and build the rest of it. We will keep doing this until the package does not raise an error during testing.

```
from feedparser import parse as feedparse
from itertools import islice
from itertools import imap


def _filter_entry(entry):
  """Filters entry fields."""


entry['links'] = [link['href'] for link in entry['links']]
  return entry
def parse(url, size=10):
  """Returns entries of the feed."""
  result = feedparse(url)
  return islice(imap(_filter_entry,
  result['entries']), size)
```

The **doctest** needs to be adapted accordingly.

...

Each item is a dictionnary that contain the entry::

```
>>> entry = res.next()
>>> entry['title']
u'CSSEdit 2.0 Released'
```

The keys available are:

```
>>> keys = sorted(entry.keys())
>>> list(keys)
['id', 'link', 'links', 'summary', 'summary_detail',
'tags', 'title', 'title_detail']
```

The 'atomisator.db' Package

The main process of creating the 'atomisator.db' package is the same. The only important thing to discuss in this section is the tool to allow the package to interact with relational databases and use the appropriate API. For this purpose, we will be using an 'object-relational mapper' tool known as **SQLAlchemy**

The convenience provided by this tool is that by using a mapping system, we can sync Python objects to corresponding rows in the SQL table without even needing to write an SQL code. SQLAlchemy can be downloaded from the following website and a detailed tutorial on how to use it can be found on their main webpage as well.

http://www.sqlalchemy.org

Generating the Mapping for the Package

The 'atomisator.db' package's database model is relatively easy to handle since it only features a single table entry structure with links and tags.

The structure of the mapping for the package is shown below;

```
from sqlalchemy import *
```

```python
from sqlalchemy.orm import *
from sqlalchemy.orm import mapper
metadata = MetaData()
link = Table('atomisator_link', metadata,
 Column('id', Integer, primary_key=True),
 Column('url', String(300)),
 Column('atomisator_entry_id', Integer,
 ForeignKey('atomisator_entry.id')))
class Link(object):
 def __init__(self, url):
 self.url = url
 def __repr__(self):
 return "<Link('%s')>" % self.url
mapper(Link, link)
tag = Table('atomisator_tag', metadata,
 Column('id', Integer, primary_key=True),
Column('value', String(100)),
 Column('atomisator_entry_id', Integer,
 ForeignKey('atomisator_entry.id')))
class Tag(object):
 def __init__(self, value):
 self.value = value
 def __repr__(self):
```

```python
    return "<Tag('%s')>" % self.value
mapper(Tag, tag)
entry = Table('atomisator_entry', metadata,
  Column('id', Integer, primary_key=True),
  Column('url', String(300)),
  Column('date', DateTime()),
  Column('summary', Text()),
  Column('summary_detail', Text()),
  Column('title', Text()),
  Column('title_detail', Text()))
class Entry(object):
  def __init__(self, title, url, summary, summary_detail='',
  title_detail=''):
  self.title = title
  self.url = url
  self.summary = summary
  self.summary_detail = summary_detail
  self.title_detail = title_detail
  def add_links(self, links):
  for link in links:
  self.links.append(Link(link))
  def add_tags(self, tags):
  for tag in tags:
```

```
self.tags.append(Tag(tag))

def __repr__(self):

return "<Entry(%r)>" % self.title

mapper(Entry, entry, properties={

'links':relation(Link, backref='atomisator_entry'),

'tags':relation(Tag, backref='atomisator_entry'),

})
```

If you want a full detailed tutorial on how to use SQLAlchemy, then you will find everything you need to know from their official webpage;

http://www.sqlalchemy.org/docs/04/ormtutorial.html

Including the Appropriate APIs

Once we have defined the mapping system, we need to have an interface that will provide the application with a pathway to add and query entries. This can be done through the main **doctest** of the package.

==============

atomisator.db

==============

This package provides a few mappers to store feed entries

in a SQL database.

The SQL uri is provided in the config module::

>>> from atomisator.db import config

```
>>> config.SQLURI = 'sqlite://:memory:'
```

Let's create an entry::

```
>>> from atomisator.db import create_entry
>>> entry = {'url': 'http://www.python.org/news',
... 'summary': 'Summary goes here',
... 'title': 'Python 2.6alpha1 and 3.0alpha3 released',
... 'links': ['http://www.python.org'],
... 'tags': ['cool', 'fun']}
>>> id_ = create_entry(entry)
>>> type(id_)
<type 'int'>
```

We get the database id back. Now let's look for entries::

```
>>> from atomisator.db import get_entries
>>> entries = get_entries() # returns a generator object
>>> entries.next()
<Entry('Python 2.6alpha1 and 3.0alpha3 released')>
```

Some filtering can be done ::

```
>>> entries = \
... get_entries(url='http://www.python.org/news')
>>> entries.next()
<Entry('Python 2.6alpha1 and 3.0alpha3 released')>
```

When no entry is found, the generator is empty::

```
>>> entries = get_entries(url='xxxx')
```

```
>>> entries.next()
```

Traceback (most recent call last):

...

StopIteration

As a result, this package provides users with two global functions allowing them to interact with the database. These functions are; **get_entries** (which fetches entries from the database) and **create_entry** (creates new entries in the database).

The 'atomisator.feed' Package

This package makes use of the **atomisator.db** package to access the database and perform read operations on its entries. This allows the package to create an RSS compatible XML file from the most recent entries of the database. For this package, we use the **Cheetah template engine** to create an RSS template file. This file features version 2 of the RSS structure.

```
<?xml version="1.0" encoding="utf-8"?>
<rss version="2.0" xmlns:rdf="http://www.w3.org/1999/02/22-
rdf-syntaxns#">
<channel>
<title><![CDATA[${channel.title}]]></title>
<description><![CDATA[${channel.description}]]></descripti
on>
<link>${channel.link}</link>
<language>en</language>
```

```
<copyright>Copyright 2008, Atomisator</copyright>
<pubDate>${publication_date}</pubDate>
<lastBuildDate>${build_date}</lastBuildDate>
#for $entry in $entries
 <item>
 <title><![CDATA[${entry.title}]]></title>
 <description><![CDATA[${entry.summary}]]></description>
 <link><![CDATA[${entry.url}]]></link>
 <pubDate>${entry.date}</pubDate>
 </item>
#end for
</channel>
</rss>
```

This package now consists of data from the database (the entries) and the configuration files (this is additional information, such as the feed's channel title etc.). The final structure and contents of the **doctest** for the **atomisator.feed** package will be;

```
================

atomisator.feed

================

Generates a feed using a template::
 >>> from atomisator.feed import generate
 >>> print generate('feed', 'the feed', 'http://link')
```

```
<?xml version="1.0" encoding="utf-8"?>
<rss version="2.0" xmlns:rdf="...">
<channel>
<title><![CDATA[feed]]></title>
<description><![CDATA[the feed]]></description>
<link>http://link</link>
<language>en</language>

...

<item>
<title><![CDATA[Python 2.6alpha1 and
3.0alpha3 released]]></title>
<description><![CDATA[Summary goes
here]]></description>
<link><![CDATA[http://www.python.org/news]]></link>
<pubDate>...</pubDate>
</item>

...

</channel>
</rss>
```

The 'atomisator.main' Package

The **atomisator.main** package unifies every package with the help of a config file '**atomisator.cfg**'.

```
[atomisator]
```

```
# feeds to read
sites =
 sample1.xml
 sample2.xml
# database location
database = sqlite:///atomisator.db
# fields used for the channel
title = My Feed
description = The feed
link = the link
# name of the generated file
file = atomisator.xml
```

We use a module called '**config**' to read this file. As a result, we include a total of three functions in the package's main module to wrap things up.

```
from atomisator.main.config import parser
from atomisator.parser import parse
from atomisator.db import config
from atomisator.db import create_entry
from atomisator.feed import generate
config.SQLURI = parser.database
def _log(msg):
 print msg
```

```python
def load_feeds():
    """Fetches feeds."""
    for count, feed in enumerate(parser.feeds):
        _log('Parsing feed %s' % feed)
        for entry in parse(feed):
            count += 1
            create_entry(entry)
    _log('%d entries read.' % count+1)

def generate_feed():
    """Creates the meta-feed."""
    _log('Writing feed in %s' % parser.file)
    feed = generate(parser.title,
        parser.description, parser.link)
    f = open(parser.file, 'w')
    try:
        f.write(feed)
    finally:
        f.close()
    _log('Feed ready.')

def atomisator():
    """Calling both."""
    load_feeds()
    generate_feed()
```

Finally, we then include them in the **setup.py** file as 'console scripts'.

```
...
entry_points = {
 "console_scripts": [
 "load_feeds = atomisator.main:load_feeds",
 "generate_feed = atomisator.main:generate_feed",
 "atomisator = atomisator.main:atomisator"
 ]
 }
...
```

We should note that in order for the application to install successfully, we need it to include the other packages as its dependencies. This package has already done this in the **setup.py** file through the use of the **'install_requires'** argument. So, when the **atomisator.main** package is installed, the rest of the atomisator packages are automatically installed as well.

```
...
install_requires=[
'atomisator.db',
'atomisator.feed',
'atomisator.parser'
],
```

Conclusion

We have now concluded our journey, no matter how brief it felt or how long it seemed. At the start, we learned about the tools that would help us create Python projects and learn how to use them effectively. These tools will be helpful for every type of project you handle in the future as they are the bread and butter of experienced programmers and developers. Once the book takes off, we immediately landed on arguably the most important chapters in this book, the syntaxes. Knowing the proper syntax and effectively implementing them is what sets a bad code from a good code. The syntax used by beginner programmers is cruder and has limitations while the syntaxes used by experience programmers are complex but more productive and usable. For this purpose exactly, we went through two entire chapters dedicated to only syntaxes and explored two distinct levels of implementation, below the class and above the class.

In the middle of all this discussion of detailing advanced concepts and practical implementations, we spent time learning about naming schemes in coding. Experienced programmers usually create their own custom functions, classes, and modules depending on the project's needs. Thus, naming them becomes an important factor as these names are what will be used to call these custom elements to a program. If the programmer's naming scheme does not follow a specific scheme or trend, then unnecessary complications will arise. Finally, we reached the part of the book where we learned how to use the concepts that we learned before this book and in this book. The key technique used in these chapters was the technique of building packages and how to build applications through the use of packages as well. Since this book's focus is practicality, these chapters also emphasize the process of distributing packages as well to community servers and other systems as well.

References

Expert Python Programming: Best Practices for Designing, Coding and Distributing your Python Software: by author Tarek Ziadé

www.ingramcontent.com/pod-product-compliance
Lightning Source LLC
LaVergne TN
LVHW022258060326
832902LV00020B/3148